ZOLA'S "GERMINAL"

A CRITICAL AND HISTORICAL STUDY

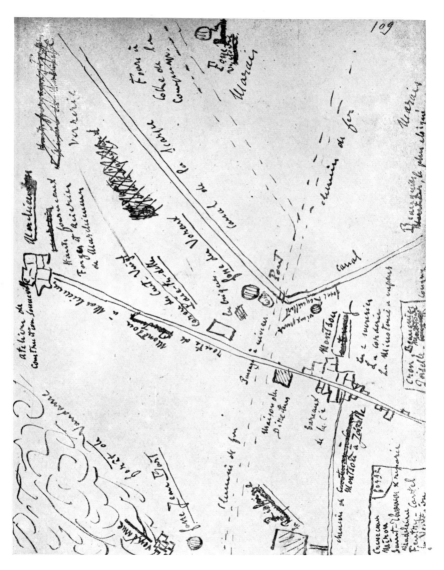

ZOLA'S MAP OF THE MINING AREA
(*Photostat by the Bibliothéque Nationale*)

ZOLA'S
"GERMINAL"
A CRITICAL AND HISTORICAL STUDY

by

ELLIOTT M. GRANT

LEICESTER UNIVERSITY PRESS

1962

Printed in the Netherlands by
Drukkerij Holland N.V., Amsterdam,
for Leicester University Press.

PREFACE

THE aim of the present volume is above all to be useful. In preparing it, the needs of the student or teacher of Zola's masterpiece have been constantly kept in mind It is hoped that all the necessary information for a sound comprehension of the novel and its composition will be found in the following pages.

Part I contains a discussion of the genesis, sources, characters, etc. of *Germinal*. There is no attempt to treat *Les Rougon-Macquart* in general or to analyze in any detail Zola's concept of the naturalistic novel. That seems quite unnecessary after so much has been said on the subject by others, especially Professor Robert and Dr F. W. J. Hemmings.

Part II consists of three sections of which the first is devoted to a reproduction of Zola's *Ébauche*, the second to several of his preliminary sketches of the novel's characters. For lack of space it is not possible to print all of the latter. Those of four important characters and one minor person of special interest have been chosen. The third section gives the Bibliography.

While some work has, of course, been done already on *Germinal*, it is scattered in various publications. This volume seeks not only to bring it together, but to supplement and complete it with additional research and new evaluation.

A study of the dossier of *Germinal* involves more than a mere consideration of Zola's documentation, important though that may be. It also permits one to observe the fashioning of the characters, the development of their particular rôle in the novel, the composition of the book, the retention or rejection of melodramatic material, etc. Such questions are treated in appropriate chapters or sections.

No attempt has been made to relate the history of the play, *Germinal*, drawn from the novel. This question, however interesting, lies outside the scope of this book.

It is a pleasure here to express the deepest gratitude to Dr Jacques Émile Zola for his kind permission to print the *Ébauche* of *Germinal* and other sections and bits of the "notes de travail," as well as for authorization to reproduce in photographic form a page of the *Ébauche*, the map which Zola made of his mining area, and a page of the actual manuscript of the novel.

Other acknowledgments are in order. To Professors Robert, Jordan, Sachs, and R. B. Grant who looked up items in Europe, I am greatly indebted. Professor Sachs did more, he read and criticized some of the chapters, kindly permitting the free use of his comments. Professors R. J. Niess and Vernon Hall also put their critical acumen at my disposal. To these three men, I am particularly grateful. At the same time I wish to make it clear that they are in no way responsible for any errors of fact or judgment that may occur in the following pages. Mr M. Hookham of the University of Leicester was kind enough to lend his copy of Mr Kleman's book which could not be found in this country or in Paris. Mr Philip Walker with great generosity lent his microfilm reproduction of Zola's "notes de travail" which I had, of course, also consulted in Paris. I am much indebted to the Baker Library of Dartmouth College which has given unstinting use of its resources and services. Last, but by no means least, I have been assisted by Mrs E. M. Grant who nobly copied newspaper articles and verified texts.

I cannot close these acknowledgments without emphasizing the generosity of the American Philosophical Society and the President and Trustees of William College. The former, by a grant of money, made the research possible, and the latter insured the publication of the volume. To both my sincere gratitude.

My special thanks to Dr F. W. J. Hemmings for encouragement and professional courtesies.

E. M. G.

Note

After the following pages were written, I learned of the forthcoming publication of two articles on *Germinal*, one by J. H. Matthews, the other by P. Aubery. Even if they are published before this volume appears, it will be impossible for me to give them greater cognizance than I am doing in these lines.

CONTENTS

PART II

ILLUSTRATIONS

PART I

CHAPTER I

THE GENESIS OF "GERMINAL"

THE *Rougon-Macquart* series was first conceived of by Zola in 1868–1869 after the composition of *Thérèse Raquin*. At this time Zola drew up a list of ten novels[1] which included one "roman ouvrier" for which the setting was to be Paris. Later, he made another list of seventeen novels where we find a "roman populaire – Gervaise Ledoux et ses enfants" and "un deuxième roman ouvrier," described as "particulièrement politique. L'ouvrier d'insurrection [outil révolutionnaire], de la Commune [. . .] aboutissant à mai 1871." [2] The first novel became obviously *L'Assommoir*, but the second novel was never composed as such. The Commune was treated at the end of *La Débâcle*, which was in fact an appropriate place for it.

Sometime after 1877 Zola moved more clearly in the direction of the novel which ultimately became *Germinal*. In 1882, Paul Alexis in his book, *Émile Zola. Notes d'un ami*, announced that the author of the *Rougon-Macquart* series would write a second novel on the working class, specifying that "les réunions publiques, ce qu'on entend par la question sociale, les aspirations et les utopies du prolétariat" would be analyzed there. And in the spring of 1883, H. Flamens, writing in *La Vérité* (7 April), said that Zola's cycle would include "ses pages noires et tourmentées, l'étude que l'auteur des *Rougon-Macquart* consacrera au rôle social de l'ouvrier." The novelist himself, writing much later to Van Santen Kolff, explained it was not till he composed *L'Assommoir*, that "unable to include there the political and above all the social rôle of the worker, [he] decided to reserve that material for another book." [3] In the same letter he stated that he came to the realization of the importance of the socialist movement in the civilization of Europe. "*Germinal*," he adds, "is, therefore, the complement of *L'Assommoir*; together they provide the two aspects of the worker."

After the creation in September, 1864, of the International, discussion of socialism had been particularly vigorous and widespread. The Commune of 1871, though not socialistic in point of accomplishment, suggested red revolution to the terrified bourgeois who, under the leadership of Thiers, repressed the Communards in a ferocious blood bath. By the end of the next decade, however, the socialists had recovered from this event, and the discussion of socialism went on apace. It was enlivened in 1882 by the split in the Fédération des travailleurs socialistes de France. In that year, at the Congress of Saint-Étienne, the majority rejected the Marxist strategy of seeking social revolution and voted in favour of a policy of gradualism. The minority, headed by Jules Guesde, and outraged by this heresy, founded the "Parti ouvrier" and preached orthodox doctrine. During the next few years these diverse opinions were aired as much as possible in view of the elections of 1885 which, in fact, did not return any member of either socialist party to parliament, but did bring into the Chamber several men of socialist sympathies like Hugues, Boyer, Camélinat, and a future socialist leader, Jean Jaurès.

Concrete and specific labour problems also came to the fore. In 1864 the so-called "loi sur les coalitions" had been voted. In reality, it merely modified an earlier statute. The new legislation abolished penalties against "la coalition sans violence" but increased them for "atteinte matérielle à la liberté du travail." [4] The right of assembly was not authorized by the law. The "coalitions" were not clearly defined, and the courts were inclined to interpret them as informal and temporary groupings rather than what we mean today by labour unions.[5] Nevertheless, the new law tended to encourage the workers, with the result that the last years of the Second Empire were marked by a number of serious strikes in the textile factories of Roubaix, in the mines of La Ricamarie and Aubin, in the metallurgical foundries of Le Creusot. After the Commune, the middle class dominated the Third Republic, but could not suppress the reappearance of labour problems. In 1874 the question of female and child labour was discussed and a law was voted which forbade the employment of women underground.[6] It also prohibited, with some exceptions, the use of children under the age of twelve in factory or mine.[7] Above that age, there were few restrictions. The twelve-hour day was common. An effort to reduce it was defeated in 1882.[8] On the other hand, labour unions were legalized without equivocation in March 1884 after a two years' debate and given the right to take counsel together for "the study and defense of their economic interests."[9]

The nihilist agitation of this period was also occupying men's minds. The various attempts on the life of Russian officials, culminating in the assassination of Alexander II in March 1881, interested and alarmed public opinion in western Europe. They led to the appearance in the French press of numerous articles on the problem of nihilism. At the same time there was an influx of Russian political refugees and agitators, including men like Bakunin, Kropotkin, and Lavrov. Zola met some of them through Turgenev, with whom he had been closely associated for several years before the latter's death in 1883. Conversations with the Russian novelist on the phenomenon of nihilism very probably occurred. As we shall see in more detail when discussing Souvarine, the nihilist of *Germinal*, these conversations conceivably played a part in the genesis of the novel.

To all these events which may well have aroused Zola's interest and stimulated his creative genius, we should add a number of minor influences in the domain of art and literature. There were really no major ones. To be sure, Zola greatly admired Balzac, whom he viewed as the father of the naturalistic novel. The author of the *Comédie humaine* was not without influence on *Les Rougon-Macquart*. But Zola, in a well-known document, took special pains to underline the differences between Balzac and himself.[10] In any case, while there is a general Balzacian influence on *Germinal* as on any of *Les Rougon-Macquart*, there is nothing specific to explain Zola's choice of subject. One finds domestic servants and peasants in the *Comédie humaine*, but with the possible exception of Jacques Brigaut (in *Pierrette*) no representatives of the proletariat. Nor are the workers in George Sand's so-called socialist novels authentic proletarians. When they are not peasants, they are much more the artisans of an earlier epoch. Certainly they do not help explain the genesis of *Germinal*.

In 1865 Edmond and Jules de Goncourt proclaimed the right of the lower classes, "les basses classes," to a major rôle in the novel, but their choice was a domestic servant. In 1874 Alphonse Daudet made some acknowledgment of the existence of the working class in *Fromont jeune et Risler aîné*. His description of the drab quarter in which Sidonie Chèbe was brought up accounts in part for her overwhelming desire for wealth and luxury. While connected with the main action and by no means unimportant, this picture of a working-class quarter is not central to the book, which remains essentially a narrative of adultery leading to disaster and death. Two years later Daudet recognized that industry could furnish material for a novelist when he introduced a metallurgical foundry into *Jack*, but his hero, forced by circumstance into a working-class career, is not thoroughly typical of the modern proletarian. In spite of these novels, it seems fair to say that Zola really broke new ground when he wrote *L'Assommoir*, for while we do not see here the modern factory worker, we do find incontestably a realistic portrayal of urban working-class men and women, a much more realistic picture of the proletariat and their *milieu* than anything Daudet attempted.

L'Assommoir was followed by publications which fall into the category of minor influences. In 1878, Hector Malot's *Sans famille* devoted several chapters to the hazards of underground work in the mines. Two years later, Maurice Talmeyr's *Le Grisou* was inspired by the mining industry. And in 1882, Yves Guyot's *Scènes de l'enfer social – La famille Pichot* related not only a mining accident, but a strike and its repression. While Daudet's novels have stylistic distinction and Malot's was widely read and extremely popular, the others are inferior productions. Still, they helped popularize the subject.[11] Then, too, a specific if minor stimulus may be found in Alfred Roll's painting, *La Grève des mineurs*, which everyone saw at the Salon of 1880. In his critique of that exhibition, Zola mentioned

Roll's work, saying that the picture revealed power – "il y a de la puissance." [12] Years later, Camille Mauclair declared with much truth that "la carrière et les impressions de M. Roll, sa façon même de peindre, l'apparentent à M. Zola [. . .] C'est la même accentuation de puissance lourde, le même désir d'exprimer par grandes masses, la même fougue, la même brutalité s'enivrant d'elle-même [. . .] La Grève de M. Roll est analogue à Germinal." [13] Quite possibly Roll's picture or one of the above-mentioned novels suggested to Zola a strike in a mining town as an appropriate subject for his second "roman ouvrier."

Then in the summer of 1883 while on vacation in Brittany he met Alfred Giard, a professor at the University of Lille and also a Deputy from the constituency of Valenciennes sitting on the extreme left of the Chamber. Conversation with Giard is another influence which may explain Zola's ultimate decision to adopt the mining area of the north as the theatre of action for his new novel. But he was still working on La Joie de vivre, the publication of which was not concluded in the Gil Blas till 3 February, 1884.

As late as 16 January, 1884, if we can believe Edmond de Goncourt, Zola had not definitely made up his mind about his new book. "Il est embarrassé," Goncourt wrote in his Journal under that date, "à propos du roman qu'il doit faire maintenant, Les Paysans." Goncourt added that the novel on the railroads appeared to be in abeyance, and that Zola "serait plus porté à faire quelque chose se rapportant à une grève dans un pays de mine et qui débuterait par un bourgeois égorgé à la première page . . . Puis le jugement, . . . des hommes condamnés à mort, d'autres à la prison . . . Et parmi les débats du procès, l'introduction d'une sérieuse et approfondie étude de la question sociale." Not long after this, Zola must have come to a decision and actually begun to pen his Ébauche.

Confirmation of this activity is to be found in certain letters, one from Charles Desmaze, another from Léon Hennique. The former wrote to Zola on 11 February suggesting books for him to consult,[14] thereby indicating that Zola was at work on the novel at that date. Hennique's note, dated the 18th, said:

"Vous n'oubliez pas, n'est-ce pas? que je vous attends demain dans l'après-midi pour aller chez Roll. Nous sommes sûrs de le rencontrer; je l'ai prévenu de votre visite." [15] A laconic remark in Zola's "notes de travail" appears to allude to this visit. At the end of a page of notes devoted to mining facts and customs, we read: "Les types vus chez Roll." [16] It seems reasonable to deduce that Zola, having decided to write on the miners, perhaps partially influenced in that decision by Roll's picture, wished to make the painter's acquaintance. Hennique's note also included the information that there would be a "conférence sur les mineurs, 11 rue d'Anjou, à la Mairie," on Thursday the 21st,—scarcely explicable information unless Hennique were aware of the nature of Zola's labors and interest.

While the novelist was thus engaged on his *Ébauche*, a strike broke out in the Anzin mines on 21 February, 1884. There had been a strike at Anzin in 1878, and another at Denain in 1880. This new conflict was more serious. It involved a larger number of workers and was to last fifty-six days. From Zola's point of view it was extraordinarily timely. On 23 February, he dropped everything and hurried to the scene of action. There, he sought out Giard who permitted him to pose as his secretary. Thanks to that stratagem, Zola was able to attend certain meetings which otherwise would have been closed to him. He stayed a week or more in the area, note-book in hand, interviewing miners and their wives, visiting their villages and the cafés they frequented. He met Émile Basly, a former miner, turned "cabaretier," who had become the "secrétaire général de la Chambre syndicale des mineurs du Nord." [17] He also obtained permission from the director of the Anzin mines to inspect all their establishments above and below ground. Guided by one of the company's engineers, a Monsieur Dubus, according to Maurice Le Blond, but possibly a Monsieur Mercier, mentioned by the novelist in a later interview and described as "un jeune ingénieur de grand talent et de grand courage," [18] he descended to the bottom of the Fosse Renard (675 metres) which he thoroughly explored. R. H. Sherard, who wrote an early biography of the novelist, went himself on a pilgrimage to this area, and relates that he met an old *porion* (inspector) who had talked with Zola and who declared that he had never heard a man ask more questions.[19] All this documentation, dictated by Zola's well-established custom, based on the theory of the naturalistic novel, and recorded in the document entitled "Mes notes sur Anzin," [20] lends great authenticity to his book.

Returning to Paris, Zola resumed his work on the *Ébauche* and started (or continued) his labour of documentation, consulting, as will be seen in another section, various newspapers and technical books. He drew up a general plan (which we shall call for convenience' sake, the *Plan par parties* [21]). In fact, he may have written a version of this plan in six parts before completing the *Ébauche*. There is evidence that the third part which concentrates on contrasting ideologies and on Étienne's growing prestige among the miners was not in the first version. The "parts originally numbered 3–6 have been renumbered 4–7, the number 3 crossed out and 4 written over it, and so on," Mr Philip Walker says correctly in an unpublished doctoral dissertation.[22] Moreover, certain characters—the Grégoires, for example—nameless in the *plan par parties*, are mentioned by name for the first time in the last section of the *Ébauche*. Then Zola went on to compose the preliminary portraits of the "Personnages" and began outlining in detail his chapters, making two outlines for each.[23] The order in which he took these last steps is open to some dispute, but an examination of his "notes de travail" shows indisputably that the portraits were composed before the second set of chapter plans,[24] and suggests that they were penned more or less simultaneously with the first set.[25] At any rate, by 16 March he was far enough advanced to be able to write to Édouard Rod: "J'ai tous mes documents pour un roman socialiste et je vais m'enfermer aux champs [that is, Médan] dès la fin de la semaine." [26] On the second of April he began the first chapter, writing the next day to Antoine Guillemet that he had set to work on a "grand coquin de roman qui a pour cadre une mine de houille et pour sujet central une grève." [27] On 8 April, while he was thus engaged, Alfred Giard and Clovis Hugues—as reported in the

Journal officiel of the following day—interpellated the government on the intervention of armed forces in the Anzin strike.
The chairman of a parliamentary committee which had been
established in early February to study the lot of industrial and
agricultural workers [28] promised to send a sub-committee to
Anzin when the strike was ended. The conflict was terminated
in April, but not before October did that sub-committee,
composed of Georges Clémenceau and Germain Casse, actually
go there. Their report could hardly have influenced the composition of *Germinal*, which was well advanced at that date,
especially as Zola did not obtain a copy till a year later. [29] But
the discussion in parliament and continued newspaper reports
of the strike contributed to the atmosphere of tension during
which the novel was planned and the first part penned.

On 16 April Zola commented on his labours in a letter to
Ernst Ziegler: "Je crois pouvoir vous promettre que mon
prochain romain n'effarouchera pas les dames. Ce sera un
pendant à *L'Assommoir*, mais sans les crudités de ce dernier." [30]
On 14 June, still at Médan, he informed Henry Céard that he
was still plunged in the labour of composing *Germinal*: "un
travail de chien comme je n'en ai encore eu pour un roman; et
cela sans grand espoir d'être récompensé. C'est un de ces livres
qu'on fait pour soi, par conscience." [31] The work went on
unremittingly till Zola and his wife left for their summer
vacation in Auvergne. From Mont-Dore he wrote to Henry
Céard on 12 August that he had not touched a pen for a week.
To Paul Alexis he wrote on the 21st that he was doing
"absolutely nothing." Leaving Auvergne on 30 August, Zola
presumably resumed work on *Germinal* as soon as he returned
home. On 18 September, *Le Figaro* published an interview
with the novelist in which the title and subject of his new
novel were announced. "L'auteur," wrote the reporter, "a
choisi pour cadre l'une des villes noires du Nord. Il étudiera
le monde des mineurs dont il établira les revendications,
les besoins." Asked whether his book would be in favour
of the miners, Zola replied: "Pas plus en leur faveur que
contre eux. Le naturalisme ne se prononce pas. Il examine.

Il décrit. Il dit: Ceci est. C'est au public de tirer les conclusions." The plan of the novel, the interviewer adds, is completed and the first half of the novel wholly written.

On 20 September, the *Gil Blas* announced that it would publish a new novel by Zola, described as being "un pendant à l'*Assommoir*" in which "la question sociale se trouve directement abordée." [32] Two months later, on 26 November, 1884, the first installment appeared, though the book was still far from finished. On 1 December, Zola lamented to Goncourt: "Je suis ici [Médan] dans une solitude complète et dans le doute de ce sacré bouquin qui me donne tant de peine. Ajoutez que je ne l'ai point fini, que j'ai encore six semaines de gros travail." [33] On 13 January, 1885 he sent two more chapters to Charpentier, stating that he still had two to write. On 18 January, he confessed to Céard that the book was still unfinished. [34] Finally, on the 25th he wrote triumphantly to Charpentier: "Enfin, mon bon ami, *Germinal* est terminé! Je vous envoie les deux derniers chapitres." [35] He had completed the last page, in fact, on the 23rd, for the manuscript bears that date. The last installment appeared in the *Gil Blas* on 25 February, 1885, and the book came out in the first week of March, though it is listed in the *Bibliographie de la France* under the date of 21 March.

The labour of actual composition which began on 2 April, 1884 and was finally completed on 23 January, 1885, was no mere mechanical elaboration of the chapter plans. It involved, as in all of Zola's novels, an intense and extensive act of creation, during which the characters took on life, the *milieu* was evoked with precision, the dialogue written, and certain details, unthought-of in the earlier stages, were added. Armed though he was with voluminous notes, Zola could not have found these tasks easy of accomplishment. While the individual chapters of *Germinal* are less than half as long as those of *La Curée* and *L'Assommoir*, they are fully as effective. *Milieu* and characters are presented in skilful arrangement, for Zola was fully aware that he was writing both a novel of action (the narrative of a strike)and a *tableau de mœurs* in which the conditions of life in a given occupation and area were being revealed to his compatriots. The welding of these two themes into an organic whole required painstaking labour as well as genuine talent. The presence of a powerful creator is felt throughout the book. GERMINAL. This now famous title was not adopted by Zola without some travail. His work-sheets contain a list of suggestions ranging from "Château branlant" and "Coup de pioche" to "Moisson rouge," all rejected in favour of *Germinal*, the significance of which is reasonably clear. It was the seventh month of the Revolutionary calendar, and one naturally thinks also of the events of the 12th of Germinal, in the third year of the Republic, when rioters invaded the Convention demanding "bread and the constitution of 1793." But Zola was thinking less of that particular day than of the period of the year (March-April). The title came to him, he says, quite suddenly, after he had hesitated over the others. At first, it seemed to him "too mystical, too symbolic." But it represented what he was looking for: "a revolutionary April, a flight of a decrepit, sick society into the springtime." "If the title is obscure for some readers," he adds, "it has become for me a flash of sunshine illuminating the whole work." [36] Just as Hugo's title *Les Misérables* underlined the humanitarian aspect of his novel, so does *Germinal* symbolize the hopes and aspirations of men for a better life this side of the kingdom of heaven.[37]

THE MANUSCRIPTS

The manuscripts, owned by the Bibliothèque Nationale, are bound in four volumes and catalogued as follows: Fonds français, Nouvelles acquisitions, 10305–10308. The first two contain the actual text as Zola wrote it for the printer; a total of 835 pages, written in ink by Zola himself. The first manuscript (10305) includes pages 1–444 covering the first four parts. Page 1 bears on the back the statement: "Commencé le 2 avril 1884." The second manuscript (10306) contains the rest of the novel, pages 445–835. On the back of 835 we read: "Fini le 23 janvier 1885." These manuscripts reveal a good many corrections, mostly of detail. Fairly frequently a part of a page has been pasted to another, indicating that a substantial modification was made; but in all such cases the original has vanished, doubtless destroyed by Zola at the moment of correction.

Page proof does not exist for *Germinal*. The manuscript just described was sent to the printer of the *Gil Blas*. Certain changes were made by Zola in proof, none of which were particularly sensational. Later in this study we shall have occasion to give a few of the variant readings.

Volumes 3 and 4 (10307 and 10308) contain Zola's "notes de travail." Volume 3 (10307) includes:

Feuillets   1– 7: plan par parties
             8–400: plan par chapitres
           401–499: *Ébauche*

As stated earlier, there are two detailed plans (with one exception) for each chapter, bound in reverse order of composition. The plans range from three to eight *feuillets* (only one being longer) per chapter.

Volume 4 (10308) includes:
Feuillets 1–95: Personnages
            f. 2 is a complete list of characters with their ages in 1866.
            f. 3 bears the heading: "Maladies des houilleurs," and gives a list of workers with an occupational malady assigned to almost every one.
            f. 4–5: a provisional list of types of workers to be included in the book.
            f. 6–95: personnages. 6–12: Étienne Lantier; 13–16: Toussaint Maheu; 17–20: Constance Maheu, dite la Maheude; 21–23: Vincent Maheu, dit Bonnemort; 24–27: Catherine Maheu; 28: Zacharie; 29–30: Jenlain (*sic*); 31: Flora (later Alzire), Léonide (later Léonore), Henri, Estelle; 32–33: Jérome Levaque; 34–35: Angéli-

que Levaque; 36: Louis Bouteloup; 37:
Philomène Levaque; 38: Bébert (Albert)
Levaque; 39–40: François Pierron; 41–43:
Suzanne Pierron, dite la Pierronne; 44–
45: Lydie Pierron; 46–47: La mère Brûlé;
48: Le père Mouque; 49: Mouquet; 50–
51: La Mouquette; 52–53: Antoine
Chaval; 54: Le père Caffiaux; 55–56:
Dansaert; 57: Richomme; 58–60: Philippe Hennebeau; 61–63: Blanche Hennebeau; 64–66: Paul Négrel; 67–73: Léon
Grégoire; 74–75: Amélie Grégoire; 76–
77: Cécile Grégoire; 78–79: Victor Deneulin; 80: ~~Georges Deneulin,~~ Lucie,
Jeanne, Maurice; 81–84: Souvarine; 85–
86: Rasseneur; 87: Marsoulan (later
Pluchart); 88: Mme Rasseneur; 89–90:
Maigrat; 91: Le docteur Vanderhagen,
L'abbé Joire; 92: Jules; 93–94: Bataille;
95: Des actionnaires que je ne nommerai
pas, etc.

      96: blank
97–106: maladies des mineurs
   107: blank
108–115: Cartes et plans
   116: blank
151–206: Les Grèves – La Ricamarie – Aubin –
         Creusot – Montceau etc. (f. 196–201:
         grève d'Anzin, 1878)
   207: blank
208–303: Mes notes sur Anzin
304–305: Notes Lévy. Anzin
306–316: miscellaneous notes on Anzin and on
         mining
317–320: Grève de Denain, 1880
   321: blank
322–323: mining terms (not in Zola's handwriting)

324: blank
325–340: Crises industrielles (Guyot)
Crise houillère de 1878 (Ducarre)
Crise houillère de 1864 (Burat)
(F. 326–329 and 332–336 are notes on
Guyot's *La Science économique*. F. 330–331
are from Burat. The remaining are presumably from Ducarre)
341: blank
342–355: Notes from Laveleye
356: blank
357–363: Leroy-Beaulieu, *La Question ouvrière*
364: blank
365–369: L'Internationale (Testut)
370: blank
371–375: Compagnie de Montsou. Compagnie
d'Anzin
376: blank
377–383: Doléances des mineurs (Stell)
384: blank
385 396: Simonin: *Le Monde souterrain**
397: blank
398–413: La Grève d'Anzin 1884 (clippings from
newspapers)
414: blank
415–453: Divers (f. 418–424: Notes sur Guesde, by
P. Alexis; f. 425–426: possible titles for
the novel; f. 427–428: letter dated 18 Feb.
1884, from a Rodney (or Rocher) telling
Zola where he can get information on
strikes; f. 434: an authorization from M.
de Forcade to visit the Anzin mines; f.
436: information from A. Pesson on the
law of 1874 prohibiting work by women
underground; etc.)

* A slip by Zola, for he used not *Les Merveilles du monde souterrain*, but
a different book: *La Vie souterraine*. Both, to be sure, were by L. Simonin.

CHAPTER II

THE COMPOSITION OF THE "ÉBAUCHE"

Zola's *Ébauche* falls into at least three sections. Approximately the first half was surely composed before he made his trip to Anzin on 23 February, 1884. The next part was composed after his return, but with the main lines of action essentially the same. The last eight pages introduce a radical change into the setup, and were clearly penned at a later date.

The first twelve pages of the *Ébauche* (f. 402/1–413/12) contain the basic subject and what Zola calls "la carcasse en grand." The conflict between capital and labour is his choice, —a broad, dramatic, and at the same time a forward-looking subject. Zola predicts that it will be the most important question of the twentieth century. Indeed, it will assume, when the novelist comes to write the book, the overwhelming quality of a cataclysm.

How to embody this conflict? For Zola was not writing a political or economic tract. The term "conflict" (*lutte*) in itself is suggestive of drama. This is clearly to be a novel in which dramatic devices will play an important part. He, therefore, envisages—naturally enough—a contest between the capitalists on the one side and the workers on the other. The workers will be miners, for even before the outbreak of the Anzin strike, let us recall,[1] Zola had picked the mining world for his theatre of action. But on the capitalist side, he is faced with the problem of choosing either a relatively small enterprise, run by an individual owner, or a corporation with a board of directors who have appointed a manager to exploit the property for them. Absentee ownership, he reflects, will permit the creation of a kind of ogre—"une sorte [. . .] de dieu vivant et mangeant les ouvriers dans l'ombre"—with whom the workers will find it difficult to come to grips. The big corporation becomes immediately a part of Zola's plan. But the introduction of a small enterprise also has advantages. Apart from the personal touch, the direct, face-to-face contact between owner and workers, it would permit the novelist to depict the competition between small and big business, to introduce the notion of a spreading strike with its threat of disaster for the small concern less able to resist. The problem of the survival of small business is still a very live issue in the twentieth century. It is remarkable to see it treated at this relatively early date, though Zola was perhaps less motivated by political or economic theory than by novelistic need. In any case, he almost immediately decided to include both types of capital in his book. And simultaneously, he visualized characters to embody them: the manager of the big corporation with his comfortable house, his pleasures, his family; the small owner defending "his skin, his life, that of his family," ruined in the end.

On the miners' side, Zola *sees* the men at work, *sees* them reduced to excessive, unbearable poverty, *sees* them go on strike, *sees* the ensuing savagery of the struggle and their ultimate defeat which nevertheless contains the seeds of vengeance. All this constitutes "la carcasse en grand." What is needed is to put characters on this stage and to make them act.

From this point on it is not desirable to try to systematize the composition of the *Ébauche*. In the first place, there are clear indications, as Professor Guy Robert has already noted, that omissions exist.[2] Furthermore, while certain sections are in themselves logically constructed, Zola did not attempt to make the *Ébauche* resemble a lawyer's brief or a geometrical demonstration. One can almost see his mind racing ahead of his pen. As an idea comes to him or a scene takes shape, he jots it down.

Nevertheless, having stated that characters are needed, Zola proceeds very briefly to create some. The Durand (later Maheu) family with two, then three of their ultimate seven children comes into existence, followed by a second working-class family still unnamed. Étienne is added to the list with some of his traits and a portion of his rôle suggested. He is to have a friend, a Russian nihilist. There is to be a member of the International, a doctor, and a priest, and, of course, specialists among the workers. On the capitalist side, he decides [3] to make the owner of the small enterprise a widower with one or two daughters and to endow the corporation manager with a wife and son (who will become a nephew). A possible marriage comes naturally to his mind. All this is still very sketchy and most of the above characters will be further developed or modified as the *Ébauche* marches on. But we shall discuss the creation of the major characters in separate sections to which we refer the reader.

What is important to note for the tone and temper of the book is that Zola, reflecting on his subject, wishes to make the conflict intense, the contrasts vivid, but at the same times does not want to blacken unnecessarily the capitalist group. The workers are the victims, not of wicked, unscrupulous, unfeeling men, but of a system. "Ne pas tomber dans la revendication bête," he warns himself. This will not, of course, lead him to soften his picture of poverty and hardships, but it will inspire him to include in both camps characters who are anything but admirable, visualizing always certain scenes or even gestures as he proceeds. Thus, the deplorable tendency of an Inspector using his position to seduce the mining girls and suffering for it an extraordinary fate, [4] the introduction of a "grosse fille [. . .] mal embouchée" with some of her characteristics, the treachery of Antoine Chaval and of Pierron, the delinquency of the "petit estropié," the immorality in the ménage of the corporation manager with a quick glimpse of the "belles épaules" of his adulterous wife, the extra-conjugal activities of the "chef-porion," are all products of this motivation.

As Zola advances in his outline, more characters are added to the picture. To help complete the capitalistic group, two shareholders in the big corporation are added. With their commonplace daughter, they represent the idle capitalist, living on inherited wealth, unproductive, but in no sense harmful. "Il faut montrer en eux la jouissance calme de la vie," he writes. An engineer (a possible husband for the daughter and a possible lover for the manager's wife) is added to the mining hierarchy. On the workers' side, the Durand (Maheu) family is sketched out in more detail, with the addition of four children. The other mining family (still nameless) is endowed with a daughter who has two children by the oldest son of Durand (Maheu), and a lodger who sleeps with the mother. Beside this "ménage à trois" Zola places a third mining family. The wife is to be the mistress of the "chef-porion" and the complacent husband a company stool pigeon, denounced by his mother—"mère terrible"—, rewarded by the corporation in the end. The person and character of the nihilist are briefly sketched with equally brief allusions to his past and to his act of sabotage. Two old men, "le vieil ouvrier et le raccommodeur," are mentioned. Zola, typically, *sees* them, "fumant, hochant la tête, élevant leurs mains tremblantes." They will ultimately, after considerable hesitation and modification, be transformed into Bonnemort and Mouque.

The representative of the International, mentioned early in the *Ébauche*, becomes, quite obviously after Zola's trip to Anzin, a "cabaretier" inspired by Basly whom the novelist met during his visit.[5]

Last, but in a sense not least, there are the animals. With Zola's love for them, it is not astonishing to find references in the *Ébauche* to the horses of the mine. They are mentioned in the first section, given even greater space in the second. Their work, the death of one and his removal from the mine, the dream of the other, the survivor's part in the catastrophe are all briefly indicated.

At the same time, pictures, scenes, and actions enrich these sections of the *Ébauche*. Zola *sees* Étienne on the road to Marchiennes, warming his hands a moment later at a fire, he *sees* Catherine "frêle," "poussant les chariots les plus lourds"; he *sees* the half-rotted ladders in the old mine (i.e. Requillart) and the young trees at the mouth, from which one has to drop; he *sees* Jeanlin kill the young soldier, jumping on his back "comme un chat sauvage"; he *sees* the "beau geste" of La Mouquette saving Catherine's life and telling her that for a long time she hasn't been Étienne's girl. This kind of visualization is found on almost every page of the *Ébauche*. Zola also suggests scenes, topics, and actions: the army arriving after the rioting; the cave-in of the mine (later in the *Ébauche* attributed to sabotage) with everything "coulant à l'abîme"; the rivalry of two men for Catherine; the death of the Durand son killed by "le grisou" while trying to save his sister; the violence of Chaval when he follows Catherine to her home; the workers' arduous escape via the ladders from Deneulin's mine; the rôle of the shopkeeper in shutting off credit as ordered by the corporation; the notion of holding a meeting in the forest; Étienne's yielding to the "grosse fille" and the scene when Catherine surprises them in an embrace; the hereditary weakness of Étienne; a vision of the dénouement.

Zola also discusses in the first two parts of the *Ébauche* the timing of the action and the placing of the accidents. As we have shown elsewhere,[6] he thought in the *Ébauche* of having the action of his novel occur in 1865, "l'année qui a suivi la loi de 64 sur les coalitions," but finally opted for 1866–1867. The two accidents also gave him pause. His first idea for the "accident qui estropie le petit" was to place it in the opening chapter. But when he visualized Étienne's arrival in the area stricken by an industrial depression, his meeting with the old miner, and his subsequent employment, he found that quite superior as an *entrée en matière* and postponed the accident to a little later, still placing it, however, before the outbreak of the strike. The greater accident, resulting from sabotage, he thought momentarily of placing before the strike with the idea of attributing the latter to the corporation's efforts to recoup financially after its terrific loss. He wisely abandoned this notion as being too exceptional a cause for a strike. The catastrophe is, therefore, placed after the strike. He was perhaps confirmed in this decision by the fact that an accident—a minor one, to be sure—occurred at Anzin in 1884 just after the defeated miners returned to work.[7]

That the catastrophe should result from sabotage rather than from a cave-in is obviously due to the presence of a nihilist in the scheme, as well as to the fact that Zola doubtless wished to avoid an accident that would resemble too closely the first one. This catastrophe is to be far greater, permitting the author to display all his powers of dramatic and epic narration. It appeals as a spectacle, gigantic and horrifying, but the human aspect is equally attractive to the novelist. For Étienne is endangered by a man whom he thought of as a friend. Then too it allows the Catherine-Étienne-Chaval triangle to come to its dénouement in particularly striking circumstances. The engulfment of Le Voreux helps, in addition, to redress the balance at the end of the strike. The workers have lost and Denoulin is ruined. While the big corporation has won, its triumph is, in some degree, a pyrrhic victory. The destruction of this mine is a serious and costly blow from which it will take time and much capital to recover. Perhaps above all, Zola was led to this arrangement by a conscious or unconscious desire to wind up his narrative with a great, symbolic catastrophe. Professor Guy Robert speaks of the "mythe de la Catastrophe qui pèse sur la Terre, comme sur la plupart des Rougon-Macquart à partir de Nana." He surely had Germinal as well as such books as La Bête humaine and La Débâcle in mind. These novels march more or less inevitably toward some great disaster, although one must not forget that a vision of hope characterizes the final page of La Débâcle and Germinal.

In the last part of the Ébauche (f. 492/89–499/96), composed later, probably after he had given names to some of the anonymous characters and sketched them in his "Personnages," Zola had a great inspiration: to give Étienne a much more central rôle by making him the leader of the strike. We shall discuss the importance of this change as it affects Étienne in another chapter. It suffices here to indicate that this requires other changes of importance. While Étienne is still, as before, a rival of Chaval for the hand of Catherine, he now becomes a competitor of the "cabaretier," dubbed Rasseneur and reclassified as a moderate, for the popularity of the miners.

This last section introduces a second new idea, that of making the old worker (le père Caffiaux) the father of Maheu's wife, "in order to have a whole family to place in opposition to the share-holders." This is a clear statement of the conflict between the Maheus and the Grégoires of which the latter are unaware but which the novelist intends to emphasize. The old man, Zola adds, will still have a companion "pour les montrer ensemble le dimanche."

We have sought in this relatively brief analysis, not to list every point mentioned in the *Ébauche*, but to indicate that Zola's outline gradually came to include most of the lines of action found in the novel and a suggestion of many scenes. But some things which we find in the novel are totally absent from the *Ébauche*. The violent death of the grocer, the murder of Cécile Grégoire, the death from starvation of Alzire, as Professor Robert has already stated, are unmentioned,[8]—though the concept of a man emasculated after death is already present.[9] The quarrel between Chaval and Étienne in the bottom of the flooded mine is at most only faintly suggested, for at this stage Zola thinks rather of a duel between Étienne and an unnamed inspector. The *Ébauche* contains no hint of the town festival (la ducasse) and while it states that Durand's (Maheu's) son plays lacrosse, the match between him and Mouquet is not specifically envisioned. Mme Hennebeau's adultery is there, as we have seen, but the idea of making her lover the nephew of her husband is still quite tentative.

The question of socialism is not absent from the *Ébauche*, for we find references to it even in the section composed before the trip to Anzin and important allusions thereafter. But it is true, as Professor Van Tieghem has stated,[10] though with some exaggeration, that much concerning the socialist movement was introduced in later stages of composition, one of the most obvious additions being the introduction of a socialist priest. Some of his sources were evidently read after the *Ébauche* was partially or wholly completed.[11] The socialist implications of the novel increase in number and intensity as Zola's work of preparation advances until the novel becomes, in spite of the absence of the actual expression, a narrative of the class-struggle.

The *Ébauche* is revelatory of Zola's imagination,—visual, concrete, dramatic and grandiose. We have already emphasized his capacity to *see* persons and events in specific detail. Examples could be accumulated almost without end. One of the most striking, not mentioned hitherto, is his vision of Catherine during the clash between miners and soldiers: "il faut que Catherine rôde comme un corps sans âme, insouciante du danger et cherchant presque la mort," or perhaps his picture of her mother: "Je la vois petite, carrée [. . .], blême, elle est au début d'esprit équilibré, prudente, de conseil sage, luttant contre la misère; et peu à peu je la montrerai impuissante, s'enrageant elle aussi, arrivant au cri final de désespoir et de négation." The abstract and the concrete are skilfully combined in these visualizations.

The grandiose suggests the epic and is akin to the mythical. The big corporation becomes in his mind's eye a sort of "tabernacle reculé," a "dieu vivant et mangeant les ouvriers dans l'ombre." The portrayal of the strike must go beyond the immediate and show the repercussions: "il faudrait que je fasse entendre dans le pays le retentissement d'autres ruines pendant la grève, ou à la suite." To obtain a "gros effet," the contrasts must be clear and "poussées au summum de l'intensité possible." The workers' lot must be made concrete, with the help of detailed facts, but at the same time everything must be logically connected, "se déduisant par grands mouvements humains." The catastrophe is visualized on a grand scale: "J'aimerais bien l'éboulement du puits, avec tout coulant à l'abîme." Such suggestions indicate that already in the Ébauche, Zola is going beyond the limits of a naturalistic novel and entering the realm of the epic.

Zola's imagination also tends toward the melodramatic and the terrible. This is evident already in his conception of the mutilation of the Inspector and in his view of the great catastrophe at the end. But it can also be seen in the character and rôle of Jeanlin, for in this early stage his murder of a soldier is much more horrible than in the novel. Nor do we find in the finished text the scene in the old mine where the boy lives with "une fillette de douze ans comme lui qu'il aurait enlevée" and where he appears "ivre-mort tous les soirs." This tendency toward the melodramatic and the terrible is given free rein wherever deemed desirable by the novelist, but is often held in check by the exigencies of realism. In any case, it is clearly visible in the *Ébauche*.

Zola's outline, then, sets up a broad, dramatic subject, suitable, as Professor Van Tieghem has said,[12] for epic frescoes, suggestive of scenes and characters. It includes important lines of action. It poses a problem which will require some expression of opinion or at least of sentiment on the part of the author who already begins to reveal his sympathies. But the labour of creation is not ended with the *Ébauche*. It has, in fact, only begun.

CHAPTER III

THE SOURCES OF "GERMINAL"

Zola's "notes de travail" contain clear indications of most of the sources he used in preparing his novel. Since a considerable portion of the *Ébauche* was composed before he left Paris for Anzin and since he had certainly not completed his labour of documentation before starting that document,[1] he knew pretty well what he needed, and, as Professor Van Tieghem has stated,[2] he chose from his observation and reading what was suitable or necessary to his project. Sometimes he found in his source-material even more than he had hoped for, and he did not hesitate to adopt whatever seemed appropriate.

The books recommended by Charles Desmaze, Le Play's *Les Ouvriers en Europe* and several others,[3] were apparently useless, for neither in the worksheets nor in the novel itself do we find any evidence that Zola profited from them. On the other hand, the suggestion of a gentleman by the name of Rodney (or Rocher)[4] to consult issues of *La Gazette des Tribunaux* and *Le Temps* dealing with certain strikes during the last years of the Second Empire turned out to be highly valuable.

Several sources were freely admitted by Zola himself immediately after the publication of *Germinal*. He then publicly stated that he had utilized Simonin's *La Vie souterraine*, Laveleye's *Le Socialisme contemporain*, Testut's *L'Internationale*, and Bormans' *Vocabulaire des houilleurs liégeois*.[5] His "notes de travail" and the finished novel leave no doubt of his indebtedness to Simonin and Laveleye. Testut's book was also consulted, but to a far lesser extent. As for Bormans' *Vocabulaire*, anything that Zola found there to be of interest to him, he could equally well have learned either during his visit to Anzin or from his reading of Simonin, and there is no indication in the novelist's work-sheets that he ever really used Bormans' booklet.

Additional sources, not named publicly by Zola, are found

in the "notes de travail." These, like Dormoy's *Topographie souterraine du Bassin houiller de Valenciennes*, Leroy-Beaulieu's *La Question ouvrière au 19e siècle*, Guyot's *La Science économique*, and a few others have been revealed by recent investigators.[6] They are naturally of varying importance in the construction of the novel.

Zola's description of the mining area, its geography and its sociological phenomena, is essentially the product of his visit to Anzin, recorded in *Mes notes sur Anzin*.[7] A young scholar, M. Loquet, has studied the geographical accuracy of *Germinal* and has concluded that it is essentially sound: "L'authenticité n'est pas celle du détail mais celle de l'ambiance, du cadre, du milieu naturel." [8] The novelist's picture of the village with its houses, its bits of garden, its cafés, its inhabitants, derives from the same source. At Anzin, Zola observed, for example, the lay-out of the mining village: "Les corons. Un, en longue file, deux rangs de maisons, collées dos à dos. Un petit trottoir de briques sur champ. De l'autre côté de la rue, des jardins sales, plantés d'arbustes maigres, sans allées tracées, très peu cultivés. [. . .] une église en briques, une école, etc. [. . .] Devant chaque maison des tonneaux posés pour recevoir l'eau pluviale." [9] And he jotted down some of the names, literal or ironical, given to the various groups of dwellings: "Noms des corons: les Trente, les Quarante-six, les Soixante-douze, les Cent-vingt, le coron des Bas-de-soie, le coron Paie-tes-dettes, des surnoms." [10] In his novel, the first paragraph of the second chapter (Part I) is clearly inspired by these notes, and later, in chapter 3 of Part II, the brick church and school, the rain barrels, and the ironical names make their appearance.

The same utilization of observed fact is found in the description of the Maheus' establishment. At Anzin Zola had carefully noted the sleeping arrangements in a typical miner's house: "En haut, un couloir d'abord où les enfants couchent. Puis une chambre pour le père et la mère, dans laquelle il faut bien aussi que des enfants se trouvent parfois." [11] In the novel, the Maheu family has a single bedroom on the second floor where most of the children sleep. The parents' bed is in the "couloir du palier" where they have had to put also the baby's cradle. In comparison with what he saw at Anzin, the sleeping quarters are reversed, doubtless because of the large number of Maheu children all of whom would not fit into the "couloir." Otherwise the arrangement is identical. The downstairs room is described in his notes as having painted walls and ceiling and a "sol dallé très proprement." On Sundays it is washed and sprinkled with "un sable blanc coûtant assez cher." [12] In the novel the room is depicted as "une salle assez vaste, tenant tout le rez-de-chaussée, peinte en vert pomme, d'une propreté flamande, avec ses dalles lavées à grande eau et semées de sable blanc." Once again his observation has served the novel well. The furniture, according to the notes, consists of "un buffet en sapin verni, une table, des chaises, ailleurs une grande armoire, etc. Un coucou." [13] The novel tells us that "outre le buffet de sapin verni, l'ameublement consistait en une table et des chaises du même bois" and that there is a "coucou à cadran peinturluré." All the living arrangements of the Maheus reflect the novelist's direct observations.

Zola's description of the mine, the buildings above ground, and the pit itself is clearly inspired not only by this personal visit to Anzin, but frequently also by his reading of Dormoy and Simonin. The machine which awed Étienne by its size, power, and movement [14] is copied—with stylistic improvements—from the Anzin notes [15] and owes nothing to published documents. And the three "brasiers brûlant au plein air et comme suspendus" which Étienne saw as he arrived in the area on that black March night were suggested by the "feux dans des corbeilles de fer montées sur trois longs pieds qui flambent dans la nuit pour éclairer et chauffer" which Zola also noted at Anzin.[16] But other items may come from reference books or be a combination of both. Before working on *Germinal*, the novelist presumably knew little or nothing about the mining industry, so he naturally looked for accurate information. He began this process before the strike at Anzin broke out on 21 February. As we have seen, he left promptly for Anzin learned all he could during the days he spent there, and returning to Paris continued his planning which included finishing the *Ébauche*, completing his documentation, outlining his chapters, etc. In his search for information he sometimes discovered only a confirmation of what he saw at Anzin, sometimes something new. He observed, for example, the existence of firedamp (*le grisou*) at Anzin, and he found confirming information about it in Simonin's book and in the Encyclopédie Roret. His description of *le grisou* in the novel is doubtless a combination of what he saw and what he read. He may have learned the word *rivelaine* (a miner's pick) during his stay at Anzin, though it is not recorded in his notes, but he certainly could have got it either from Bormans' little book or, more probably, from Simonin's volume where it is not only verbally described but actually pictured.[17] At Anzin, he descended into a mine, recorded in great detail what he saw and experienced,[18] then reproduced much of it in his novel.[19] He found a confirmation of his impressions in Simonin's book and incorporated some of what he read into his text.[20] During his Anzin experience he doubtless learned the arrangements for escape in case of accident, but he found additional details in Simonin's pages. He observed at Anzin the method of propping (*boisage*), but Dormoy's book gave him further information some of which passed into the novel. At Anzin he saw with his own eyes the "cuvelage" (tubbing, or wooden lining of the shaft), but he found in Dormoy a precise technical description of this construction as well as geological data on the underground waters called "le niveau" and "le torrent."[21] In the novel, Souvarine will weaken the *cuvelage* at the point where pressure from the *Torrent* is a constant menace. Again, in Dormoy's volume, Zola found details on miners' wages, pensions, and what we call today fringe benefits, some of which made their way, occasionally modified or dramatized, into his novel. The whole first part of the *Topographie souterraine* was devoted to the historical background of the mining industry. It ran to a good many pages, from which Zola took material to furnish the factual substance of less than two pages of the novel, just enough to make the history of the Grégoire fortune (in chapter 2 of Part II) credible. Indeed, throughout, Zola used technical lan-

guage and information with restraint,[22] frequently leaving aside
as much as or more than he actually adopted. His documentation, motivated by a desire to tell the truth, to reproduce
reality, was held in check by the knowledge that he was
writing a novel, not a sociological tract.

Books like those of Dormoy and Simonin not only gave him
information, they also stimulated his imagination It is more
than possible that the whole episode involving Le Tartaret and
Catherine's work next to the "corroi" (a technical word provided by Simonin) [23] would never have been composed, had
Zola not read *La Vie souterraine*. The great catastrophe at the
end of *Germinal* was also suggested to a considerable extent by
his reading of Simonin's volume. Of course, he intended from
very early in his planning to put a terrible catastrophe, one
caused by sabotage,[24] into his novel, and did not need a documentary source to think of that. But the grim experience of
Étienne and Catherine trapped in the bottom of the mine is
indisputably modelled on Simonin's accounts of somewhat
similar events near Bessèges (Gard) and at Marles (in the Pas-de-
Calais), the only difference being that the catastrophe in
Germinal is caused by an act of sabotage rather than by a cave-
in. Like the people at Bessèges, who fled before the waters to
the top of a gallery (where they were finally found) and there
were forced to dig with their hands a little seat in the schist
with the water lapping at their feet, Étienne and Catherine
retreat before the invading flood and finally by digging in the
schist fashion "une sorte de banc élevé" where "l'eau ne glaçait
plus que leurs talons." [25] When the unlucky pair are forced to
eat rotted wood and chew bits of Étienne's leather belt, and
when, as they drink, Chaval's corpse floats up close to them,
they are again having the same experiences as the people in
Simonin's account endured.[26] Clearly, *La Vie souterraine* fulfilled
a double purpose. It gave authentic information and it provided
events and experiences that were picturesque and exciting even
to the point of being almost incredible. One is reminded of
Corneille's concept of the improbable but true. Such items
undoubtedly appealed to Zola as being good material for this

novel, for we have seen in discussing the *Ébauche* that his imagination tended toward the grandiose and the melodramatic.

On the question of socialism Zola, rather surprisingly, also relied heavily on documentary sources. He had lived through the period of the founding of the International, and a few years later as a reporter for *La Cloche* had been present when the French parliament was debating the so-called iniquities of that organization.[27] He had witnessed the development of socialist theory and discussion, had seen the break between the Marxists and the gradualists. He had surely not been unaware of the propaganda and activities of the anarchists. He must have learned something about the Russian nihilists from articles in the French press of the 1870s and 1880s supplemented perhaps by conversations with his friend Turgenev. He himself had written for *Le Figaro* an article on "La République en Russie" in which the nihilists did not go unmentioned. But when he came to write his novel, he apparently judged all this as insufficient and therefore sought specific information. Henri Barbusse maintained that Zola consulted Jules Guesde.[28] That cannot be true, for Zola did not meet the leader of the Parti Ouvrier till after *Germinal* was published. Furthermore, the notes on Guesde, compiled for him by Paul Alexis and preserved in the dossier of *Germinal* at the Bibliothèque Nationale,[29] remained unused as far as *Germinal* is concerned. The principal source of the passages in the novel dealing in any way with socialism, anarchism, or the International is not his memory but rather Laveleye's *Le Socialisme contemporain* (2nd. edition, 1883), and secondarily, on the International, Testut's book.[30] Laveleye's, in particular, fulfilled in this domain a function comparable to that performed by Simonin's on the mining industry. On the one hand, it was a reference book; on the other, it was a source of ideas. Zola found there, for example, a definition of Ricardo's iron law to which the working-class is supposedly subjected under the capitalistic system. He introduces it, without mentioning Ricardo, in the third part of the novel. The definition given there by Souvarine of this *loi d'airain* comes almost

textually from Laveleye's pages.[31] Would Zola have thought
of including this particular law in the discussion without the
stimulus of Laveleye's book? We are inclined to doubt it.
Then, when he attributes to his Russian nihilist the determina-
tion to have "ni femme ni ami" in order to be "libre de son
sang et du sang des autres," the sentiment comes almost verbatim from Laveleye's treatise.[32] Étienne's speeches in the forest
contain sections that are strongly reminiscent of Laveleye's
pages on the collectivists. Quoting from Malon's *Histoire du
socialisme*, Laveleye states that collectivist principles require
among other things the "substitution d'une famille égalitaire et
libre à la famille morale et oppressive qui fait de la femme et de
l'enfant les esclaves du mari et du père" and demand "égalité
civile, politique et économique de tous les êtres humains."
Étienne forecasts that the reforms to be realized by the people
will be: "retour à la commune primitive, substitution d'une
famille égalitaire et libre à la famille morale et oppressive,
égalité absolue, civile, politique et économique [. . .].[33] The
language is virtually identical. Laveleye's chapter on "Les Socialistes catholiques" also provided Zola with information, but
quite possibly offered a stimulus as well. One may question
whether the radical priest, Ranvier, would have appeared in
Germinal, had Zola never read this volume.[34] It will be seen in
our next chapter that Ranvier was not thought of in the early
stages of Zola's planning. As the novelist turned the pages of
Laveleye's book, the idea that his own would be incomplete
without such a character may well have come to him.

The desire for the colourful which at the same time would be
authentic accounts for Zola's utilization of numerous episodes
in the strikes at La Ricamarie and Aubin in 1869. At La Ricamarie there was a crowd of miners "qui a parcouru les divers
puits du bassin en arrêtant le travail, avec menaces, voies de fait
ou intimidation." When Zola read that in *La Gazette des
Tribunaux* of 5 August, 1869, he at once seized on it for his
novel. In the early pages of the *Ébauche*, to be sure, he had
envisaged such a scene.[35] The newspaper item either justified this
action or suggested it. It is impossible to say just which for we

do not know the exact date when Zola wrote this section of the
Ébauche or the date when he consulted the newspaper file. In
any case, this was both authentic and colourful material. The
same issue of the *Gazette des Tribunaux* gave him the episode of
a miner being forced by other strikers to drink from a trough.
This, too, in a slightly modified form went into the novel. At
La Ricamarie and at Aubin, a clash occurred between the
striking workers and the troops sent to protect industrial property. Some of the details of these clashes were adopted by Zola.
When he attributes to the strikers such a statement as "lorsqu'on
avait fait la guerre de Crimée, on ne craignait pas le plomb." [36]
he is repeating almost verbatim a sentence reported on 13
November 1869 in *La Gazette des Tribunaux*. When Levaque
seizes the bayonets thrust toward him and Maheu presses his
bared chest on the points of other blades, they are doing what
some of the strikers did at La Ricamarie as related in the
6th August issue of *La Gazette des Tribunaux*.

Zola's narrative of the strike is a composite of the Anzin
strike of 1884, the conflicts at La Ricamarie, Aubin, Fourchambault, and Le Creusot in the last years of the Second
Empire, with a detail or two suggested by the strike at Montceau-les-mines in 1882. The cause of the fictional walk-out at
Montsou, its length, and its conclusion are essentially the same
as at Anzin. The strike there began in February, and Zola
merely moves the date ahead a couple of months in order to
make sure that the hardships of the winter season will last to the
end. But since the Anzin strike did not furnish enough colourful
details, the novelist turned to the conflicts of 1869–70. He could
doubtless have invented what he needed, but actual events lent
authenticity to his book.[37]

At the same time, the rôle of personal invention in the narrative of the strike is by no means negligible. The march of the
mining men and women and some of the attendant details may
have been suggested by events at La Ricamarie and elsewhere,
but no such blazing narrative and description as we find in
Part V of this novel can be found in the newspapers of the
period. Nor was the climax before the house of M. Hennebeau

with the final savagery of Maigrat's mutilation born anywhere but in Zola's own mind. His narrative of the clash between miners and soldiers at the end of Part VI is a combination of what he read and what he invented. The conclusion is, therefore, inescapable that his strike is far more than a patchwork of historical facts, it is also a work of creative imagination.

The dossier of *Germinal* includes clippings from various newspapers. A column from *Le Gaulois* of 27 February, 1884 which dealt with the labour leaders at Anzin, Basly and Fauviau, interested the novelist. What was said about the latter may well be the source of Zola's statement that Étienne Lantier's reading was ill-digested [38] for it informed its readers that Fauviau was "un garçon qui a lu pas mal de livres révolutionnaires sans en comprendre autre chose que les passages déclamatoires qu'il sait par cœur et qu'il débite." From *L'Événement* of 2 March, 1884 Zola clipped an article on the Anzin strike which was sympathetic to the strikers and suggested that the Company "foresaw and desired" the walk-out. The dossier also contains a document which gives a short report of a speech by Giard in the Chambre des Députés (6 March 1884). Zola's acquaintance said: "La Compagnie désirait donc la grève, elle la voulait, je dirai plus: elle l'avait préméditée depuis longtemps." Is it any wonder then that the workers of *Germinal* are of the same opinion? [39] But even when Zola did not clip articles or take notes for his dossier, newspaper items may have remained in his memory. When, for instance, Souvarine denounces those French workers who decided to live in idleness after winning the grand prize in a lottery, Zola is probably remembering some "fait divers" reported in the French press.[40] Reality lies behind more paragraphs and sentences of *Germinal* than one might think.[41]

Zola's knowledge of the miners' maladies has been shown by Professor Frandon to have been culled from the *Traité pratique des maladies, des accidents et des difformités des houilleurs* by Dr H. Boëns-Boisseau, a book which the novelist re-entitled as the *Hygiène du mineur*. Like Simonin's volume, it gave him both authentic and picturesque material. The scrofula from which

Jeanlin and others suffer, Catherine's anemia and her slowness in
coming to maturity are examples of the former; Bonnemort's
famous "crachats noirs," an example of both. The Belgian
doctor was also concerned about cleanliness and sexual promiscuity in the mining area. He called attention to "les lits mal
faits et dont on ne renouvelle pas assez fréquemment les draps."
Readers of the novel will recall that even in the reasonably
clean Maheu household the sheets served for a full month and
that the Levaque woman changed hers only once in three.[42]
At Anzin, Zola became aware of the sexual promiscuity brought
about by the living conditions of the miners. He found full
confirmation of that in the treatise by Boëns-Boisseau.[43] What
is more, this source-book not only shows that Zola's references
to chlorosis, ephemeral fever, asthma, gingivitis, scrofula,
grisou burns, and stunted bodies among the miners were based
on reputable medical authority, but suggests, in Professor
Frandon's words, that "la diversité des types dans *Germinal*,
n'est donc pas habileté ou art de romancier; elle est imposée
pas les 'considérations générales' d'un traité médical." [44] Moreover, as Mlle Frandon does not fail to point out, Zola found
in this volume a confirmation of his theory of the "action
sociale et physique des milieux."

As for economics, Zola was influenced in his views by several
writers. On the question of costs of production he noted from
Amédée Burat that large production was required to lower the
"prix de revient" (cost price).[45] Leroy-Beaulieu's book informed him that in modern industry the capital investment is so
great that the equipment has to be used, in other words, that
industry is less and less capable of surviving a prolonged
strike.[46] From Yves Guyot's book, *La Science économique*, he
seems to have adopted the highly debatable notion that industrial depressions are caused "non par excès de production, mais
par excès de consommation." [47] It explains to some extent
Deneulin's remarks on the current crisis.[48]

The sources indicated so far are reference books or newspapers. Were there perhaps borrowings from other French
novels, in particular, those mentioned in our first chapter as

being a possible explanation of Zola's interest in the subject? In spite of the absence of any such indication in the "notes de travail," Professors Moreau and Frandon tend to think so. The question involves three different books: Hector Malot's *Sans famille* (1878), Maurice Talmeyr's *Le Grisou* (1880), and Yves Guyot's *Scènes de l'enfer social—La famille Pichot* (1882). Mlle Frandon has analyzed the relevant part of *Sans famille* and concludes that any resemblance between that book and *Germinal* is due to the fact that both authors drew from the same source: Simonin's *La Vie souterraine* (1867). In this she concurs with Zola himself who declared in the same interview in *Le Matin* already referred to: "A la fin de mon roman il y a une situation identique à celle du roman de M. Malot, *Sans famille*. Il y a une bonne raison à cela, c'est que tous deux nous l'avons prise dans la *Vie souterraine* de Simonin."

In this interview Zola denied any dependence on Talmeyr's *Le Grisou*. While Professor Frandon states that the relationship between *Le Grisou* and *Germinal* is limited, she obviously thinks it real. Both novels, she notes, begin with the hero on foot seeking work. True, but is this really more than mere coincidence? The *Ébauche* shows that Zola came to this arrangement rather slowly. It was partly dictated by the necessity of explaining Étienne Lantier's departure from Lille where *L'Assommoir* had left him. Both novels end with the hero walking on the highway. Here, as Professor Frandon admits, there is a great difference, for Lantier is headed for Paris and new activity, while Jean Jacquemin is on his way to death. Other details in the two novels are similar, and Mlle Frandon lists them with care. But practically all, such as the "doubles tartines de beurre et de fromage," the furniture in the miner's house, the portraits of sovereigns on the wall, the women working in the depths of the mine clad in masculine attire, the moral consequences of promiscuity, could have come just as well from Zola's own *Notes sur Anzin*. Mlle Frandon admits as much, but her admission is relegated to the notes placed at the back of the book. There is also in each novel a cave-in which breaks the legs of Toubeau in *Le Grisou* and of Jeanlin in *Germinal*. But surely this kind of accident does not require a source; in a novel dealing with mines, it is "tout indiqué."

Professor Frandon makes much of the fact that Ghilaine in *Le Grisou* is raped by Jacquemin who accidentally caused an explosion and then took advantage of her in the ensuing confusion. A child is born, and for thirty odd years Ghilaine, mentally affected, lives a wretched life, forced even to beg in order to avoid starvation. Says Mlle Frandon:

> *L'Ébauche* manuscrite de *Germinal* atteste le souvenir dominateur de cet épisode. Zola songe à un personnage qui serait "une femme d'âge, mendiante, à moitié folle, quarante ans [c'est presque l'âge de Ghilaine dans la 2ᵉ partie du roman de Talmeyr] devenue muette à la suite d'un coup de grisou [...] elle mendie dans les rues [MS. 10307, f. 443] *L'Ébauche* attribue à Catherine [Maheu] seize ans, "Catherine serait une yercheuse, écrit Zola, roulant la houille dans les galeries basses." C'était l'âge et le métier de Ghilaine au moment du drame souterrain, et Zola, dans cette note, écrit "yercheuse" avec l'orthographe du *Grisou*.[49]

While these facts are correct, the *rapprochement* is very misleading. The "femme d'âge, mendiante, à moitié folle," etc. mentioned in Zola's *Ébauche* was thought of in connection with a personal drama for Jeanlin, and was in no way linked in Zola's mind with Catherine or Étienne. A glance at the complete text will show that Zola hesitated between giving Jeanlin "un petit ménage, une fillette de douze ans comme lui," etc. and giving him for mistress "une femme d'âge, mendiante, à moitié folle."[50] We know that he rejected the second idea in favour of the first. The "femme d'âge, mendiante, à moitié folle" was never incorporated into the novel.[51] The one really significant fact, cited by Mlle Frandon, is that Zola did write "yercheuse" in describing Catherine in his *Ébauche* (f. 440), whereas he customarily wrote the word with an "h". This would seem to prove that Zola had at least seen the text of

Le Grisou and the other details suggest that he had read it. But there is no proof here that he used it.

Other resemblances between *Le Grisou* and *Germinal*, such as the question of wages and the humanitarian and social theories expressed do not prove that the former is the source of the latter. The measures taken at Anzin to reduce the cost of the coal (the "prix de revient") readily explain what happens in *Germinal*.[52] And Zola's reading of Laveleye's *Le Socialisme contemporain* as well as his own liberal tendencies accounts more than adequately for the views expressed by Étienne and others. We find it difficult to agree with Professor Frandon that Zola owes much of anything to Talmeyr's novel. To read a book is not necessarily to use it.

Guyot's novel is a much more likely source. Some of the similarities, to be sure, result from the choice of subject. In a novel dealing with mines, an accident caused by an explosion of fire-damp (*le grisou*) or by a cave-in is practically inevitable and is in itself no proof of indebtedness. In a book relating a strike, a clash between the workers and the public authorities is again highly probable. Professor Morceau's contention[53] that the roving mob scene and the clash between miners and soldiers in *Germinal* were borrowed from *L'Enfer social* seems exaggerated. The first item is the product of Zola's imagination at work on material that he got from the *Gazette des Tribunaux* and from his own visit to Anzin. His "notes de travail" not only prove that, but also show pretty conclusively that the clash between miners and soldiers was strongly affected by similar episodes at La Ricamarie and Aubin in 1869. The fact that the soldiers fire spontaneously in *Germinal*, as they did at La Ricamarie, indicates that Zola did not use Guyot's text where the officer deliberately orders the volley.

Professor Frandon's statement that "c'est de *L'Enfer social* que procède, dans *Germinal* et déjà dans l'*Ébauche* manuscrite, cette évocation reprise plusieurs fois du 'dieu inconnu' suçant 'la vie des meurts de faim qui le nourrissaient,'[54]" also appears exaggerated, in view of the fact that the idea was a commonplace of socialist oratory and also in view of the fact that

Guyot identifies this god with Onésime Macreux, the owner
of the mine. The latter, as Mlle Frandon points out, is too
much a caricature to be effective. Zola's "dieu inconnu" is
rather the big corporation, the trust, which seems like a
remote and mysterious force to the ignorant miners.

But it is possible, as Mlle Frandon suggests, that Guyot's
unscrupulous grocer Pierre Consigne who refuses credit and
seduces girls, and his violent death at the hands of enraged
women may have influenced Zola's sketch of Maigrat, though
the author of *Les Rougon-Macquart* certainly outstripped Guyot
in horror when he thought of the mutilation scene. The sale
of house furnishings, in particular a clock, calls to mind a
similar occurrence in *Germinal*. The threat of importing foreign
strike-breakers is common to both books. And the moment in
Germinal which depicts the miners on their way to the night
meeting in the forest is strikingly similar to the corresponding
scene in *L'Enfer social*.[55] It is difficult to avoid the conclusion
that *Germinal* owes something to Guyot's novel, though
L'Enfer social was possibly even more useful, as Mlle Frandon
says, in showing Zola certain pitfalls to be avoided. In any
event, we agree that in comparison with *L'Enfer social*, *Germinal*
is characterized by "une ampleur aisée qui donne un rythme
plus large, plus naturel, plus vrai au déroulement de la vie des
mineurs," that while both books reveal a sincere concern for
human suffering and injustice, Zola's possesses in addition
"le sens de la vie et le don de l'exprimer." [56]

While *Germinal* is admittedly a heavily documented novel,
owing much to a multiplicity of sources, it is nevertheless far
more than a compilation of natural and social history. The
sources themselves indicate that although, in accordance with
naturalistic theory, Zola wanted facts, he was also concerned
with the colourful, the dramatic, the picturesque, the effective.
He always kept in mind the intellectual and the artistic need
of the individual chapter or part. In a given paragraph or page,
the documentation may be dominant, but if we look at the
whole, we see that the novelist is always in command, always
alert to create the total as well as the immediate impression he

wishes to convey. A comparison of almost any one of the sources reveals this preoccupation. Just in the matter of geography, purely physical details have been adjusted to the philosophical and dramatic requirements of the book.[57] The volumes of Laveleye, Simonin, and Dormoy, the newspaper reports of the 1869 strikes, and other documents are handled in comparable fashion.[58] If *Germinal* were but a piecing together of facts and quotations, it would not be the work of indignation, compassion, and, in the last analysis, hope, that most literary critics have proclaimed it to be.

CHAPTER IV

ZOLA'S CHAPTER PLANS

W HILE the *Ébauche* included the main lines of the action and established many of the characters —though it did not give names to all—the division of the novel into parts and chapters had still to come. We find this activity going on in the *Plan par parties* and the two sets of chapter plans. The portraits of the *Personnages* also contribute some items to the action, and Zola frequently refers to them in his chapter outlines. But, of course, no labour of chapter construction is found within these preliminary portraits which in general are devoted to the characteristics and physical appearance of the actors in the drama. Because of that (and because it is impossible to generalize with certainty about the time of their composition, except to state that they were composed after the *Plan par parties* and before the second set of chapter plans,[1]) discussion of them is reserved for the next chapter.

The *Plan par parties*, expanded, as we have seen, from six to seven parts, gives only thumbnail outlines of individual chapters. The first batch of regular chapter plans does more. We frequently find here the substance of a chapter though the material is often set down without regard for the exact order in which it will appear in the finished product. The second chapter plan usually attends to that, rearranging and coordinating the data of the earlier plan, correcting it and adding new material when desirable. While both sets represent a labour of organization more than of creation, there is nearly always, naturally enough, an advance toward perfection from the summary outline in the *Plan par parties* through the first detailed plan into the later one. A few examples will serve as illustration.

The opening chapter of the book is outlined in the *Plan par parties* as follows: "Arrivée d'Étienne. Conversation avec le vieil ouvrier. Celui-ci entièrement posé. Toute son histoire et celle de la mine [les accidents*].[2] Le dieu capital au fond inconnu. Description de la fosse la nuit. Poser l'Internationaliste." At the top of the *feuillet*: "Premiers jours de mars 66, un lundi." (MS. 10307, f. 1). While these lines do not evoke the windswept plain, while they say nothing of the industrial depression, while they fail to identify the "vieil ouvrier," they give, even at this stage, some of the essential elements of the chapter.

The earlier of the two detailed plans [3] begins to fill in lacunae and develop the data so briefly presented. The novelist emphasizes here certain descriptive elements of the chapter: the solitary walker on the road from Marchiennes to Montsou, the blackness of the night, the icy wind over the vast plain, the fantastic aspect of the mine looming up in the darkness.[4] The old worker is now identified as Bonnemort and some information about him added: "Il s'est nommé, il a dit que son grandpère a été un des premiers à forer l'autre puits, le vieux, la fosse Réquillard (*sic*), lui a travaillé au Voreux et maintenant on a fait de lui un charretier." [5] The "dieu capital" of the *Plan par parties* is characterized a little more specifically: "Capital, actionnaires: tabernacle reculé, dieu vivant et mangeant les ouvriers dans l'ombre" (f. 15). With regard to the history of the mine, Zola tells himself that it should be "telle qu'elle doit être dans la bouche du vieux" (f. 14). Then some of the conversation between Étienne and Bonnemort is indicated, in particular, the question of ownership is raised: "Quand Étienne demande à qui appartient le Voreux, Bonnemort répond: Je ne sais pas. Histoire de la Cie. Finir par les actionnaires inconnus là-bas qu'il désigne d'un geste vague dans la nuit noire [le dieu capital, inconnu, accroupi*]." [6] The two men also speak of the industrial depression: "Une conversation triste sur la crise qui s'étend partout, nommer des industries, des usines." But Zola takes care to add: "La crise posée, non expliquée, mais posée comme elle doit l'être entre les deux personnages." [7] Then he wonders whether to introduce Rasseneur's "cabaret". A "non" written in the margin gives the answer. As for the Internationaliste (*i.e.* a representative of the International) suggested in the *Plan par parties*, no reference is made to him now unless it is included in the question concerning Rasseneur's "cabaret", for in the *Ébauche* (f. 456/53–457/54) the "cabaretier" was a member of the International. A few other details are added to the above so that in the four *feuillets* devoted to this chapter, one observes a substantial start toward the final accomplishment.

The later plan not only arranges this material more carefully, setting up the order which will be followed in the finished chapter, but it brings additions and improvements. Étienne's search for work during the preceding days and his destitution are sketched with greater exactitude and fullness than before: "depuis quinze jours[8] il rôde, allé et repoussé partout. On lui avait parlé de Marchiennes. Il est allé dans les ateliers de constructions Sonneville. Rien. Arrivé le samedi, cherché partout, achevé son pain le dimanche soir et reparti dans la nuit, le lundi matin, ayant couché dans un coin de chantier et renvoyé par un surveillant. Il n'a plus de pain, plus rien devant lui, que deviendra-t-il?"[9] This is not only situated in its definitive place in the chapter, but is closer to the final text than the corresponding lines of the earlier plan.[10] Then Bonnemort's history is more completely outlined: "Galibot, puis herscheur, puis mineur, puis remblayeur et raccommodeur, et enfin charretier."[11] His nickname is to be explained: "Son rire, pourquoi il s'appelle Bonnemort." To emphasize the effect of years underground, the phenomenon of his black spittle, his *crachat noir*, is introduced. The fate of his father "tué à la mine" is added. His comings and goings, while Étienne waits in the darkness, are specified.

On the question of ownership this later outline brings the planning a step closer to the final text: "Le vieux redescend lorsqu'il nomme le directeur M. Hennebeau. La mine est à lui, demande Étienne.—Oh! non.—A qui est-elle alors?—Ah, on ne sait pas, à des gens! Et son geste dans l'horizon noir, le dieu capital, inconnu, accroupi—Le tabernacle, le dieu qui devore les ouvriers dans l'ombre."[12] Some of this language will survive into the finished product.

At the end of this plan, the chapter is well organized, ready for the labour of creation.

An even more striking illustration of the progress toward perfection in Zola's planning is seen in the history of chapter 7 in Part IV.[13] The paragraph in the *Plan par parties* says briefly: "La réunion dans le bois, [Rien que des mineurs*] au milieu de laquelle ils [*i.e.* the lacrosse players] tombent. Jenlain s'y grise (son meurtre). [Le vieil ouvrier, épisode. Le dieu capital*]. Réunion très violente. [Le mouchard. *Antoine poussant chez le patron*]. La violence résolue. On arrêtera le travail. Ouvriers du patron. Montrer l'ingénieur. C'est là que reparaissent les actionnaires." [14] Zola quickly discarded the notion of bringing the engineer and the shareholders into the scene and he soon included women and children as well as miners.

The big difference between the two detailed outlines is that the earlier one (f. 210–216) forecast a meeting by day rather than at night. The second (f. 205–209) not only envisages a night meeting in the forest, but indicates very specifically the importance of the growing light of the rising moon. Étienne's first words are to be delivered in relative darkness ("Tout de suite un premier discours d'Étienne, lent et froid, (obscurité encore)" (f. 206), then, "sa voix se hausse, il se livre tout du coup, tandis que la lune commence à l'éclairer sur son tronc d'arbre." Bonnemort is to be spot-lighted by the moon. "Et l'épisode du vieux Bonnemort dans la pleine lune: le vieillard silencieux qui a une seconde crise de bavardage, opposition: tout ce qu'il dit, le passé, ce qu'il a souffert" (f. 208). Étienne is to be carried away by the situation and his emotions: "Étienne est-il débordé? Non, emporté lui-même." And the moonlight still sheds its mysterious, hypnotic radiance at the end: "Finir par un grand cri qui se perd sous la lune." [15]

The skeleton outline quoted from the *Plan par parties* gives little idea of the effectiveness of the final arrangement. The addition of the women and children makes the collective emotion, culminating almost in hysteria, more impressive, more disturbing than it would be without them. The shift from a day meeting to a night meeting in the growing moonlight is a stroke of genius, for it enables Zola to bring into his chapter a theatrical effect otherwise difficult to achieve. It will permit him to play on that contrast of light and dark, white and black which in one way or another is a fairly constant characteristic of the book. Without these changes and improvements the finished chapter might well lack the dramatic tension which it clearly possesses.

Readers of the novel will recall that chapter 5 of Part V [16] is devoted in part to Hennebeau's painful discovery of the scandal in his house and in part to the march of the mining men and women as seen through the eyes of Négrel, Mme Hennebeau, and the girls. The chapter evolved quite slowly in Zola's planning. First of all, it simply does not exist in the *Plan par parties* where the fifth chapter contains the material found in the first part of chapter 6 of the completed book. Furthermore, nowhere in Part V of the *Plan par parties* is there any mention of Hennebeau's discovery of his wife's infidelity.

Of the two detailed outlines, the earlier one (f. 260–264) shows Zola uncertain and groping as far as the arrangement and even the content of this chapter are concerned. He thinks (f. 260) of beginning the chapter with the return trip of Mme Hennebeau, the three girls, and Négrel from their excursion, including of course at this point the march of the mining men and women [17] while the four women and the engineer remain hidden in a shed. He even seems uncertain of the method to use in revealing Mme Hennebeau's adultery to her husband for he writes (f. 261): "Il peut avoir surpris sa femme avec son neveu, ou se douter de quelque chose." The next *feuillet* suggests that his wife and her companions return before the end of the chapter and that his house is already surrounded and under attack. The last *feuillet* (264) includes the notion (which Zola had jotted down much earlier) [18] of the "objet perdu par Madame Hennebeau dans le lit de Paul: un flacon d'or," but the novelist wonders at the same time whether it should go into this chapter or the next. This *feuillet* (264) is, in fact, puzzling, for, in addition to various

uncertainties, it contains at least one item, the death of
Maigrat,[19] which makes one suspect that it may have been
penned later, *after* the first plan for chapter 6.

The later plan (f. 252–259) indicates that Zola has made up
his mind on the principal events of chapter 5 and their order
of presentation. The outline begins: "M. Hennebeau resté chez
lui. Le prendre, lorsque Mme Hennebeau est partie pour
chercher Cécile. Il peut être neuf heures du matin [. . .]"
The return trip of Mme Hennebeau, Négrel, and the girls,
with the march of the mining men and women is placed much
later in the chapter as it will be in the novel. While this outline
is very complete, it does not include Hennebeau's beating the
bed with his fists. That is a "trouvaille" of the moment of
final composition. But this later plan represents a marked
advance in effectiveness over its predecessor. It is noteworthy
that in both plans Zola wants to show that social revolution,
however important, will not guarantee human happiness.[20]

The final chapter of Part V in the published novel not only
throws together the material of the last two chapters in the
Plan par parties, but brings the violence which has finally
broken out in this strike to the extraordinary climax which no
reader can ever forget.

The initial outline [21] for this chapter states almost at once
that "Cécile affolée ne veut pas rester." She wishes to rejoin
her parents, and the outline implies (in accordance with f. 262)
that Mme Hennebeau and the others have already returned
from their excursion and are inside the General Manager's
house. Leaving it, accompanied by a maid, she is threatened by
the mining women who take her for a relative of Mme
Hennebeau. Old Bonnemort tries to save her, but she imagines
that he wants to kill her and screams with terror. Rescued by
the opportune arrival of her parents and Deneulin, she is led
back to the house. The miners hurl stones at the dwelling until
the report of the imminent arrival of the "gendarmes" scatters
them. But the outline goes on to show Zola's preoccupation
with the question of violence. On f. 274 he writes: "Comme
intensité, il faudrait pour finir que la bande se livrât à une

véritable sauvagerie." On the next *feuillet* the notion of the
emasculation of the corpse of a "surveillant," which he had
thought of as he penned the *Ébauche* (f. 425/24–426/25) comes
to his mind as a fitting climax. The second plan will assign
that fate to Maigrat who was absent from the *Plan par parties*
and the initial outline for this chapter, although, as we have
seen, his death was mentioned on f. 264 of chapter 5.

The second plan rearranges the material quite radically. The
chapter will open with the mob of miners before or close to
Hennebeau's house where Mme Hennebeau and the girls have
not yet returned. Étienne is there, and Souvarine and Rasseneur
make their appearance. The Grégoires calmly cross to Hennebeau's dwelling as they will in the novel. Maigrat is placed in
the kitchen, which he leaves to go protect his store. Then the
plan calls for the return of Mme Hennebeau and the girls with
the scene involving Cécile coming next. This time Bonnemort,
"pris d'une fureur sombre," really tries to strangle her. The
outline then says: "Étienne, à ce moment, s'apercevant de ce
qui se passe et voulant les jeter sur le magasin. Mais Deneulin
[à cheval (?)*] a paru, Paul revient, Hennebeau lui-même sort,
et la bataille où l'on ne sait plus qui veut sauver Cécile et qui
veut la perdre." [22] After her rescue, we have the scene of
Maigrat's fall, his death, the emasculation of his corpse, and the
triumphal parade of the women. The chapter is to end with the
flight of the miners before the imminent arrival of the "gendarmes," the delivery of patty shells to the Hennebeau's kitch-
en, the vision of a fire in the Vandame forest, and a glimpse of
the "paysage industriel sous le ciel étoilé." This second plan
forecasts the chapter very much as we know it. Only a few
minor differences exist. Once again a chapter evolves from very
tentative beginnings to a skilful and impressive completion.

Organizational difficulties were apparently quite serious for
the novelist throughout the last two parts of the novel. The
Plan par parties forecast seven chapters for both parts instead of
the five for Part VI and six for Part VII [23] that finally emerged.
Aside from that, several interesting developments may be
noted. In the second (*i.e.* later) outline for chapter 1 of Part VI

the radical priest is mentioned, without name, for the first time.[24] Quite possibly this is the precise moment of his creation. To be sure, he is referred to in the published novel in chapter 5 of Part IV where we are simply told that abbé Joire has just been appointed elsewhere and that his successor is "un abbé maigre, aux yeux de braise rouge." But there is no reference to him in the preliminary outlines for that chapter. Nor did he exist in the *Ébauche* or in the *Personnages*. It seems probable that he must have been created while Zola was composing the second set of chapter plans and in all likelihood when he penned this particular outline.

While the earlier detailed plan for chapter 2 suggests the utter misery of the Maheu family, it does not pick on Alzire as the child to be ill,[25] nor does it include anything about the rows between the women of the *coron* or Dansaert's scandalous conduct. The later plan attends to these points, though even here Alzire is not represented as actually dying.[26] In chapter 3 the item on Pologne, cooked and served to Souvarine without his prior knowledge, was not thought of by the novelist till he came to write his second outline.[27] But perhaps the most important developments occur in connection with chapter 6 which relates the clash between the miners and the soldiers guarding the pit. Not only did Zola divide this narrative into two chapters in the *Plan par parties*, but in his first detailed plan he concluded that two chapters would really be preferable.[28] By the time he penned his second plan he had definitely decided on a single chapter which, on the whole, he arranges as we find it in the book. One important difference, however, between the novel and the preliminary plans is that in the earlier stages Zola, influenced by events at La Ricamarie, intended to have the soldiers try to remove their prisoners from the vicinity of the mine. At La Ricamarie the troop had attempted to take them to St Étienne via "le sentier creux du Brûlé." They were stoned by the miners while on their way. In the second plan Zola writes: "Le cortège s'est organisé, mais il doit passer sous la pente qui conduit au coron, dans une sorte de chemin creux, à côté des deux tas de briques. Et le combat à coups de pierre." [29]

In the final composition, while keeping the idea of having the soldiers take some prisoners, Zola abandoned this march in favour of a stationary scene.

In the last part of the novel,[30] devoted to the great catastrophe, some of the individual chapters underwent marked change in the course of the novelist's planning. The earlier plan for chapter 1 makes no mention of the dinner at La Piolaine which will be carefully arranged for in the later.[31] Souvarine's act of sabotage is indicated in both detailed plans for chapter 2 but the earlier plan displays hesitation on Zola's part on the question of motivation and on whether the nihilist realizes that his act will probably kill some of his comrades. As Zola finally works it out, Souvarine's chief motive is to "attaquer le capital." [32] He knows in advance that some miners will be below [33] but is not aware till after his sabotage that Étienne and Catherine will be among them.[34] In neither plan do we find any reference to the execution of Souvarine's mistress. The earlier detailed outline for chapter 3 is brief and indicates that the chapter itself was to be brief: "Chapitre court, d'une belle horreur" (f. 355). In the final composition it became one of the longer chapters of the book. On the last *feuillet* of this outline, Zola thought—apparently for the first time—of leaving Chaval below ground and having him killed by Étienne. The later plan, with one or two exceptions,[35] forecasts the chapter very much as we know it.

In all the stages of planning the central episode of the fourth chapter was to be the rescue operations with the heroism and death of Zacharie. In the *Plan par parties* and the first detailed chapter plan, the rescuers try to reach the trapped miners by digging toward them from the Jean-Bart mine; in the later plan, they start from Réquillart. Obviously before composing the last plan, Zola had looked at his map. But the chief difference between the outlines involves the fate of Cécile Grégoire. In the earlier one, Zola was inclined to go ahead with the marriage and to predict that Mme Hennebeau would console herself with Deneulin's son returned from Africa.[36] In the later plan, the murder of Cécile is decided. Her death, says Zola, is to be a part of the social conflict: "Mais surtout bien montrer cette résultante des Maheu contre les Grégoire, faire sentir le dénouement tragique." [37] It also fits in with the lugubrious scenes going on at the pit-head and underground.

That underground scene, treated in the next chapter, gave the novelist, in some respects, considerable trouble. In the early stages the problem of Chaval was bothersome. Unmentioned in the *Plan par parties*, Chaval appears in the first detailed outline, but his fate remains uncertain. "Étienne doit-il tuer Chaval, là, ou même à la fin?" [38] And in the final plan the novelist writes: "Et faire revenir dans la tête d'Étienne l'idée du meurtre. Son besoin de tuer (sans ivresse, pourtant). Sa physiologie [. . .]. Enfin [Il finirait donc en assassin. Son besoin de meurtre satisfait*] comment il le tue, soit en combat, soit en se jetant sur lui (exaspéré par un fait et Catherine applaudissant). [Chaval voulant allumer le grisou peut-être*] Il a osé cette fois. Il jette le cadavre dans le plan incliné. [Chaval a des chandelles qu'on lui prend ou des provisions*]." [39] In the novel, Catherine's attitude is different, and Étienne's act is less in the realm of a hereditary psychosis than all the early planning would lead one to expect.

Had Zola clung to the arrangements found in the first detailed outline for the final chapter, the dénouement of *Germinal* would have been perceptibly different from what is. For in this early outline the Maheu's humpbacked daughter is still alive; Cécile Grégoire as well. Chaval, far from dead, is a *porion*, lording it over La Maheude and Étienne who, wishing as much as ever to kill him, decides to leave "enragé, prêt à toutes les luttes," and "pour faire cesser les cancans." [40] The later outline forecasts the chapter very much as we know it. The "dieu capital, accroupi" was not forgotten in any of the plans nor in the book. But in the later plan, as well as in the finished product, it is clearly subordinated to the theme of germination. This last chapter, like those discussed above, is a good example of the continued labour of creation which persisted, really, till *Germinal* appeared in volume form in 1885.

*   *   *

We find in the chapter plans an occasional bit of dialogue, a striking phrase, or descriptive word which Zola will incorporate into his final text. In the opening chapter, Étienne's question to Bonnemort about the ownership of the mine and the old man's reply is one such example. The "plaine rase," "le vent qui souffle, glacial," the "vision fantastique de la fosse" looming up in the darkness appear in identical or only slightly varying form in the chapter plans and in the printed text. Catherine's remark "Il ne faut pas boire" during her conversation with Étienne (ch. 4, Part I) is another. Her indignant exclamation: "Vous êtes tous des lâches" when Chaval is mistreated (ch. 4, Part V) is still another.[41] In the same category are the naive words of the Grégoires' maid: "Ils ne sont pas méchants" (ch. 6, Part V). The image of the mole ("les lâches ont donc reparu, les taupes, les chauve-souris") used by Chaval in his insults to Étienne (ch. 3, Part VI) is found in the preliminary plans as well as in the book. His final remark to Catherine in the same chapter plan: "Reste avec lui, puisque tu en veux et ne refous pas les pieds chez moi, ou malheur!" has passed with little change into the final text. Of course, these things are put in the novel in a fuller and more perfect context, but basically they are retained. When Souvarine leaves Montsou after his act of sabotage, some of the phraseology used by Zola in his early planning [42] reappears in the completed version, for here, too (though it is chapter 3 rather than chapter 2), the Russian goes off into the night, into the unknown, without casting a glance behind him. The very last sentence of the book contains a similar phenomenon, for in both chapter plans Zola wrote: "La terre grosse d'une sourde rumeur, et le siècle futur encore en germe dans le sillon, faisant déjà éclater le sol." [43] The definitive sentence is a little longer, a little more menacing with the introduction of the "armée noire, vengeresse," but it nevertheless retains elements of the planning stage.

While Zola's planning seems extremely, indeed, almost incredibly complete, we discover that here and there such is not the case. Take, for example, chapter 3 of Part III. The finished chapter, as we have it, opens and closes on the situation between

Catherine and Étienne now that he is not only living in the same house but sleeping in the same room with her. The second (*i.e.* later) detailed chapter plan establishes the definitive order of events in this chapter, but concerning the end says: "Finir en revenant à Catherine [. . .] Voir à trouver un épisode la nuit, qui terminerait le chapitre." (f. 126) So that the novel's final paragraph, beginning: "En octobre" and ending: "Plus ils vivaient côte à côte, et plus une barrière s'élevait, des hontes, des répugnances, des délicatesses d'amitié, qu'ils n'auraient pu expliquer eux-mêmes." This charming and rather touching paragraph was "found" at the time of actual composition.[44]

Other examples of incomplete planning or of arrangements changed at the moment of composition may well be cited. In the third chapter of Part IV the preliminary outlines (f. 168–171 and 172–175) state that part of Étienne's prestige at this point is due to a newspaper he receives, the paper not being named in either plan. Only when he came to write the chapter did Zola bestow upon it the name of *Le Prolétaire* which he changed before it went to the printer to *Le Vengeur*.[45] Hennebeau's most violent outburst of emotion in chapter 5 of Part V did not come to Zola's mind, as we have seen, in the planning stage. He thought of this gesture (the beating of the bed) as he penned the text of his chapter. The death of Alzire in chapter 2 of Part VI was apparently decided upon at the time of composition. In the fourth chapter of that same Part Zola intended, according to his second outline, to include the phenomenon of Catherine's first menstruation, brought about by the violence of her emotion when she is ejected by Chaval: "Dans ce tourment affreux je veux qu'elle se règle, trempée, etc." [46] But when he sat down to pen the chapter, he obviously decided that it was not the best place for this intimate event and postponed it to the first chapter of Part VII. And we noted the important change he made, at the moment of writing, in the arrangements for the last chapter of Part VI.

The final part of the novel gave Zola less trouble in composition than it had given in the planning stage, but even here the text reveals some changes or additions. In the first chapter, for instance, the setting for the conversation between Étienne and Souvarine is along the canal instead of at Rasseneur's and in that conversation Zola includes the narrative of the execution of Souvarine's mistress which was absent from the preliminary plans. In the fifth chapter, Zola's hesitations on Étienne's motives in killing Chaval are finally resolved only as he composes his definitive text.

*   *   *

Let us not forget that quite apart from the establishment of a given item or a given motive, the actual writing of the text is an act of literary creation, not a merely mechanical task. While the chapters of the novel are much shorter than those of *L'Assommoir*, for example, they are still three or four times longer than the average chapter plan. In the final stage of composition, the characters take on life, the dialogue is really perfected, the narrative thoroughly unfolded, the stylistic effects weighed and adopted. In a later chapter of this study some of these accomplishments will be analyzed. Here, we wish simply to give an example of the transformation of a brief paragraph in one of the preliminary plans into the finished product.

Chapter 3 of Part IV was to end, according to Zola's second outline, by Étienne's decision, made after leaving the Maheus' house, to send for Pluchart.

> "Finir par une promenade d'Étienne, ce qui me redonne le coron et le Voreux surtout. Ce soir-là, la machine d'extraction peut s'arrêter. Rencontrera-t-il Souvarine qui quitte sa machine? [Maheu rencontré, pas de poisson*]. Il se décide à ce que Pluchart vienne pour une réunion privée, espoir que l'Internationale les soutiendra s'ils adhèrent. Mais un brusque doute surtout, la peur de mener les camarades à la misère et à la mort, cela dans le crépuscule. Mais ne pas finir sur le doute, finir au contraire sur l'espoir de l'Internationale [bouffée d'orgueil en lui*], sur l'ambition, etc. en entrant peut-être chez Rasseneur." [47]

Now when the novelist came to write the last section of the

chapter, he began, in accordance with his plan, by Étienne's walk: "Dehors, la nuit tombait déjà, une nuit glaciale, et la tête basse, Étienne marchait, pris d'une tristesse noire." The mood, induced, in part, by the preceding scene in the Maheus' house, is reinforced by the black, icy night, reminiscent of the bitter night of the opening chapter. As forecast in the plan he sees the *coron*, but here Zola shifts from the exact order of his outline, for before permitting Étienne to move on to Le Voreux, he uses the vision of the mining village to raise up in the young man all that distressing doubt which in the planning stage was to be placed after the decision to send for Pluchart. Sixteen or seventeen lines, developed from a brief sentence of twenty-two words, are devoted to an acute analysis of Étienne's thought and emotion. The passage is packed with phrases and words, all tending to the same effect: "le coron sans pain, [. . .] ces petits qui ne mangeraient pas, [. . .] la mélancolie affreuse du crépuscule, [. . .] la vision du désastre: des enfants qui mouraient, des mères qui sanglotaient, tandis que les hommes, hâves et maigris, redescendaient dans les fosses." He is so disturbed that "ses pieds butaient sur les pierres," and the idea that he may have caused the misfortune of his comrades filled him with an "insupportable angoisse."

Then it is that he finds himself before Le Voreux. The paragraph which Zola now writes is extremely effective. Here, too, the "masse sombre des bâtiments" heavy under the "ténèbres croissantes" recalls the grim scene of the opening chapter. Only here there is no hum of activity. In this deserted coal yard, lying there under great motionless shadows, this mass of buildings seemed like a corner of an abandoned fortress (au milieu du carreau désert, obstrué de grandes ombres immobiles, on eût dit un coin de forteresse abandonnée). And here there is a special anguish, for with the stopping of the "machine d'extraction," life seems to have departed from the very walls. Not a voice could be heard, not a lantern seen. As Zola puts it: "l'échappement de la pompe lui-même n'était qu'un râle lointain, venu on ne sait d'où, dans cet anéantissement de la fosse entière." In such words there is a suggestion of a larger phenom-

enon, of something mysterious and awesome. This eloquent
paragraph, be it noted, was inspired by a sentence and a half
(with a maximum of eleven or twelve words) in Zola's plan.

A second thought now crosses Étienne's mind. This idle
machinery means that the company is suffering too. And Zola
proceeds to put into effect his intention of closing on a note of
hope. He, therefore, fills the young man's mind with a resurg-
ence of optimism, unrealistic and romantic. If the company
cannot be defeated, at least its victory would cost it dear. The
miners might as well die straight away as die little by little of
starvation and injustice. Ill-digested readings in which examples
of people "qui avaient incendié leurs villes pour arrêter l'ennemi" or of men letting themselves die of hunger "plutôt que
de manger le pain des tyrants" helped replace his gloom and
doubt. In this re-awakening of his faith "des bouffées d'orgueil
reparaissaient et l'emportaient plus haut." Romantic visions of
personal success as "a triumphant leader renouncing power and
placing all authority in the hands of the people" ("son refus du
pouvoir, l'autorité remise entre les mains du peuple, quand il
serait le maître") filled his revery.

Étienne is brought out of this trance-like meditation by
Maheu who (in contrast to the item in the outline) has caught
and sold a magnificent trout. But still buoyed up by new hope,
he enters Rasseneur's "cabaret" to announce his decision to
send for Pluchart. "Sa résolution était prise, il voulait organiser
une réunion privée, car la victoire lui semblait certaine, si les
charbonniers de Montsou adhéraient en masse à l'Internationale."

Thus does Zola build two substantial and frequently eloquent
pages from a brief, pedestrian outline. Other examples could be
cited in abundance, for every page of the finished novel reveals
the creative work that went into the composition. The mind
and hand of a powerful artist are present throughout.

CHAPTER V

THE CHARACTERS OF "GERMINAL"

To discuss the origin, the formation, the significance not only of the important characters of *Germinal*, but also of some of the minor ones is the aim of the present chapter. Are these characters entirely the products of creative imagination, or do they reflect to some extent people of flesh and blood whom Zola knew or met or read about? What is their rôle in the novel? Are they individuals or mere types? Are they credible or incredible? The answers to such questions can help in the evaluation of Zola's art as a novelist.

Most of the characters of the book were born as Zola composed the *Ébauche*, Étienne Lantier being the great exception. Undoubtedly the eldest son of Gervaise Macquart was destined for a rôle in *Germinal* before the first line of the *Ébauche* was written.[1] The others do not share that honour. Some, like the Durands (later, Maheus), were soon conceived of and immediately named; many remained nameless to the very end of that preliminary draft. The principal actors in the drama, whether named or not, are already characterized and their rôles sketched out. Further details and developments are found in the chapter plans and in the portraits which we find under the heading of *Personnages* in pages 6–95 of manuscript 10308. We recall that these portraits were composed before the second set of chapter plans,—more or less simultaneously with the first.[2]

The preliminary portraits give us a physical and psychological picture of the character in question, his age, his connection or rivalry with other participants in the action. Sometimes his rôle in the book is completed or modified. Occasionally, as Van Tieghem says,[3] the novelist comments on some bit of action in which the person will be involved or sets limits to his state of mind; more than once the analysis evokes a scene. In many cases the final text of the novel contains few surprises for the reader of these character sketches. Not in all, however.

It is, therefore, desirable to study in detail Zola's creation of a number of characters and to reproduce the text of some of the portraits.

Zola's theory of the naturalistic novel contains the central notion that men are the product of their environment and their heredity. This is pre-eminently the case with the miners of *Germinal* and, on the capitalist side with the Grégoires. Both are clearly molded by the condition of their way of life. The miners would have to possess a powerful and unlikely streak of enterprise and ambition in their heredity to enable them to rise above that condition. Much the same can be said of the Grégoires. Their ancestor's spirit of enterprise apparently died with him, and the present family lives on the fortune created by others. At the same time neither the miners nor the capitalists are all alike. Without analyzing the heredity of men like Chaval or Levaque, Zola presents them as being quite different from Toussaint Maheu. In similar fashion Hennebeau and Deneulin are not identical with Léon Grégoire. The novelist is aware that all the miners are not angels and that the capitalists are not necessarily devils. Individual differences exist. Considerable variety is therefore found in the portraits of both picture galleries.

The Maheu Family

Originally named Durand and expanded in the course of the *Ébauche*, as we have seen, from four to ten members, the Maheu family stood in Zola's plans for the principal working-class representatives on whom he intended to concentrate interest. "Voilà la famille qui va crever de faim," he wrote in an early paragraph, immediately followed by a page in which he envisioned the husband's death, shot by the soldiers, and the widow's forced return to the mine. Simultaneously he thinks of Catherine's rôle, links Étienne emotionally with her, places them—only momentarily as it turns out—in the "petite mine," imagines a rivalry for her with a consequent fight, possibly a murder, alludes cryptically to her earnings, foresees her death, but not, he says, in the fashion of Miette, the "guerrière" of *La Fortune des Rougon*. All this is a nucleus to which the novelist adds as he advances in the *Ébauche*.

Reserving Catherine for special consideration, let us see how Zola fashions the other members of this central family. In the *Ébauche* and particularly in his portrait in the *Personnages*, Toussaint Maheu acquires greater importance and prestige as the novelist's plans develop. At first a second-rank figure, definitely under his wife's thumb, he is described as "ignorant, brutal," and mildly "alcoholic." [4] But about midway in the *Ébauche*, Zola decides to do a little better by him. While still dominated by his wife and still scarcely able to read and write, he is presented as a typical miner and as a "brave homme" who hates injustice.[5] Later, we are told that, like his wife, his anger is aroused by the poverty and hunger they experience.[6] To this basic conception, the portrait in the *Personnages*, written after Zola's visit to Anzin, adds a bit more. His physical appearance is carefully depicted [7] and does not differ essentially from what we find in the novel. Morally, he remains about the same; less alcoholic if anything. Sexually, he is above average, for he stays away from prostitutes. There is less emphasis on his subservience to his wife. He begins to emerge, as he will in the book, as much more the authentic head of his family than in the early pages of the *Ébauche*. Above all, he is a good workman and a reasonable man, angered only by injustice. The novel will show him to us as the sober, hardworking head of his mining squad. He is esteemed by his comrades and, therefore, chosen to be their spokesman.[8] One of the admirable scenes of the book is the meeting of the delegation of miners with Hennebeau, when this "quiet and orderly man" somehow finds the words with which to state the workers' case.

On Constance Maheu (called Mme Durand through most of the *Ébauche*) Zola planned to cast a fairly strong spotlight. While he finally let her husband share some of that illumination, he never pushed her into a dimmer background. From the beginning he wanted her to be an "original and living creation" (une création originale et vivante) [9]. Married after the birth of her first child, she is what her work and her life have made her: "hard toward her children, selfish, demanding that they work as she does." She is angered by the loss of their wages when they leave the family circle. She drinks but not to excess.[10] If she is "mauvaise," it is because of the life she has led. Zola adds that it is logical for character to result from work and poverty.[11] It is part of his concept of the naturalistic novel. This early sketch of La Maheude (as she is called in the last section of the *Ébauche*) is soon modified. Her moderate drinking becomes the still more venial vice of coffee-drinking. She is presented as being "raisonnable," "un peu bavarde," above all "pratique," but still made hard by her environment. Little by little during the strike she is carried away by her emotions.[12] She urges her husband into the battle and she is absolutely ruined in the end.

The portrait in the *Personnages* confirms and completes the above. The description of her physical appearance which Zola had postponed till he could visit a mining area[13] is now carefully set forth: "a long Flemish face, thick lips, big nose," etc.[14] At Anzin Zola had seen a mining wife, "la gorge abandonnée dans un corsage de laine." [15] He, therefore, attributes to La Maheude drooping breasts "roulant dans le corsage de laine." It suggests to him her casual display before Étienne and then the moment when Chaval twits her about it. The portrait insists, however, on her sexual decency, her fidelity to her husband. As the portrait was written before Zola made up his mind exactly what to do with Étienne, the question is raised as to whether she should become Étienne's mistress after the death of Maheu and Catherine. That problem is solved by the larger rôle given to Étienne and the final reasons adopted for his departure at the end of the book. With the completion of the *Ébauche* and the portrait in the *Personnages*, Constance Maheu is essentially the woman we see in the novel: a decent, hard-working miner's wife, struggling against heavy odds, reasonable, but capable of being inflamed and driven to violence; somewhat animalistic, to be sure, as a result of the near starvation level at which she is forced to live.

Of her seven children, five presented no serious problem to Zola. Except for his courage and devotion in attempting to save his sister and others trapped in Le Voreux mine, Zacharie, the oldest, is a third-rank figure. He is, at the end of Zola's planning and in the novel, what he was in the beginning, an unreflecting, commonplace fellow who has but one day of glory. The three youngest children, Lénore (first called Léonide), Henri, and Estelle require no comment. Alzire,[16] alone, gave Zola a moment's hesitation. She is an eight-year-old humpback. There was a humpbacked girl in Guyot's novel,[17] and Zola also saw one at Anzin during his visit, recording that fact in his notes.[18] His first notion was to make her vicious,[19] but he quickly gave that up in favour of casting her in the rôle of a precocious, charming little girl, serious beyond her years. Her death was not included in the *Ébauche* and merely predicted in the portrait in the *Personnages*. Her death scene in the novel was apparently a last minute "trouvaille," for it is not specifically mentioned even in the second set of chapter plans. While she is not treated brutally, like little Lalie in *L'Assommoir*, Alzire's life and death exploit very much the same sort of pathos.

Jeanlin has a complicated history. From the outset, Zola saw him as crippled in a mining accident, hesitating only on where to place that incident and on how serious to make it.[20] More important are the novelist's modifications of the boy's character. He seems, God wot, thoroughly delinquent in the novel, fully realizing Zola's intention of endowing him with all the vices.[21] But the fact is that he appears even worse in the *Ébauche*. At one point Zola thought of giving him as mistress an older woman, half crazy, rendered dumb by a "coup de grisou," reduced to begging in the streets.[22] Killed in the clash with the soldiers, her body would be dragged away by the boy during the night and thrown into the old, abandoned mine. This whole fantastic notion was wisely discarded by Zola. Another bit of excessive melodrama appears in the

Ébauche à propos of the murder of Jules. In this early stage, the youngster not only stabs him, but hurls the body, not yet dead, into the same pit.[23] This was wisely modified, for in the novel, Jules' body is lifeless when Jeanlin and Étienne lower it into the Réquillart mine. The plan of giving the boy a "petit ménage" which also appeared in the *Ébauche* is retained, but Zola abandoned the idea of making him syphilitic [24] and transmitting the disease to his even younger girl-friend who would die of it. In spite of these modifications, the boy is surely enough of a little monster to satisfy Zola's basic intention of showing in him "le total dégénéré de tous les vices des houillères".[25]

On Catherine Maheu Zola lavished more thought and care than on any other character of *Germinal*, save Étienne Lantier. Certainly there are more and longer references to this girl in the *Ébauche* than to most of the other actors in the drama. The portrait in the *Personnages*, however, shows that by then Zola had pretty well made up his mind about her.

From the outset Zola intended to have Catherine leave her family for a "galant," [26] to have Étienne attracted to her,[27] and to bring about her death. But she must die, he says, not in the clash with the soldiers, but rather from poverty,[28]—in other words, from the mine itself. Pregnant perhaps? In any case, she will die in Étienne's arms at the end of the book. At this point, Zola decides to make her, instead of the strong 18-year-old girl he had originally pictured, a combination of physical frailty and nervous energy,[29] lowering her age to 16. As the result of a last minute change, she becomes even younger in the novel.[30]

She is moreover, at this stage, a girl with the intellectual limitations of her environment. Zola first writes that she has "religious ideas," but immediately changes that to "superstitious." [31] While he does not insist on this trait in the *Ébauche*, he does not forget it. It appears very clearly in the novel.[32]

The vision of Catherine's death leads Zola, after some hesitation, to the notion of placing her and Étienne in the same group of miners at the time of the great catastrophe.[33] They would then be logically together when she breathes her last.

The *Ébauche* soon reveals, however, that Zola is still concerned about her rôle, fearing lest it be static. Seeking an active drama for her, he now conceives the idea of a rivalry between two men for her, a "brutal" and Étienne. "I will give her," he writes, "an almost unconscious tenderness for Étienne," and envisions already, for the end of the book, their "nuit de noces" in the mine.[34] The theme of combined love and death, of "noces consommées en présence de la mort," as Professor Robert has expressed it,[35] is present here in germ.

The next pages of the *Ébauche* (f. 438/37–439/38) show the author uncertain and groping with regard to the precise arrangements for this rivalry, and it is not till we reach f. 465/62 that we see Zola's ideas crystallizing in fairly definite form. Her rôle in the first three parts is pretty well established, though the novelist in a later stage of composition (after expanding the book from six to seven parts) will slow down the action, placing Catherine's departure from home in the last chapter of Part III rather than Part II. This will permit him better to depict the growing but partly unconscious desire of Étienne and Catherine for each other after he becomes a lodger in the Maheu household.

Catherine's growing fondness for Étienne is now the principal development of Zola's thoughts concerning her. He carries it somewhat farther in the *Ébauche* than he will in the novel, for in the former he suggests that in the 5th part "elle pourrait s'offrir." [36] In the novel, she will betray her preference by an involuntary act (chapter 3, Part VI). This is a much more effective arrangement. Her refusal to live with Étienne after the battle between the two men, her decision to return to Chaval's room, the moment when she looks out the window to tell Étienne that Chaval has not returned are all clearly forecast in the *Ébauche*. Her rôle in the clash with the soldiers, and her decision to return to work in the mine afterwards are equally well established. At the end of the *Ébauche*, her character and rôle will need little additional thought and labour. She has become and will remain a pathetic and attractive figure, "un produit et une victime du milieu," as the portrait in the *Personnages* soon puts it.

This portrait in the *Personnages* gives her physical appearance, emphasizing her delicacy and charm. It adds that she is anemic with difficulties of a female order which react on her character. Professor Frandon has explained that the source of this phenomenon is Boëns-Boisseau's book on miners' maladies. At the end of the portrait Zola adds that she knows how to read and write.

At this stage of Zola's planning, Catherine Maheu is and will remain one of his more attractive heroines, a creation of his sympathy, his compassion, and his affection.

The oldest member of this working-class family, Vincent Maheu, called Bonnemort, was in a sense the last born.

In the first half of the *Ébauche*, the man whom Étienne meets on the road to Marchiennes is not Bonnemort, but Toussaint Maheu.[37] In the second part of the *Ébauche*, we find a reference to a "vieil ouvrier" who has some of the characteristics that Vincent Maheu will ultimately have but who is not yet Vincent Maheu, for we are told that he lives alone in a hovel by the road.[38] Later in the *Ébauche*, the novelist gives this "vieil ouvrier" (whom Zola thought of calling le père Caffiaux) a comrade, a "raccommodeur," and evokes a picture of the two old men "smoking, their hands trembling and their heads wagging, walking in the midst of the events." [39] At length, in the concluding section of the *Ébauche*, as stated earlier, Zola decides to make his "vieil ouvrier" the father of La Maheude.[40] This is almost definitive. Finally, in the latter part of the appropriate portrait in the *Personnages*, the old man becomes the father of Toussaint Maheu and the oldest surviving member of a family which has worked in the mines since 1760.[41] Nowhere in the *Ébauche* or the portrait does he try to strangle Cécile. On the contrary, at the end of the *Ébauche* and in the first outline for chapter 6 of Part V he tries to save her. She mistakenly fears that his intentions are malevolent. Not till Zola composed his second set of chapter plans did he determine on the strangulation. A remnant of indecision about

Bonnemort's motives in the scene before Hennebeau's house lasted even into the manuscript text of the novel where the author says that "Bonnemort was unaware whether he wanted to strangle or help the girl." [42] This was corrected in proof, for by that time Zola had definitively mapped out the scene in chapter 4 of Part VII where there is no doubt about the old man's intention. There, his act is an essential part of the social conflict, the climax of the clash of classes as represented by the Maheus and the Grégoires. Of course, Bonnemort is presented throughout as a product of nearly fifty years' labour in the mines.

Étienne Lantier

When Zola began to map out in the late 1860's the *Rougon-Macquart* series, he assembled some of his ideas in a document entitled "Notes sur la marche générale de l'œuvre." There, he said that he intended to study "les ambitions et les appétits d'une famille lancée à travers le monde moderne, faisant des efforts surhumains, n'arrivant pas à cause de sa propre nature et des influences, touchant au succès pour retomber, finissant par produire de véritables monstruosités morales (le prêtre, le meurtrier, l'artiste)."[1] Then, in the "Premier plan remis à l'éditeur A. Lacroix," we find a brief summary of a novel on "le monde judiciaire," the hero of which was to be Étienne Dulac, the third child of a working-class couple. "Étienne," the author says, "est un des cas étranges de criminel par hérédité, qui, sans être fou, tue un jour, dans une crise morbide, poussé par un instinct de bête. De même que ses parents misérables et devenus vicieux, lèguent le génie à son frère Claude, ils lui lèguent le meurtre. Il y a des cas très saisissants de pareils faits."[2] It seems reasonably evident that this Étienne Dulac was to embody the "meurtrier," one of those moral monstrosities of the "Notes sur la marche générale de l'œuvre."

Long before Zola conceived of *Germinal*, Étienne Dulac had become Étienne Lantier. He was "born" in 1846, the son of Gervaise Macquart and her lover Lantier. He appeared as a child in *L'Assommoir* (1877) where he served as apprentice for

a while to Goujet, but then left Paris to learn a trade in Lille.³
In the last chapter of that novel he is reported as sending his
mother a "pièce de cent sous de temps à autre." ⁴

Zola's conception of Étienne in *Germinal* is partly con-
ditioned by the above, partly by the brief description which
appeared in the "Arbre généalogique" published in *Le Bien
public*, 6 January, 1878 (reproduced in *Une page d'amour*, the
same year), and is developed further in the *Ébauche* and in the
portrait in the *Personnages*. The latter was written in two stages:
f. 6–11 inclusive were probably composed after the first two
sections (*i.e.* f. 402/1–491/88) of the *Ébauche* were penned;
f. 12 after the last section (*i.e.* f. 492/89–499/96) was added.

Étienne's rôle in the novel, as outlined in the *Ébauche*, was
markedly modified sometime after Zola's trip to Anzin.
Before that trip and for a short but indefinite period after his
return to Médan, Zola thought of Étienne as being merely one
of the workers, not as one of the leaders. This is equally true
of the portrait in the *Personnages* up to the final paragraph
(*i.e.* f. 12). We shall therefore first discuss his personality and
rôle as Zola sketched them out during this early stage of
planning.

The physical appearance and certain tendencies of Étienne
are supposedly—in accordance with Zola's concept of the
experimental novel—governed by his heredity. The brief description in the "Arbre généalogique" states: "Élection de la
mère. Ressemblance physique de la mère, puis du père.
Hérédité de l'ivrognerie se tournant en folie homicide. État de
crime." In *L'Assommoir* Étienne clearly resembled his mother.
In *Germinal*, physically at least, he resembles rather more his
father. This is not mentioned in the *Ébauche*, but is spelled out
in the *Personnages*. Here, Zola states that Étienne first resembled
his mother (presumably in *L'Assommoir*), then his father, that
he is a good-looking fellow, rather short, dark, with a straight
nose, round chin, a gallant smile on white teeth; a Provençal,
to boot, somewhat dark-skinned with curly hair. He is clean
shaven but for a mustache. Zola adds: "Buisson le tambourinaire." ⁵ The allusion to Buisson indicates that in addition to

hereditary traits for Étienne, Zola had in mind the person who served Alphonse Daudet as model for Valmajour in *Numa Roumestan* and whom Zola had met.[6] Daudet describes his musician as "un beau garçon, la tête régulière, le front haut, barbiche et moustache d'un noir brillant sur le teint basané, un de ces fiers paysans de la vallée du Rhône qui n'ont rien de l'humilité finaude des villageois du centre." [7] Take away the "barbiche" and you have pretty much the portrait of Étienne Lantier.

More important is the question of alcoholism in Étienne's heredity. Not only is it mentioned in the description quoted from the "Arbre généalogique," but it is emphasized in the "notes de travail." Fairly early in the *Ébauche* Zola says: "Ne pas oublier que j'ai fait d'Étienne dans la famille un maniaque de l'assassinat. *Il faut que je termine* en indiquant cela." [8] He thinks almost immediately, but only temporarily, of having Étienne kill one of the daughters (of Deneulin or Hennebeau?) by pushing her into the old pit (i.e. Réquillart). Later in the *Ébauche* we find a new allusion to this trait: "Ne pourrais-je mettre un inconnu terrible chez lui, la névrose de la famille qui un jour se tournera en folie homicide [...] Une violence de bête fauve qui s'éveille en lui par moments, un besoin de manger un homme." [9] He finds this a good idea: "Cela serait très bon." This unhappy trait crops out again in Étienne's fight with Chaval and also when he sees Jeanlin kill the young soldier. And finally on *feuillet* 483/80 of the *Ébauche*, Zola attributes his departure from the mining area to his fear of murdering Chaval. Apparently Zola was thinking even in 1884 in terms of the moral monstrosities of the early notes. But, while, at first, Étienne may still be seen as the "meurtrier" that Dulac was to have been, modifications of that conception began to creep in. His resistance to violence is one such modification. Then, too, it is notable that never in the *Ébauche* or elsewhere is Étienne tempted to kill Catherine. On the contrary, her influence calms him: "et j'imaginerai alors qu'un amour heureux avec Catherine aurait pu l'adoucir." [10]

Most of these ideas are repeated in the portrait in the

Personnages. Here, Zola has more to say on the question of drink, instilling in Étienne such a fear of the effects of alcohol that in general he abstains from its use. It literally drives him crazy, arousing ideas of death for himself and for others. But the novelist plans to show him once under the influence of alcohol. Where and when? During the "ducasse"? Or in a spot where it would serve the dramatic action? [11] In the finished novel it comes in Part V when the gin Étienne drinks leads him to a violence of which he would not otherwise be guilty. Even here his drinking does not result in murder.

The "lésion nerveuse" with which Étienne is by heredity afflicted would be more important than it actually is, if Zola had maintained his original idea of using Étienne again in a novel on the Commune and/or in a novel on the railroads. The first plan for chapter 5, Part VII, shows that he was still thinking of that possibility.[12] But he gave up that notion and transferred the "besoin de tuer" divorced from any immediate alcoholic stimulus, which constitutes the most extreme aspect of this "lésion nerveuse," to a newly created brother of Étienne, Jacques Lantier, the hero of *La Bête humaine.* In the completed version of *Germinal*, this hereditary trait plays a part, but a relatively minor one. When Étienne finally kills Chaval, he acts almost as much in self-defense as under the domination of an irresistible, hereditary impulse.

From the earliest mention of Étienne Lantier in the *Ébauche*, Zola intended him to be in love with Catherine.[13] Like the novelist himself in his youth, Étienne is timid in his relations with girls. As Zola puts it in the *Personnages:* "Avec les filles il est un peu timide, avec des idées de violences, de les prendre et de se satisfaire." [14] He has had in the past only prostitutes. He wants Catherine honorably, at the same time strongly. No love *à la* Goujet, says Zola. "Idée de possession avec un fond d'honnêteté, de mariage possible. Une ou deux délicatesses peut-être, mais l'idée du mâle lâché, contrarié par des timidités premières." [15] Only at the end, in the bottom of the mine, after Chaval's death and just before her own, will Étienne possess her.[16]

Étienne's interest in Catherine is of double importance, as revealed in the *notes de travail* and confirmed by the novel. It provides, through his rivalry with Chaval, some of the human drama of the book. While the eternal triangle may be trite, it frequently produces excitement. It certainly does so in *Germinal*. But Étienne's love for Catherine, as finally worked out by Zola, is also a relatively pure and delicate phenomenon. It stands in marked contrast to the brutality that dominates much of the book. There is even genuine tenderness in Zola's analysis of their unspoken love.

Equally important in the early stages of composition is Zola's concept of Étienne as a reactor to the mining scene. The first mention of Étienne in the *Ébauche* says: "Il me faut arranger Étienne pour qu'il travaille au fond." [17] Here and a little later in the *Ébauche*, the novelist plans to use him as a "mécanicien." That is, after all, his trade. But the necessity of bringing him into closer contact with Catherine and the desire to show through Étienne's observation and experience the hardships endured by the men who actually get out the coal, led Zola to abandon that plan and to make him a miner. About midway in the *Ébauche*, Zola comes to the view that the best thing is to have Étienne dismissed from a railroad for insubordination, with the result that he is unable to find work in the railroad world. Nor can he find a factory job because of the industrial depression. The novelist then sees him tramping on the highway to Marchiennes where he meets "mon mineur" who helps him to find employment. "Voilà donc Étienne dans la mine." [18] Except for the fact that Étienne meets Bonnemort rather than Maheu, this plan remained unchanged, and Étienne is already in Zola's mind the "lien conducteur pour exposer toute la mine, l'enfer d'en bas." [19] He is, moreover, to be of a slightly superior education "pour les réflexions", and the book is to be in part "l'éducation de révolte du jeune homme," [20] who witnesses all the social injustices and is embittered by them. The fact that Étienne was not originally a miner, that he comes in from the outside permits a critical observation of the mining world that would have been much less likely and perhaps less convincing had the novelist chosen a life-long miner as his observer. It is a skilful arrangement.

On *feuillet* 435/34 of the *Ébauche* Zola raises the question of Étienne's survival or death in the great catastrophe. The problem gives the novelist little pause. Étienne must live, in order to represent "the eternal threat to capital, to society." As frequently in the *Rougon-Macquart* series, events are determined by what Professor Robert calls "leur valeur d'enseignement." [21]

Zola sums up in *feuillets* 482–483 of the *Ébauche* his conception of Étienne at this point of his planning. His early sentiment of revolt finds a more definite expression, indeed, a programme, at the time of the public meeting (at the Bon Joyeux). His feelings turn toward violence during the meeting in the wood and the events of the following day. His hereditary madness is aroused in his fight with Antoine and later in the presence of Jeanlin's murder of the soldier. He is driven to violence during the clash with the troops. At the end, he flees to avoid murder. Yet all that is accompanied by his affection and his tenderness for Catherine. There is, says Zola, an almost continual struggle in him between the two sides of his nature. He is, in short, an "homme très complexe dans une nature simple."

This view of Étienne is wholly confirmed in the portrait in the *Personnages* (up to the final paragraph) where Zola also includes other points we have previously mentioned, and where he explains a little more clearly that while Étienne is slightly better educated than the other workers, he still does not know much. He can read and write. He wants to learn. He reads some newspapers,[22] possesses a book or two. The nihilist and Rasseneur teach him socialism. His experience teaches him as well. "In short," says Zola, "Étienne, in *Germinal*, gets his socialist education." ("En somme, Étienne, dans *Germinal*, fait son éducation socialiste"). But he remains just one of the miners.

Then comes an important development. In a new section of the *Ébauche*, clearly written later, as we indicated, and in a new final paragraph added to the portrait in the *Personnages*, Zola conceived the notion of making Étienne the leader of the strike. It is for him a much more central and significant rôle. He arrives in the mining area as before and finds work. Then, as Zola puts it: "He has been a good worker, he talks, indulges in propaganda, and has acquired little by little great influence over his comrades. He is then a leader, not determining the strike, but accepting it, wishing to control it at first, then carried away himself, then going beyond what he wanted. And finish by the discredit into which he falls, the suspicions cast upon him, the end of his popularity, his complete downfall." [23] This arrangement, Zola adds, will permit a study of ambition, struggle, and ignorance in one of these "chefs de bagarre." It also permits the novelist to create a third ideological attitude in the miners' camp, for while Souvarine is still an anarchist, Rasseneur becomes a possibilist, and Étienne a "collectiviste autoritaire." Some of the traits of Basly, the secretary of the miners' federation of Anzin, whom, we recall, Zola met in February 1884, and to whom the novelist referred in the Ébauche (f. 456/53–457/54) are now redistributed. Instead of making the local "cabaretier" the secretary of the miners' group and placing him in communication with an official of the International, Zola transfers those functions to Étienne. Professor Frandon has quite correctly called attention to that development.[24]

This distinction among the three men is logical and clear. But in the course of further planning, it became more complicated. For Étienne, attracted by Souvarine and by some aspects of the latter's philosophy, is momentarily won over to an extreme position. While, in the plan for chapter 4, Part IV, Zola says: "Et là tout Souvarine [. . .] ses idées, compléter la théorie anarchiste, Étienne ne va pas encore jusque là," [25] in the plan for chapter 7 (Part IV) which is devoted to the night meeting in the wood, Étienne does go to greater extremes. His programme, says Zola, is "en partie le programme de Souvarine." [26] Later, in the plan for chapter 3, Part VI, we find a statement which not only complicates but confuses the situation, for Zola writes: "Rasseneur c'est Darwin, c'est Karl Marx, et c'est lui qui est vaincu par Étienne, Bakounine." [27] This is, indeed, extraordinary, for Rasseneur, a possibilist, is certainly not a Marxist, and Étienne, who is not really a disciple of Bakunin in spite of his speech in the wood, is close to the Marxist position. Happily, this confusion did not last into the novel where Étienne is only momentarily converted to Souvarine's ideas. His silence in chapter 3 of Part VI when the Russian again advocates destruction is in contrast to Zola's statement in the plan for that chapter. His citation of Darwin in chapter 2 of Part VII in a final discussion with his anarchist friend indicates clearly that he is still basically of the same opinion that he expressed in the fourth chapter of Part IV when he declared that assassination and arson, justified by this disciple of Bakunin, were monstrous. At the end of the book, he leaves Montsou, not to scatter dynamite like Souvarine, but to rejoin Pluchart in the hope of becoming like him a labour-leader and helping to organize the victory of the working class. This is a socialist, not an anarchist, intention.

The Soviet critic, M. K. Kleman, considers that Zola failed to make Étienne Lantier an authentic Marxist. Dominated by the communist ideology and dialectic, Kleman believes that since Zola, himself, was a "petit bourgeois," convinced of the possibility of evolution without violence, it was impossible for him to rise to a proper comprehension of scientific socialism.[28] Now it is doubtless true that Zola was not a good political theoretician. His momentary identification of Étienne with Bakunin, to which we called attention a little earlier, is perhaps a measure of his inadequacy in such matters. In later years he seems to have been attracted to Utopian socialism, for *Travail* clearly reveals the influence of Fourier. This might prove to the Marxists that he was never a reliable "scientific socialist." Nevertheless, *Germinal* has been frequently dubbed "socialistic." Conservative critics have long denounced it as such, and would surely be amazed by Kleman's view. They presumably base their judgment on the fact that, in spite of Zola's attempt at impartiality and objectivity, his sympathies clearly lie with the workers. They are doubtless impressed by the ideas expressed at the end of the book, for Étienne Lantier, having learned from experience, leaves Montsou in the firm conviction that a revolution, "la vraie, celle des travailleurs," is not far off. It may be achieved, he speculates, by a general strike; it may be made possible by more favourable legislation than existed in the Second Empire or even in the early 1880s. But that it will come, bringing with it a new society, juster than the old, he does not doubt. Is this vision incompatible with the dreams, programs, and aspirations of Marxist socialists of that day? We doubt it.

Is Étienne Lantier, Marxist or not, the contemptible character that Professor Hemmings has proclaimed him to be?[29] We assume that this judgment is inspired, not by Étienne's "lésion nerveuse" which is his misfortune rather than his fault, but by the fact that the young man is at moments motivated by personal ambition and pride. He becomes aware of the limitations of his fellow workers and feels superior to them. He is tempted by certain bourgeois refinements. This is to say that Étienne Lantier is not perfect. But to call him contemptible seems very harsh, indeed, for he is sincerely and genuinely revolted by the hardships of the miners and the injustices they endure. He pays for his pride in his fall from popularity. Before casting such a judgment, let us remember that "tous hommes n'ont pas bon sens rassis." Let us furthermore recognize that Zola deserves credit as a novelist for not oversimplifying the man. "Homme très complexe dans une nature simple," it will be remembered that he wrote in the *Ébauche*.[30] Far from arousing disgust and contempt, he inspires compassion, sympathy, and, in spite of some weaknesses, even a measure of respect and admiration.

Souvarine

Hardly had *Germinal* rolled off the press when the book reviewer of *Le National* (8 March, 1885) reproached Zola for introducing a "violent anachronism" into his book in the personage of Souvarine. "Ce n'est pas à la fin du Second Empire," he wrote, "qu'ont commencé en Russie les attentats contre le czar et les répressions sanglantes qui ont empli d'exilés les terres de l'Occident." Now even though one can cite in justification of Zola, Karakazov's attempted assassination of the emperor in

1866 and the fact that men like Bakunin and Nechayev were preaching anarchism before 1870, the question arises as to why and how Zola came to include this Russian anarchist refugee in his work. The class struggle which he was determined to depict involved the introduction of extremists as well as moderates if it were to be at all complete. This is undoubtedly one reason for the existence of Souvarine. But are there more specific reasons? Is it possible to discover what influences came to bear on his creation?

When Zola began to compose *Germinal*, nihilism, as we stated earlier, was still a subject of interest in western Europe. The terrorist campaign in Russia during the years 1877 to 1881 had not been forgotten. The attack on General Trepov in 1877 and the subsequent trial and amazing acquittal of the would-be assassin, Vera Zasulitch, the murder of General Mezentzov in 1878, of Prince Dmitry Kropotkin,[1] Governor-General of Kharkov, in 1879, the various attempts on the life of the Czar in 1879 and 1880, culminating in the successful assassination of 13 March, 1881, could not fail to arouse the curiosity and the apprehension of western Europeans. Not only were these attempts reported as news, but they also inspired discussions of the nihilist movement. *Le Voltaire*, for example, (in which Zola published *Nana*) ran articles on Russia and the nihilists from 1878 to 1881. In November 1879 *Le Temps* published three articles entitled "En cellule. Impressions d'un nihiliste," by J. Pavlovski, a friend of Turgenev's and an acquaintance of Zola's.[2] That year saw the appearance of E. Lavigne's *Roman d'une nihiliste*, followed in 1880 by his *Introduction à l'étude du nihilisme*. A. Leroy-Beaulieu devoted an article to "Le Parti révolutionnaire et le nihilisme" (*Revue des Deux Mondes*, 1880); J. Vilbort published two articles on the burning question in the *Revue politique et littéraire* (also 1880); and J. B. Arnaudo's book came out in a French translation entitled *Le Nihilisme et les nihilistes*. The various outrages against Russian officials and some of the subsequent executions were reported in *L'Illustration*, often with appropriate pictures. *Le Figaro*, in February and March of 1880, ran a series of articles on nihilism and the nihilists, inspired by the explosion in the Winter Palace on 17 February. The assassination of Alexander II was naturally front-page news for all the Paris press. Zola, himself, devoted to the Russian question one of the articles he was writing that year for *Le Figaro*. Entitled "La République en Russie," [3] it discussed among other things the nihilists' recruitment and their aims. We cannot assert that either the text of this article or that of *Germinal* was directly influenced by any of the publications just listed. They prove merely that the topic was a lively and current one which aroused general interest and could not fail to attract Zola's attention.

Some twenty-five years ago, M. K. Kleman, a Soviet citizen, offered a double solution to the problem of Souvarine's presence in the novel. In the first place, he saw in the friendship of Zola and Turgenev one explanation. He quoted a well-known Russian exile of the 1870s and 80s, P. L. Lavrov, as stating that Turgenev was planning just before his death—which occurred in 1883—a new novel in which a Russian revolutionary and a French radical would be contrasted.[4] The Soviet critic conjectured, reasonably enough, that Zola was cognizant of Turgenev's plan and after the latter's death incorporated the idea in *Germinal*. Kleman also felt that Souvarine's existence and to some extent his character are to be explained by the fictional nihilists of Turgenev's novels, *Virgin Soil* and *Fathers and Sons*, and to a still greater extent by the real nihilists of the years 1878 to 1881. These contentions are interesting and partially sound, but the problem is far more complex than Kleman realized.

The name of Zola's nihilist comes—as Kleman also indicated [5] —from the editor of a Russian paper, *Novoie Vremia*, A. S. Suvorin, the French form being Souvorine. He was introduced by Turgenev to Zola in 1879 or early in 1880. This is possibly confirmed by a notation in Zola's own handwriting on the back of a letter by Turgenev, preserved in the Bibliothèque Nationale; it reads: "Le Nouveau Temps, rédacteur Souvorine, à Saint-Petersbourg." [6] Zola, who at first thought of calling his character Nicolas,[7] apparently remembered the meeting and adopted the name which he kept in its original spelling,

Souvorine, in the early stages of composition.[8] Then, perhaps to avoid complete identification with the editor of *Novoie Vremia* but still liking the name, Zola shifted from 'o' to 'a' dubbing him Souvarine.[9] The change from Nicolas was surely a good one. "Nicolas le nihiliste" might have produced a comic effect which Zola did well to avoid. Souvarine is an impressive name for a character who is anything but comic. And while it is amusing to realize that the real Souvorine was the editor of a conservative paper, the average reader of *Germinal* was and is unaware of that fact.

The person and character of Souvarine are the products of more than one source, some of which can be identified. Was he as strongly influenced by Bazárov, the nihilist of *Fathers and Sons*, Nezdánov, the nihilist of *Virgin Soil*, and the afore-mentioned Lavrov as Kleman thinks? The nihilists of Turgenev are not terrorists. While they reject authority and have critical minds, they are really examples of philosophical nihilism. Souvarine, on the other hand, while ordinarily peaceful, is not only capable of destructive action, but has a record of terrorist activity and before the end of *Germinal* gives the reader a concrete example of his capacity. Bazárov and Nezdánov seem very tepid in comparison. The latter, to be sure, is in part an aristocrat, the illegitimate son of a prince. "Everything about him," writes Turgenev, "betrayed his high breeding: his small ears, hands, feet, his rather small but delicate features, his soft skin, his soft, abundant hair, his very voice, which was rather lisping but agreeable." Souvarine's "figure fine," his "air de fille," his "mains petites de bourgeois" may possibly have been first suggested to Zola by the nihilist of *Virgin Soil* but it is by no means certain. Then the flesh-and-blood Lavrov, also put forward by Kleman as a model, is described in a letter by Turgenev as being "a dove trying to pass as a vulture," a man whose words are "frightening" but whose "glance remains gentle" and whose "smile is full of kindness." [10] Souvarine, too, has an "air de douceur," and, in that respect, resembles Lavrov as well as Nezdánov, but Kleman forgets that Souvarine is also posses-sed of eyes of steel ("yeux d'acier") which belie his gentle manner. Lavrov, moreover, was 61 years old when Zola began to write *Germinal*. It seems unlikely that he was the model for Souvarine.

Nor is it probable that Bakunin was the prototype. He was in his late fifties when Zola began composing the first of the *Rougon-Macquart* series and he died before the publication of the first proletarian novel, *L'Assommoir*. His big physical frame is in contrast with Souvarine's slight build, and while their ideas are naturally similar, as the novelist intended his character to be a disciple of Bakunin, this relationship in itself implies that Souvarine is not meant to be Bakunin.

A more credible model, if any given individual influenced Zola, would be the anarchist-prince Peter Kropotkin who was 42 years old at the time of the composition of *Germinal*, far closer in age to the thirty-year-old Souvarine than Lavrov.[11] Kropotkin was known to Turgenev and possibly through him to Zola. Only a year before the latter began working on his novel, Kropotkin's name was prominent in the French press as one of the anarchists tried at Lyons for belonging to a subversive organization. Kropotkin was convicted and sentenced to five years in prison. Zola says in his preliminary portrait of Souvarine in the *Personnages* that he was a disciple not only of Bakunin, as stated above, but also of Kropotkin.[12] This, too, would seem to suggest that he was not intended to be Kropotkin himself. But in the same portrait he is called a "prince raté," and in Zola's manuscript plans for chapter 1, Part III, where Souvarine appears for the first time, he is characterized as a "prince réfugié." [13] Kropotkin was certainly a refugee and a prince. Whether he could be justly called a "prince raté" probably depends on one's point of view. He was, moreover, editor (with Élisée Reclus) of *Le Révolté*, and Professor Pierre Aubery has suggested,—at the same time overlooking other possibilities[14]—that some of Kropotkin's ideas, as expressed in *Le Révolté*, find an echo in Souvarine's conversation. The pictures we have of Kropotkin in his youth [15] show him not unlike Souvarine. Both are slim, both possess a thin mouth and nose, both have a light beard. But other details cannot be determined.

The blondness, the pink complexion, the white, pointed teeth with which the novelist endowed Souvarine are not revealed in these black and white pictures of Kropotkin. All things considered, one may conclude that Peter Kropotkin remains a possible but uncertain model of Zola's Russian refugee.

As for Souvarine's mysticism, it is unnecessary to attribute it to Kropotkin, Lavrov, or the heroes of Turgenev's novels. The notion that the Slav is mystic in contrast to the rationalism of the Frenchman was so widespread as to be commonplace. In 1881 Zola gave utterance to it in the article already referred to, "La République en Russie," where he wrote: "Les nihilistes font profession de ne croire à rien. Mais j'imagine que dans ce doute fervent il y a une bonne part de mysticisme. Nous sommes là aux frontières de l'Asie, l'Inde est derrière, et je vois je ne sais quelles extases bouddhiques, sous l'illuminisme de ces héroïnes nihilistes, qui semblent agir dans une crise d'hystérie révolutionnaire."

Kleman's final contention that Souvarine is connected with the terrorist campaign in Russia is undeniably sound. The Soviet writer has clearly established the connection between the events of Souvarine's past and those of 1878 to 1881. The "chef de police" whom Souvarine killed or helped to kill [16] is indubitably General Mezentzov whose name, in fact, is given by Zola in his preliminary portrait of Souvarine in the "notes de travail." [17] The attempt made to blow up the emperor's train (*Germinal*, ed. Bernouard, p. 471) was inspired by a similar attempt on 1 December 1879, near Moscow. The "mines chargées sous les palais du tzar" (*Germinal*, p. 256) clearly allude to the explosion in the Winter Palace (Feb. 17, 1880). And the statement that Souvarine lived for a month "dans la cave d'un fruitier, creusant une mine au travers de la rue, chargeant des bombes" reproduces one of the episodes of the preparations of the Executive Committee of Narodnaya Volya for the execution of Alexander II. Zola does not include in *Germinal* the successful assassination of Alexander II. That would have been much too obviously an anachronism in a book dealing with the Second Empire. But he did include, as we have shown elsewhere,[18] the execution of Alexander's assassins, for the death of Annouchka, Souvarine's mistress, is modelled after that of Sophia Perovskaia.

These events explain to some extent Souvarine's character, for a man capable of such deeds will not recoil before the sabotage of a mine. But there is a still more important source, unknown to Mr Kleman, revealed by recent scholars: Laveleye's *Le Socialisme contemporain*,[19] To be sure, Zola showed in 1881 in the article already mentioned ("La République en Russie") that he was aware of the social origins of the Russian nihilists—"fils de prêtres," "petits gentils-hommes," "étudiants," "employés"—and that they were followers of Bakunin, "l'exterminateur." Those facts he may have learned from conversations with Turgenev or from articles in the French press. But Laveleye's chapter on "L'Alliance universelle de la démocratie et l'apôtre du nihilisme" was indubitably the main source of certain characterizations of Souvarine in the text of *Germinal*. When Souvarine says: "Tous les raisonnements sur l'avenir sont criminels parcequ'ils empêchent la destruction pure et entravent la marche de la révolution" (*Germinal*, ed. Bernouard, p. 257), Zola has attributed to him a sentence taken verbatim from Laveleye. When Étienne asks the Russian how the desired results are to be obtained, he replies: "Par le feu, par le poison, par le poignard. Le brigand est le vrai héros, le vengeur populaire, le révolutionnaire en action sans phrases puisées dans les livres. Il faut qu'une série d'effroyables attentats épouvantent les puissants et réveillent le peuple." This, too, comes almost verbatim from Laveleye's chapter.[20] Souvarine's fanaticism, his detachment, his indifference to women (since the death of Annouchka), his courage are reflections of the "Revolutionary Catechism" drawn up by Bakunin (or possibly by Nechayev) and included by Laveleye in this same chapter. A few extracts will suffice as illustration:

> Le révolutionnaire est un homme voué. Il ne doit avoir ni intérêts personnels, ni affaires, ni sentiments, ni propriété. Il doit s'absorber tout entier dans un seul intérêt

exclusif, dans une seule pensée et une seule passion: la
Révolution [. . .] Il n'a qu'un but, qu'une science: la
destruction. [. . .] Il méprise et hait la morale actuelle.
Pour lui, tout est moral qui favorise le triomphe de la
Révolution, tout est immoral et criminel qui l'entrave.
Entre lui et la société, il y a lutte et lutte à mort, in-
cessante, irréconciliable. [. . .] Tant pis pour lui s'il a dans
ce monde des liens de parenté, d'amitié ou d'amour!
Il n'est pas un vrai révolutionnaire si ces attachements
arrêtent son bras.

Can there be any doubt that these phrases influenced Zola's
creation?

The "Revolutionary Catechism" also speaks of the importance of women in anarchist activity and Laveleye adds that
in all the conspiracies "on trouve des femmes riches et in-
struites, même des filles de fonctionnaires, de militaires et de
nobles." He is thinking of women like Vera Zasulitch and
Sophia Perovskaia, and we have seen that Souvarine's Annouchka is modeled, at least in her death, on the daughter of
the Governor of Saint-Petersburg.

But however much Laveleye's book accounts for Souvarine's
character and for Zola's knowledge of the anarchists, one detail
remains a puzzle. In chapter 3 of Part VI, Souvarine is reported
as saying that

En Russie, rien ne marchait, il était désespéré des nouvelles
qu'il avait reçues. Ses anciens camarades tournaient tous
aux politiciens, les fameux nihilistes dont l'Europe trem-
blait, des fils de pope, des petits bourgeois, des marchands
ne s'élevaient pas au delà de la libération nationale,
semblaient croire à la délivrance du monde, quand ils
auraient tué le despote; et dès qu'il leur parlait de raser la
vieille humanité comme une moisson mûre, dès qu'il
prononçait même le mot enfantin de république, il se
sentait incompris, inquiétant, déclassé désormais, enrôlé
parmi les princes ratés du cosmopolitisme révolutionnaire.

Where did Zola get this information? Few in western Europe

were aware of the limitations of the nihilists' aims. For they sought, apparently, neither a communist dictatorship nor even the immediate establishment of more or less autonomous communes, but land and liberty. Even after the assassination of Alexander II the Executive Committee of the People's Will (Narodnaya Volya) demanded only political amnesty and the calling of a Constituent Assembly. A modern historian of the movement, Avrahm Yarmolinsky, says flatly that "the People's Will did not share the anarchist animus against all centralized authority" and calls attention to the opening statement of its official Programme: "According to our fundamental convictions, we are socialists and populists." [21] This attitude ran counter to Bakunin's position, and his disciple Souvarine would logically view it as a fall from grace.

None of the possible documentary sources which we listed earlier—Arnaudo, Vilbort, Lavigne, A. Leroy-Beaulieu, and others—could have enlightened Zola on this point, for none of them mention it. Nor does Zola himself discuss it in his article of 1881. Was his source of information Turgenev? Quite possibly. But his "notes de travail" contain one hint which, alas, cannot help us. In his manuscript plans for this chapter in which Souvarine gives utterance to his disillusion, Zola says: "Tout rappeler, sa fraternité [. . .] son détachement de tout, des femmes, des amis. Très exact au travail, donné en exemple. *Et reprendre les notes de P.* parler du nihilisme en Russie, puis ce qu'il a lu dans un journal [. . .]" [22] The "notes de P." may well have been Zola's source of information. But these notes have disappeared. They are not in the dossier of *Germinal* at the Bibliothèque Nationale. Dr Jacques Émile Zola disclaims any knowledge of them. Who was "P."? Paul Alexis? The only notes by Alexis in the dossiers of *Germinal* are those on Jules Guesde. And it is more likely that if Zola were referring to Paul Alexis he would have written "les notes d'A." P. may possibly be Pavlovsky, that friend of Turgenev's who was an acquaintance of Zola's. [23] The "notes de P." remain an unsolved, and, we fear, insoluble mystery in the composition of *Germinal*.

To sum up: Most questions raised by Souvarine's presence in the novel appear to be reasonably well solved. Possible conversations with Turgenev and a knowledge of the latter's plans may account in part for Zola's decision to include a Russian nihilist in his work. But the activities of the Russian terrorists from 1878 to 1881, and the discussions of their deeds and ideas in French newspapers, periodicals, and books can also explain much of Zola's interest. To the extent that Souvarine is connected with these activities and published discussions, Zola is guilty of anachronism. They were, however, fairly plausible in a novel dealing with the Second Empire in view of the fact that one attempt was made on the Czar's life in 1866. In a work devoted to the class struggle in which intellectual currents of the nineteenth century were embodied in certain characters, it was natural for Zola to include an anarchist. If a living model for this anarchist must be sought, the anarchist-prince Kropotkin appears to be the most likely candidate. Souvarine's character, however, is clearly accounted for by the texts we have quoted, the primary and principal source being undoubtedly the chapter on Bakunin in Laveleye's *Le Socialisme contemporain*. Finally, let us note that Zola seems to have been well satisfied with his creation, for years later in the "notes de travail" for *Paris* he wrote: "Je vois déjà que l'anarchiste étranger [. . .] sera venu chez Guillaume, causer science et anarchie. Pas un Souvarine, car il faut que je laisse intact mon Souvarine." [24]

One problem still remains: the history of Souvarine's exact rôle in the novel.

Fairly early in the *Ébauche* we read: "Un ami à Étienne. Un nihiliste, un petit Russe, mécanicien, un russe réfugié, et les conversations du soir," [25] This first notation suggests that the nihilist's rôle is to be purely intellectual. The second reference in the *Ébauche* a few pages farther on introduces the name of Nicolas and attributes to him destructive activity as the scene of sabotage is sketched out.[26] The third reference evokes his person: "blond, délicat," etc.[27] At the same time Zola not only alludes to his past history in Russia but raises the question of what to do with the man after the accident. Momentarily, he thinks of having him commit new violence. In any case the nihilist coldly accepts the fate of his friend Étienne caught in the bottom of the mine. Finally at the end of the *Ébauche* the name Souvorine (with an 'o') appears and Zola conceives of letting him have the last word: "Tout détruire." [28] While this notion for the dénouement was wisely abandoned and other modifications were made, it is clear that the essentials of Souvarine's rôle were established in Zola's mind at the end of the *Ébauche* and confirmed by the portrait in the *Personnages*.

Examination of the chapter plans, the manuscript, and the printed text of *Germinal* reveals the changes made by Zola. In the second set of chapter plans he is always called Souvarine (with an 'a'). In the outline of chapter 1, Part III, it is suggested that Étienne first met him at Lille whereas in the novel their friendship dates from Étienne's employment by the Montsou Company. In Part IV, chapter 4 (at the Bon Joyeux) Souvarine is present not only before the arrival of Pluchart, as in the novel, but according to the manuscript[29] he remains all through the following scene displaying his interest in Rasseneur's defeat and Pluchart's success. Sometime between penning the manuscript and sending it to the *Gil Blas*, Zola eliminated him from the second part of the chapter. The same phenomenon occurred in the famous night scene in the woods (ch. 7, Part IV). In the chapter plans and in the manuscript [30] Souvarine is present and applauds. In the novel (both *feuilleton* and volume) he is merely recalled: "Souvarine, s'il avait daigné venir, aurait applaudi [. . .]."

When we come to Part V and the scene before Hennebeau's house, the chapter plans and the manuscript again place Souvarine in the thick of things, for he is present with Rasseneur and others in the "estaminet Tison." He advocates blowing up Hennebeau's establishment with a barrel of powder and draws from Étienne the reproach that he talks a lot but does nothing.[31] Both the *feuilleton* and the printed volume omit the Russian completely from the chapter.

Part VI continues the same type of evolution. In the latter

section of the first chapter, according to the manuscript and hints in the chapter plans, Étienne runs into Souvarine who has just completed his night service. A fairly long conversation takes place in which Souvarine speaks of the "mauvais état du cuvelage," adding that it is "imprudent de ne pas le refaire en entier, ce qui, du reste, aurait fermé la fosse pendant deux mois." He goes on to express his pity for the horses underground, and again suggests the use of a barrel of powder. As before, Étienne rebukes him for his inactivity and this time Zola suggests that the Russian has something destructive in mind: "Souvarine ouvrit les lèvres, le regarda en face, puis s'éloigna silencieux, comme obsédé par une idée fixe dont le clou d'acier semblait luire au fond de ses yeux pâles." [32] All this was dropped from the *Gil Blas* version as well as in the volume.

In chapters 3 and 5 the manuscript text alluded again to Souvarine's *idée fixe*, but in the first case the sentence was immediately crossed out by Zola and in the second it was eliminated by the time the *Gil Blas* came off the press.[33]

Again, in the second chapter of Part VII, the manuscript included a hint from Souvarine of intended action, for when he says to Étienne: "Vous êtes tous trop lâches," the Frenchman cannot help asking: "Mais toi que ferais-tu?" Souvarine indulges in a violent gesture and replies: "On verra." [34]

The conclusion to be drawn from these modifications and eliminations is fairly obvious. Whereas in the manuscript version, Souvarine had a slightly more active rôle in the first six parts, in the printed versions, he is strictly limited to the rôle of social theorist, detached from everybody and everything, almost a passive spectator of the mining scene, expressing violent opinions but never indulging in anything that could even remotely be labelled action. Nor is he allowed by Zola in the published texts to give the slightest hint of his ultimate intentions. Then in Part VII, he at last comes into his own, performs his sabotage which is the more dramatic as it has not been forecast but which is perfectly credible in view of his Russian past and his expressed opinions. For this destruction he received the accolade of *Le Révolté, organe communiste-anarchiste* which cited him as an example to be followed: "Le Souvarine de Zola, dans *Germinal*, parle peu, et quelle besogne révolutionnaire il accomplit!" [35] We can hardly share this admiration, but we can doubtless admit that Zola's arrangement lends to Souvarine's departure after his abominable act of courage and the engulfment of Le Voreux a dramatic quality which makes it one of the most effective moments of the book.

Rasseneur

In that article in *Le Gaulois* (27 February, 1884, shortly after Zola left for Anzin) to which reference has already been made,[1] information was given on two labour leaders at Anzin, Basly and Fauviau. The article stated that Basly was about thirty years old, that he was the secretary of the workers' organization and a "cabaretier" whose well patronized establishment was located on Villars street in Denain. It added that Basly received five francs a day as secretary, that he travelled everywhere in the coal-mining area making speeches, and created for himself a fairly agreeable existence. After Zola arrived at Anzin, he met Basly and visited his cabaret. Whether he met Fauviau, also described in *Le Gaulois* is unknown. But that he was impressed by Basly is clear. He devoted a paragraph to him in "Mes notes sur Anzin," [2] and mentioned him by name in the *Ébauche* where he appears as the prototype of the representative of the International who was to be introduced into the novel, and then as the "secrétaire d'une société de secours mutuelle." [3] After Zola decided to give Étienne a more important rôle, he changed his "cabaretier" from a member of the International (and a Marxist) to a "possibiliste," as we have seen. In the final composition, Rasseneur still resembles Basly in that he is a former miner, dismissed after a strike, now turned "cabaretier," but he no longer resembles him ideologically.[4] He has, like Basly, a wife who runs the cabaret. In the very brief portrait [5] that Zola composed for her, we learn that she is "beaucoup plus avancée que son mari" and

that she is in agreement with Étienne. This is confirmed in the
finished novel.

Basly's cabaret was called *Au dix-neuvième siècle*.[6] To Rasseneur's Zola gave the fictitious name, *A l'Avantage*.

The Grégoire Family

Before Zola's planning was completed, the Grégoire family
assumed in his eyes a kind of symbolic value. The Maheus
versus the Grégoires, the poverty and industry of the former
versus the wealth and idleness of the latter, but ultimately
tragedy for both; to this arrangement Zola gradually came.

Relatively little space is devoted in the *Ébauche* to the
Grégoires, but the first reference indicates either that Zola had
them well in mind or that some paragraph of the *Ébauche* in
which they were described has been lost, for he writes: "Mes
deux actionnaires [. . .]" [1] as if they already had an existence.
This first allusion presents husband and wife as old, seventy
and sixty, Flemish in appearance, calmly enjoying life. A word
sums up their family history: from father to son they have
done nothing. In the same paragraph, Zola gives them a
daughter, equally calm, peaceful, and happy. He projects a
marriage between her and the young engineer, then hesitates,
thinking it would be more distinguished to avoid it.

Only at the very end of the *Ébauche* is this family mentioned
again, this time by name. Here Zola speaks of three scenes:
the visit of La Maheude to the Grégoires' house early in the
book, the moment when Cécile finds herself threatened and
even in danger during the mob scene, and finally the Grégoires'
visit to the Maheu establishment at the end.[2] But, as stated
earlier, neither here nor elsewhere in the *Ébauche* is there the
slightest hint of the dreadful fate that ultimately overtook the
daughter.

The history, character, and rôle of Léon Grégoire are much
more thoroughly sketched out in the preliminary portrait in
the *Personnages*.[3] His age is definitively fixed at 60, and his
calm, peaceful, undistinguished personality is still more carefully set forth than in the *Ébauche*. His attitude toward inherited

wealth is clearly indicated; he is disturbed by no doubts whatever; the legitimacy of his fortune is as certain in his mind as his own existence. Zola sums it up by saying: "Un bourgeois naïf et effroyable." His wife echoes his sentiments and ideas.

In Léon's portrait Zola relates his family history without, however, going into the detailed history of the Montsou mines as he will do in the novel. That aspect of the problem, as Mlle Frandon has admirably shown in one of her best chapters, was taken from Dormoy's account of the Anzin mines. But in this preliminary portrait Zola is satisfied briefly to explain the origin of Grégoire's fortune. For a moment he toys with the idea of having Grégoire sell his shares, but decides against it, preferring to present him as an "actionnaire bonhomme."

While Grégoire and his wife offered no serious problem, the daughter Cécile was more difficult. We have discussed this question in an article in *French Studies*[4] to which we refer the reader, and therefore find it sufficient to say that her ultimate fate puzzled the novelist for some time. Should he have her marry Négrel or not? If not, for what reason? Her lot was not decided till he came to write the second set of chapter plans for Part VII. Then he determined on her strangulation by Bonnemort. Her death, as he indicates clearly, becomes an element of the social conflict, an almost inevitable part of the dénouement.

Professor Hemmings has made valuable, interesting, and possibly controversial comments on the Grégoire family. He views them as "avowedly comic characters." The humour which envelopes them "has its source in irony," an irony which "disturbs more than it amuses, being morose, tinged at moments with a sardonic savagery." In fact, he adds, it is "little different from Flaubert's *grotesque triste*." [5] There is much in support of Mr Hemmings' opinion. The restrictions which M. Grégoire smugly puts on his charity, his stupefaction at Négrel's remark that he represents "l'infâme capital," his naïve astonishment at the thought that the miners could possibly resent the fact that his family lives comfortably on the proceeds of their work, his incredible statement during

the mob scene before Hennebeau's house that when the miners
have shouted enough, "they will go eat their supper with all
the more appetite,"—all that certainly verges on the comic
or the ironic or both.

The Grégoires' punishment at the end of the novel is judged
by Mr Hemmings to be a miscalculation on Zola's part, for it
"weakens the caricatural unity of the Grégoire figures." But
Cécile's death is justified by Zola, as we stated above, from
the point of view of the social conflict. He wished to "bien
montrer cette résultante des Maheu contre les Grégoire." [6]
And he doubless felt, as Mr Hemmings says, "under compul-
sion not to leave any of his characters unscarred by suffering."

The essential decency of the Grégoires as well as the final
tragedy makes it a little difficult to accept without any reservation their classification as "avowedly comic characters."
While they are naïve and at times fatuous, they are law-abiding
and peaceful citizens. But above all, they form a part of the
economic picture which Zola is painting,—an essentially
serious picture with some pretensions to objectivity. All share-
holders are not of the "bloated capitalist" type, like the
"grand seigneur", the largest stockholder in the Montsou
company, guilty of spending his dividends in scandalous
fashion. The Grégoires prove it by their example, and M.
Grégoire takes pains to condemn such a manner of living.[7]
In the midst of our smiles and laughter, let us render this
justice to the master of La Piolaine.

Hennebeau and his wife

In the same camp as Léon Grégoire we naturally find Hennebeau. Nameless throughout the *Ébauche* and the *Plan par parties*,
the general manager of the Montsou mines is identified in the
Personnages and in the chapter plans. His character, his past
history, his rôle in the action of the novel, his domestic situation
were pretty well suggested in the *Ébauche*. A paid employee
rigorously carrying out the orders of the Régie, a disciplined
man, a cog in a vast machine, a decent fellow withal who has

no personal desire to crush the workers, an unhappy husband, —this sketch of Hennebeau in the *Ébauche* [8] is confirmed in the preliminary portrait in the *Personnages*, in the various chapter plans, and finally in the novel.

Not that Zola failed to exhibit some hesitation. His first thought was to give him two daughters with a possible marriage or seduction for one of them. Perhaps even, the younger daughter might contribute to her own seduction and her lover be killed in the end. Something of this sort would enliven one side of the action. Then a switch in Zola's mind turned the daughters [9] over to the individual *patron* (who will be named much later Deneulin), and the general manager is temporarily awarded, as we saw in an earlier section, a son. A momentary drama, in which this son becomes engaged to one of the *patron*'s daughters killed during the strike comes to Zola's mind. This is later modified by the notion of giving the manager a vice which would lead to a "mariage malpropre" between the son and the *patron*'s daughter with a dowry stolen from the company or sweated out of the workers.[10] Such an arrangement would permit the novelist to show the rottenness of the ruling class. But all this melodrama was wisely abandoned by Zola in favour of making Hennebeau an upright man whose only weakness is his desire for his unfaithful and unworthy wife. This weakness provides, as Zola says in the portrait, a "human drama" placed in opposition to the "social drama." [11] Or, as he wrote later to Édouard Rod: "Il m'a semblé nécessaire de mettre au-dessus de l'éternelle injustice des classes l'éternelle douleur des passions." [12]

Hennebeau is the only contact the Montsou workers have with their employers, for Zola deliberately refrained from introducing a shareholder who could make any claim to control of the company. Grégoire does not own enough stock for that. The only other shareholder mentioned in the plans or in the book is an "actionnaire grand seigneur, grand propriétaire, ministre, pot de vin." [13] But he is kept in a remote background. Indeed, in the novel he is simply alluded to by Grégoire during the dinner at Hennebeau's house. The big corporation remains throughout the book essentially impersonal, a far-off, mysterious force, represented by a general manager.

A less important figure than her husband, Blanche Hennebeau remains virtually unchanged during Zola's planning. His only hesitation was whether or not to make her adultery incestuous. In both the *Ébauche* [14] and the *Personnages* [15] he wonders whether to put her into Négrel's bed, and decides in the latter that he will. When criticized by Édouard Rod for introducing this particular adultery into his novel, Zola, in the letter already mentioned, replied: "Cet adultère banal n'est là que pour me donner la scène où M. Hennebeau râle sa souffrance humaine en face de la souffrance sociale qui hurle!"

A selfish, vicious, and ignorant woman, Mme Hennebeau represents some of the worst features of the capitalist side.

Deneulin

In commenting on the *Ébauche* we noted that Zola quickly determined to include in his novel not only a big corporation but a small enterprise run by an individual owner destined to be ruined by the spreading strike. If the strike itself is both a nineteenth and twentieth century phenomenon, the theme of a small company suffering from competition with a huge concern, being forced to the wall and finally swallowed up is no less so, for it is a familiar occurrence of our day.

We also saw in discussing Hennebeau that Zola decided to transfer to the *patron* the daughters he originally thought of giving to the general manager. Later in the *Ébauche* we learn that the *patron* (a widower) is to be Grégoire's brother [16] who has sold his share of the property and become a mine operator himself. Furthermore, at this point Zola conceives of endowing him with two or three worthless sons in addition to the girls. The sons were eliminated, though one (named Georges in the *Personnages* [17]) survived in the plans for quite a while as a possible lover of Mme Hennebeau in replacement of Négrel.[18] When Zola rejected the marriage between the engineer and Cécile Grégoire, Georges no longer had any reason for existence.

The portrait in the *Personnages* gives us the *patron*'s name, his age, and informs us that he is Grégoire's cousin rather than his brother. Like his cousin, he had owned a "denier" in the Montsou company, but had sold it, hoping with the purchase and exploitation of the Vandame concession to make a fortune. The portrait goes on to outline in some detail the competition he suffers from the Montsou company and sketches for us his personality. He has, says Zola, the manner of a cavalry officer, quick tempered, brusque, hard-working, and courageous. He is good to his men. But he is a poor administrator. All the details of this portrait are confirmed in the book.

B. OTHER CHARACTERS

Négrel

Since Zola was guided during his inspection of the Anzin mines by the company's engineer,[1] who apparently served him well, Professor Moreau reproaches the novelist for making Négrel, the engineer of the Montsou mines, antipathetic.[2] M. Moreau is doubtless not implying that Zola's guide was the model for Négrel, because that is not very probable. *Before* leaving for Anzin, in the section of the *Ébauche* already penned, Zola had thought of including an engineer in his book and of having him sleep with the general manager's wife.[3] To be sure, his contact with the company's engineer did not alter that notion, but neither did it create it. Furthermore, Négrel's courage at the time of the great catastrophe was suggested to Zola by the engineer of the Marles pit in the Pas-de-Calais, whose exploit in descending into the mine after the terrible cave-in of 1866 was related by Simonin.[4] This seems to be the source both of Négrel's action and of his courage,—however brave the engineer of the Anzin mines may have been. We are inclined to believe that neither the good nor the bad in Négrel's character stems from any one whom Zola knew personally. He was created independently.

Apart from the incestuous adultery tentatively thought of in the *Ébauche* [5] (and ultimately adopted), and his courage first set forth in the second plan for chapter V of Part I,[6] the most important aspects of Négrel's character are outlined in his portrait in the *Personnages*.[7] Here Zola states that he wishes to depict in Négrel "un enfant de cet âge." Négrel is sceptical, unscrupulous toward women, liberal, republican even, but without profound convictions. His very "insouciance," however, suggests (by way of contrast) to Zola a concrete scene, thus illustrating a phenomenon of composition to which we called attention earlier. In a kind of sudden vision, the novelist sees Négrel beholding the spectacle of social revolution and experiencing an unusual moment of fear. The scene pleases the author who calls it "excellente," necessary to complete the book. He wonders where to put it. After some hesitation between chapters 4 and 5 of Part V, he decides on the latter.[8]

Chaval

Antoine Chaval was conceived in Zola's mind when the plan to make Catherine Maheu the object of rivalry between two men, a "brutal" and Étienne, came into being.[9] Almost immediately, the novelist saw him working in the "petite mine" after successfully seducing the girl.[10] About midway in the *Ébauche*,[11] the man receives his baptismal name, and is characterized as gallant, brutal, and good-looking. His origin (from the Pas-de-Calais) is mentioned, his treachery forecast, and his reward—a promotion to the rank of porion—is indicated.

The *Ébauche* displays hesitation concerning Chaval's activity during the strike. While the violent scene between him and Catherine (chapter 3, Part IV in the finished novel) is clearly pictured,[12] and his part in the night meeting in the wood hinted at,[13] along with confirmation of his treachery, there is a momentary repugnance to make the man a traitor. Zola suggests that if he has him persecuted by the other workers, he can avoid "le côté traître" which he calls "commun et enfantin." [14] This scruple did not last long in the novelist's mind.

The *Ébauche* continues with the fight between Antoine and Étienne in the cabaret (the Bon-Joyeux) which ends with the former's defeat.[15] Will he play a treacherous rôle in the clash with the soldiers? Zola raises the question, only to say that if he does, it must be "quelque chose de très discret." [16] The *Ébauche* concludes Antoine's rôle by saying that the company has named him a "porion" and that he has resumed work in the "petite mine" at the end (f. 478/75).

It is noteworthy that neither in the *Ébauche*, nor in the *Personnages*, nor in the *Plan par parties* is there any reference to Chaval's death. It appears to have occurred to Zola as he penned the first plan for chapter 3 of Part VII where he says: "Si je laissais Chaval dans l'accident, je pourrais le faire tuer par Étienne, le meurtre, il voit rouge, il le tuerait, avant ou après la mort de Catherine. Avant."[17]

The portrait in the *Personnages* characterizes the man quite carefully, adding physical details that were not in the *Ébauche*: "Un garçon blond, aux traits accentués, nez fort, bouche forte, joues coupées déjà de deux grands plis. Les yeux bleuâtres—barbe rouge, moustaches et bouquet au mention. Taille moyenne, gros os, roulis des épaules." [18] Zola sums him up, physically and morally, by saying that he represents "la brute dans l'ouvrier." [19] Does his very name imply that he has an animalistic nature? Some critics have thought so, but the choice seems odd, for the horse is presented in *Germinal* as being lovable, and one can hardly say as much of Chaval. In any case, Zola finally sensed that he was in danger of making the man too ignoble. He therefore determined in his outline for chapter 2 of Part V to permit Chaval to display a little concern and even affection for his mistress when she is overcome in the bottom of the Jean–Bart mine.[20] His "élan de tendresse," apparently real, is nevertheless short-lived.

At only one point does the finished novel depart from all these preliminary indications. It gives this character a touch of the diabolical in the first scene underground. There, when Chaval, stimulated by Étienne's presence, seizes Catherine and kisses her, Zola writes: "Ses moustaches et sa barbiche rouges *flambaient* dans son visage noir, au grand nez en bec d'aigle."[21] As the whole underground scene is described, both in the

Ébauche and the novel, as a veritable hell, the application of this comparison to Chaval is not inappropriate. It remains temporary, for this man has not the majestic qualities of Satan.

La Mouquette

If there is a touch of the comic in the Grégoires, there is more in the presentation of Mouque's daughter. Her enormous "derrière," deliberately displayed to indicate her scorn or contempt, recalls the kind of exaggeration for comic effect that one finds in Rabelais.

She first appears in Zola's planning on *feuillet* 425/24 of the *Ébauche* where the novelist writes that he will put another girl into the mine, a "grosse fille" with big breasts, crude in her language, shameless in her morals, ready to give herself virtually in public. It is noteworthy that Zola penned this description before making the trip to Anzin.

La Mouquette clearly represents SEX in its most elemental form. We agree with Mr Walker that she and Catherine are the "two sides of the subject of proletarian love." [22] La Mouquette gives us the gross; Catherine, if not the pure, at least something more delicate and touching.

The *Ébauche* forecasts the brief liaison between La Mouquette and Étienne, although at first Zola does not think of involving her emotionally, for he says: "elle-même n'y tient pas." [23] And the *Ébauche* also foresees her heroic self-sacrifice in saving Catherine's life at the cost of her own. The gross girl of the early pages dies the death of a proletarian heroine (if I may use Mr Walker's phrase) at the end.

She has not, however, been completely visualized in the *Ébauche*. The portrait in the *Personnages* adds a great deal: her facial features as we shall find them in the novel, her gayety, her good nature. "Très brave fille," says Zola,[24] and except for a momentary hesitation when he thinks of having her support her father during the strike by accepting money for her favours [25]—a notion quickly abandoned—he made no change in that characterization. But her famous gesture was not put on paper till late in the planning stage. It was not mentioned in the preliminary portrait nor in the plans for chapter 6 of Part I, where in the novel she first indulges in her peculiar expression of scorn. The second outline of chapter 5 of Part V contains Zola's initial written reference to it. There, as he jots down his vision of the roving mob scene, he writes: "Et finir par des dames qui reviennent de Montsou, et auxquelles la Mouquette montre son derrière. Ce derrière, pas cochon, farouche." [26] In the finished novel, this particular display is described as not being laughable. In this chapter and circumstance, it certainly is not. Later, in the chapter on the clash with the soldiery, it provokes "un rire de tempête," in which the reader, if he be not too Victorian, tends to join.

On one occasion, Zola eliminated her gesture from his final text. At the end of chapter 7 of Part IV, in describing the excitement produced in the women by the inflammatory words of Étienne and others, he first wrote: "La Mouquette [. . .] la jupe par-dessus la tête, parlant de démonter" [27] etc. This he corrected in proof.

In spite of this restraint, unknown of course to the reader, many were shocked as well as incredulous at the girl's gesture and promiscuity. Interviewed in *Le Matin* (7 March, 1885), Zola, in defense of his work, quoted a Dr Gally who wrote: "Le fait de la fille du houilleur qui s'écarte un peu de la bande pour se livrer sans honte ni pudeur, presque sous les yeux de ses compagnons de travail, est d'une entière vérité." Like other characters in the novel, she is, to a large extent, the product of her environment.

La Brûlé

A minor character in the novel, la mère Brûlé is one of Zola's most striking and successful portraits. In the *Ébauche* (f. 487/84) he identified her as the mother of his third miner, "mère terrible qui combat et qui accable son fils de sottise sur sa lâcheté." He already foresaw a part of her rôle in the rioting of the fifth part and her death at the end. Then when he came to compose the preliminary portraits, he made her, without discussion, the mother-in-law, rather than the mother, of Pierron.

At this point he sees her as a "vieille énergumène," [28] and as "une grande femme maigre, avec des cheveux blancs. Le nez en bec d'aigle, de gros sourcils blancs, la bouche pincée, sans dents." [29] Her violent character—"très violente, très exaltée"— is partially explained by her past misfortunes, her husband having been killed in the mine. The visual image in these lines of the preliminary portrait stayed in Zola's mind throughout the novel. The physical traits, repeated, with some addition, will result in a vivid, unforgettable picture.

The first time we see this woman in the finished novel is in chapter VI of Part I. Quarreling with Philomène Levaque, la Brûlé is depicted as "une vieille sorcière [. . .] terrible avec ses yeux de chat-huant et sa bouche serrée comme la bourse d'un avare." The mouth, described more picturesquely than in the planning stage, is nevertheless the same, but the hoot-owl eyes are an appropriate and effective addition. If the "nez en bec d'aigle" is not specifically mentioned in this first glimpse of the woman, the reader doubtless thinks of it, for the witch is traditionally thus endowed.

Zola speaks of her again in the third chapter of Part II in connection with her daughter. Her past misfortune is related, her anger when Suzanne marries a coal-miner is set forth. Her continued violence stands in contrast to the daughter's calm: "il n'y avait que la mère Brûlé qui hurlât avec son enragement de vieille révolutionnaire, ayant à venger la mort de son homme contre les patrons." We are thus prepared—even if we have not read the "notes de travail"—for some of La Brûlé's later activities.

Another quarreling scene occurs in chapter V of this Part where she shouts her reproaches at Pierron for his weakness toward an inspector. Étienne overhears them and watches the old woman disappear in the distance "avec son nez d'aigle, ses cheveux blancs envolés, ses longs bras maigres qui gesticulaient furieusement." The hooked nose is now specifically mentioned, and with her unkempt hair and her skinny, waving arms, suggests the old witch of the first sketch.

In Part III we see her very briefly in chapters II and IV where she appears in characteristic poses, shouting and gesticulating in the first instance on discovering that Lydie, whom she wanted to keep at home, has managed to escape, and in the second, taking a prominent place—"maigre et droite," "le poing tendu vers Montsou"—among the angry women of the *coron* on that disastrous pay-day which preceded the strike.

In the night meeting in the forest, eerily lighted up by the moon, La Brûlé is again the old witch. "Les femmes déliraient," writes Zola, and among them we are not astonished to see "la vieille Brûlé, hors d'elle, agitant des bras de sorcière." And again, at the end of the meeting, "les femmes s'enrageaient," among them, naturally, La Brûlé with characteristic anger and gestures.

That La Brûlé should play a prominent rôle in Part V is now expected by any reader. He is not disappointed. She assumes the lead at Jean-Bart in putting out the furnaces: "La Brûlé, armée d'une grande pelle, accroupie devant un des foyers, le vidait violemment." Lest there be any doubt concerning her witch-like appearance, Zola adds that the women—for others had joined her—were all "sanglantes dans le reflet d'incendie, suantes et échevelées de cette cuisine de sabbat." At La Victoire, La Brûlé leads the others to destroy the lamps. At Gaston-Marie, she forces Chaval to drink from a puddle. During all the march of the mining men and women, one feels her to be present—even if not always mentioned by name—among these old, frightful women ("vieilles, affreuses") uttering their cry for bread. Before Hennebeau's house, Étienne himself is dismayed by the violence of the women, "agitées d'une fureur meurtrière, les dents et les ongles dehors, aboyantes comme des chiennes, sous les excitations de la Brûlé, qui les dominait de sa taille maigre." She is one of the furies threatening to strip Cécile Grégoire of her clothes, and she is naturally, inevitably, the one to emasculate Maigrat's corpse and to carry her booty on the end of a stick in a procession reminiscent of bloody revolution.

Finally, in the clash with the soldiers, we find La Brûlé characteristically in the thick of things, indeed taking the lead. Her arrival is the signal for a flood of invective far worse than what had occurred before. "Une vieille femme déboula," writes Zola, "c'était la Brûlé, effrayante de maigreur, le cou et les bras à l'air, accourue d'un tel galop, que des mèches de cheveux gris l'aveuglaient." And without waiting, she fell upon the army, "la bouche noire, vomissant l'injure." She it is who begins the "battle of the bricks." "Ce fut la Brûlé," we are told, "qui se campa la première. Elle cassait les briques, sur l'arête maigre de son genou, et de la main droite, et de la main gauche, elle lâchait les deux morceaux." Here again, Zola places her among the "furies." Her death comes soon after. A bullet brings her down, "toute raide et craquante comme un fagot de bois sec, en bégayant un dernier juron dans le gargouillement du sang." The physical and the psychological traits are in conformity with the original picture. At one point in his planning, Zola had thought of putting La Maheude among the "pétroleuses."[30] But if anyone in the novel, apart from Souvarine, merits the appellation of "pétroleur" or "pétroleuse," it is surely La Brûlé. She reminds us throughout of those gaunt, haggard women of the French Revolution who appear in many of the paintings and sketches of the period of the Terror and who impart to it some of its more repulsive characteristics.

This woman is neither an agreeable nor an admirable person. Her intelligence is limited, her emotions anything but subtle. The old revolutionary, the "vieille énergumène," the woman with an eternal grudge, the wiry witch, the mutilator of Maigrat, with her lean body, gleaming eyes, tightly pressed lips, wild words and gestures, is nevertheless one of the most clearly drawn characters of this novel. A good example of the way in which Zola can paint an effective picture from a very slight preliminary sketch, La Brûlé remains fixed in the reader's visual memory.

Maigrat

The *Ébauche* indicates that from an early moment Zola visualized a scene of emasculation [31] performed on the corpse of a hated individual. But nowhere in the *Ébauche*, nor in the *Plan par parties*, nor in the portrait in the *Personnages* is it suggested that the grocer is to suffer that fate. The earliest mention of Maigrat's death is in the first detailed plan for chapter 2 of Part II where Zola writes: "Préparer Maigrat pour sa mort. Couche avec les filles, il faut envoyer les filles pour obtenir du crédit."[32] Neither the manner of his death nor the treatment of his corpse are related.

When we come to chapter 6 of Part V, we see the novelist groping in the first plan for a way to end that chapter effectively. "Comme intensité, il faudrait pour finir que la bande se livrât à une véritable sauvagerie." [33] His initial thought, doubtless suggested by the *Ébauche*, is to finish the chapter with the death and mutilation of a "surveillant" who is thus punished for his "débordements de mâle." He finally decides to assign this fate to the grocer.[34] All the details of this extraordinary scene are listed in the second plan for the chapter.

✳   ✳   ✳

A number of miscellaneous characters remain to be discussed. Those on the workers' side do not in general differ markedly from their description in the *Ébauche* and in the *Personnages*. Mouque,[35] somewhat like Bonnemort, represents the worker who has been brutalized and stupefied by long years in the mines; his son, Mouquet, the thoughtless, indifferent worker. Levaque, to be sure, is less politically minded and less coldly cruel than Zola originally intended,[36] but he is still far from an admirable figure. The "ménage à trois" which he tolerates is part of the *tableau de mœurs*, something which Zola might easily have invented, but which he learned about during his visit to Anzin.[37] The wife, the lodger, the daughter, the son Bébert, the daughter's children provide no surprises for anyone familiar with the "notes de travail." Much the same can be said of the Pierron family, even though Zola had a moment's hesitation concerning Pierron himself, for in the *Personnages* the novelist thinks of not making him a "mouchard." [38] In the end he returns to the original plan of the *Ébauche*.[39] These two families furnish the two children, Bébert and Lydie, who in company with Jeanlin depict the ravages of environment on youngsters "mis au travail trop tôt, galopinant ensuite, coulant au vice par la promiscuité avec les parents." [40]

If Zola did not know anything about the organization of mining personnel before going to Anzin, he learned a good deal about it there. Among other things he discovered that every pit had a "chef-porion" and several "porions." So Le Voreux will have Dansaert and Richomme. They occupy an intermediate place between the workers and the capitalists. Dansaert, by virtue of his position as head inspector, is more remote from the miners than the "porion" Richomme and therefore belongs, in their view, in the other camp. Unless he derives in part from the Inspector mentioned on *feuillet* 426/25 of the *Ébauche*—an uncertain hypothesis—he was created briefly on f. 455/52 and 457/54, his affair with Suzanne Pierron coming simultaneously to Zola's mind. Again characterized toward the end of the *Ébauche* (f. 490/87), his cowardice at the time of the great catastrophe was not conceived of by Zola till much later. As for Richomme, because of his lower rank and his decent character, he is closer to the workers. Zola says in the portrait in the *Personnages* that he is "le type d'un vieux militaire, celui que j'ai vu à Saint-Louis.[41] Tout blanc, cheveux courts, et grosses moustaches en brosse. [. . .] Très juste, très bon." [42] He remains in the novel pretty much as depicted in the *Personnages*, his fate also unchanged.

Pluchart,[43] the abbé Joire, Dr Vanderhaghen, the young soldier Jules, the military captain (called Duvillard in the "notes de travail" but anonymous in the novel) are not quite supernumeraries for they all talk. In fact, Pluchart talks long and well. They play minor but significant rôles, created by the needs of the plot, sometimes specifically suggested by Zola's reading. Had Zola not read in Laveleye's book of the danger of the army's being infected with socialism, he might well not have created Jules or the scene between him and Étienne. Had he not consulted the *Gazette des Tribunaux*, he might not have fashioned the military captain exactly as he did. Had he not heard at Anzin of a sardonic remark made by the Company's doctor,[44] Dr Vanderhaghen might still have existed but perhaps with a slightly different manner. Whether the abbé Joire had a prototype at Anzin or elsewhere is unknown. As for Pluchart, he had to be created if the International was to be brought into the narrative in any direct, concrete way. In the "notes de travail" he is an unsuccessful lawyer propagandist and agent for the International. Only in the final stages of composition was he described as Étienne's "contremaître" at Lille [45] This brought him closer to the working class.

That last-minute creation of Zola's, l'abbé Ranvier,[46] stands in contrast to l'abbé Joire and symbolizes the element in Roman Catholic circles that saw the danger of widespread poverty and wished to do something about it through cooperation or alliance between the church and the working class. Ranvier's transfer at the end is also symbolic, proving, as it does, the influence and power of the bourgeoisie. Was his name suggested to Zola by that of a member of the Paris Commune, Gabriel Ranvier? There is no evidence to that effect, but it would not be wholly unlike the novelist to give ironically the name of a notorious Communard to a Catholic priest. The fact that the priest had socialist leanings would make it seem a little more appropriate. This, of course, is sheer speculation.

If we include Bataille and Trompette in a discussion of characters, we are merely following Zola's example, for page 93 of MS. 10308 contains a "portrait" of Bataille and an allusion to a second horse, obviously Trompette, whom Zola dubbed for some time [47] Merveille. The "portrait" contains nothing not found in the novel. It is a good example, however, of Zola's thoroughness in planning, of his well-known affection for animals and his tendency to treat them almost as human beings. Like some of the other portraits, it includes bits of action clearly visualized. Here, as in the *Ébauche*,[48] Zola *sees* the horses in the mine, beholds the removal of the one who dies, and evokes the panic and death of Bataille in the great catastrophe: "Bataille galopant, puis mourant avec des hennissements terribles." [49]

And Le Voreux? some one may ask. Indeed, several critics

hold that the principal character of *Germinal* is the mine itself. They are not entirely wrong, for Zola uses a vocabulary in describing Le Voreux that makes it seem like a living creature. *Bête goulue, bête méchante, corne menaçante, le puits dévorateur, gueule gloutonne, boyaux géants, ogre* [...] *que rien ne pouvait repaître* are some of the epithets. After Souvarine's sabotage the final engulfment of the machinery is represented in similar terms: "on vit la machine, disloquée sur son massif, les *membres* écartelés, lutter contre la mort: elle *marcha*, elle détendit sa bielle, *son genou de géante*, comme pour se lever; mais elle *expirait*, broyée, engloutie [...] C'était fini, *la bête mauvaise, accroupie* dans ce creux, *gorgée de chair humaine*, ne *soufflait* plus de son *haleine* grosse et longue. Tout entier, le Voreux venait de couler à l'abîme." Throughout the book the mine has been more than a material phenomenon; it has been an evil and living force with which human beings have had to struggle. It is, therefore, not inappropriate to place it among the characters of the book, though we do not share the belief that it is the chief protagonist. Without contesting the mine's importance, we persist in thinking that for Zola men and women came first, that they were central to his narrative.

C.   CONCLUSIONS

Mr Martin Turnell is representative of a certain attitude when he says that in Zola's work "the individual as such has virtually ceased to exist and become the mere incarnation of herd instincts like lust, avarice, or hate." [50] At the same time, Turnell thinks that the naturalistic novel, instead of being, like *Mme Bovary* for example, a combination of Art and Truth, eliminates Art and becomes only an amalgam of Truth and Natural-and-Social History. Now it is true, of course, that according to Zola's theories, men are products of their heredity and environment. But does this mean that they cannot then be symbolic, like Mme Bovary, of something important in human nature or human society? Emma Bovary, as Mr Turnell correctly says, is not only a woman, but also "a symbol of the thwarted Romantic whose desires and aspirations are continually cheated by reality." [51]

No character dominates *Germinal* as Emma Bovary dominates the novel bearing her name. Nobody in *Germinal* is spotlighted, examined, analyzed as old Goriot and Rastignac are in Balzac's novel. There is even less concentration on individuals in *Germinal* than in some of Zola's other novels, like *La Curée* and *La Conquête de Plassans*. But the characters take on symbolic value without losing individual identity. Étienne Lantier is not only a man with passions and desires (to say nothing of his well-known weakness, his "lésion héréditaire"), but he represents the worker who aspires —legitimately, be it added—to a place in the sun, and he comes more and more in the book to represent the Marxian socialist. The Maheus are clearly drawn, and at the same time symbolize the willing worker who seeks nothing more than a decent life. Deneulin, the small entrepreneur in competition with the great corporation and doomed to disappear, is obviously a social type, with, however, certain traits of character not necessarily connected with that rôle: his desire to treat his men as well as he reasonably can, his frankness in admitting, as he does, that in the given economic situation the worker pays for "les pots cassés." Souvarine is doubtless more a symbol than an individual, but he is not devoid of personality. Other characters in the book share this duality; they are human beings as well as symbols. If they remain, in spite of these reservations, less complex than they might be, it is partly because of Zola's emphasis on action, partly because of the material and economic forces—the ogre-like mine and the distant god, capitalism—with which the workers are struggling. In other words, the explanation lies in the fact that the novel is a social narrative in which, as Zola himself put it, "chaque chapitre, chaque compartiment de la composition s'est trouvé tellement resserré qu'il a fallu tout voir en raccourci. De là, une simplification constante des personnages." [52]

Zola succeeds in *Germinal* in interesting the reader in the fate of his protagonists. Furthermore, unlike some of his other novels, *Germinal* contains characters whom we can like, esteem, or even admire. In *La Curée*, the three principals are in varying ways and degree contemptible. *Nana* suffers from the same kind of defect. In *La Terre*, only Jean Macquart retains our esteem to the end. Even when allowance is made for the fact that Zola was using a *fer rouge*, such novels seem quite one-sided in their presentation of human nature. In this respect *Germinal* is certainly superior. It has its share of unpleasant people; witness Chaval, Jeanlin, Maigrat, Dansaert, Mme Hennebeau. But others are not all bad. Souvarine slaughters the innocent, but in his dreadful way he is idealistic. Négrel is anything but admirable in his sexual life, but he is a courageous man. Grégoire is lazy and fatuous, but respectable. La Mouquette is promiscuous, but good-natured and capable of self-sacrifice. Zacharie, trivial though he is, displays rare courage and devotion in trying to save his sister's life. Then there are characters with whom we can sympathize. Not that any—with the possible exception of little Alzire—are saints. Étienne, as we have seen, has defects as well as good qualities. Toussaint Maheu and his wife are honest, hard-working people, but they are painfully limited. Deneulin, enterprising and energetic, is brusque and administratively ineffective. Hennebeau, while upright, is disgracefully weak before his wife. Catherine, essentially good and kind as well as hard-working, is superstitious and possibly too non-resistant to the mores of her environment. But she seems thoroughly individualized, even though she has obviously been molded by the *milieu*. After all, she and La Mouquette are markedly different from each other.

While these characters are not subtly or minutely analyzed, while they are lacking in greater or lesser degree in depth, they hold our interest, and many arouse our compassion. Maheu and his wife, Catherine, and Hennebeau are surely more sinned against than sinning. In the end Grégoire inspires pity. The weaknesses of La Mouquette and Zacharie are overlooked in the moment of their death. Étienne, while far from a hero in our eyes, has gone through an ordeal which moves us to compassion and sympathy. The reader is not inclined to waste any indignation on his killing of Chaval. A glance devoid of bitterness or condemnation follows him into the April sunshine.

If there is a hero in *Germinal*, it is humanity itself,—humanity with its woes and sufferings, but also with its aspirations and its struggles for a better life.

CHAPTER VI

THE ART OF ZOLA IN "GERMINAL"

THE preceding sections of this study indicate how much care Zola put into his creation. But he did more; he managed to transform a subject which at first glimpse seems limited, drab, and dismal into something grandiose and, on occasion, even poetic. For Zola was a poet. Not a lyric poet, to be sure, but an epic poet. Writing in 1885 to Henry Céard, the novelist declared that his work was "une grande fresque," and that he himself possessed a poetic temperament. "Vous n'êtes pas stupéfait, comme les autres, de trouver en moi un poète," and he goes on to state categorically that exact observation is for him a springboard. "La vérité," he says, "monte d'un coup d'aile jusqu'au symbole." [1] More than one critic, of course, has noted this statement and observed Zola's procedures. Guy Robert, F. W. J. Hemmings, Marcel Girard, F. Doucet, Armand Lanoux, J. H. Matthews, and most recently Philip Walker [2] have all called attention in various ways to the poetic quality of Zola's masterpiece. They have studied aspects of style and manner, underlined certain mythical concepts, and reached the conclusion that these elements in his work lend to it much of its distinction. Without repeating all that these critics have written about this particular novel, we wish in this section to take certain portions of *Germinal* and subject them to a fairly close scrutiny for the purpose of observing the artistic devices which permitted Zola to paint a convincing picture of commonplace reality or enabled him to bestow on that reality grandeur and epic force.

A. EXAMPLES OF THE EPIC IN "GERMINAL"

The opening chapter of *Germinal*, in which nothing much happens, is nevertheless a masterly introduction. An unemployed worker, Étienne Lantier, comes to Montsou, meets an old wagoner named Bonnemort, and talks to him about the possibility of employment. That constitutes all the action of the chapter. Its richness lies in everything surrounding that action. A man walking alone in a pitch-black, starless night, whipped by the March wind "blowing in great gusts like a storm at sea," a wind made icy "from sweeping over miles of marshes and bare earth," surrounded by a flat, treeless, unending plain, advancing on a road that runs "with the straightness of a jetty through the blinding, swirling sea of darkness," [3] —such is the initial picture painted by Zola. It contains already some of the essential elements of the book: the hero (if there be one), the suggestion of storm and struggle, the grim bareness of the landscape, the emphasis on darkness which introduces the most important tone of the novel,—a tone which comes naturally enough to Zola's mind in view of the subject and which carries with it a presentiment, a foreboding, perhaps even a prediction of disaster. The only break in this almost infinite blackness comes when the traveller perceives pools of red, "three braziers apparently burning in mid-air." They seem to him like "smoky moons," and they hover over a "solid black mass, [. . .] dimly outlined by five or six dreary lanterns hanging on blackened timber-work which stands like a row of gigantic trestles." From this "fantastic, smoke-black apparition arises the heavy, laboured panting of escaping steam." Here again, the picture is prophetic, with hints of something monstrous and fearful. M. Girard has said that the predominant colours of *Germinal* are black and white, the latter being defined as "le blanc terne." He is correct, though we persist in thinking that he is more correct when he says that Zola uses them through "fidélité au réel" than when he attributes to these colours any profound philosophical significance. In any case, in this opening chapter white is absent. Red is chosen in its stead.[4] The flames playing on the black background are suggestive of Hell,—the hell which Zola stated in his *Ébauche* [5] he intended to expose.

Throughout the chapter these basic elements of darkness, cold, bareness, and storm are recalled. A paragraph introducing the wagoner and picturing a workman at the tip (*le culbuteur*)

ends with a sentence on the wind: "Up above, the icy wind
redoubled its fury with great regular gusts like the strokes of a
scythe." A moment later: "Could he (Étienne) not hear a cry
of famine borne over this bleak country by the March wind?
The gale had lashed itself into a fury and seemed to be blowing
death to all labour and scarcity that would kill countless
men. [...] Everything seemed to vanish into the black unknown." Nor is the red forgotten, for Étienne glimpses in this
obscurity "distant furnaces and coke-ovens [...] with their
sloping lines of crimson flames; whilst further to the left the
two blast furnaces were burning blue in the sky like giant
torches." The wind and the flames are again used by Zola to
introduce the paragraph relating the old man's history: "The
wind went on wailing like a cry of weariness and hunger
rising from the depths of the night. By the light of the leaping
flames the old man kept quietly on chewing over his mem-
ories." And the chapter ends with the same wind, darkness,
and flames: "Each squall seemed fiercer than the last [...] No
touch of dawn whitened the dead sky: only the blast furnaces
and coke-ovens flamed, reddening as with blood the darkness
without penetrating its mystery."

The something monstrous and fearful suggested by the first
object emerging from the blackness of the night takes on
identifiable shape and form as the traveller recognizes a mining
pit with its surface machinery. But the frightening and
fantastic aspect of the apparition is carefully maintained. The
first distinguishable workers are pictured as "living shadows."
The old wagoner is stunted and his spittle black. The mine
itself, Le Voreux, with its suggestive name, "its chimney
sticking up like a menacing horn," appears like an "evil,
voracious beast, crouching ready to devour the world." The
escaping steam of the pump with its long, heavy, monotonous
panting" is like "the snorting breath of a monster." And the
chapter ends on the same note. On this "naked plain deep in
darkness" Le Voreux inspires fear. "Huddled in its lair like
some evil beast," it "crouched ever lower and its breath came
in longer and deeper gasps, as though it were struggling to

digest its ration of human flesh." There is more than realism, there is a form of poetry in this evocation of the mining scene.

Atmosphere is not all. The chapter informs us that the traveller's name is Étienne Lantier, that he is about twenty-one years old, dark, good-looking, strong in spite of his slight build. We learn something of his past, his dismissal from his railroad job after striking his boss, his week-long endeavour to find work, his total destitution. We realize that as an outsider, coming into the mining area, he can observe the scene more effectively than one long familiar with it. His conversation with the old wagoner establishes the latter's identity, situates by an allusion to the Mexican expedition the action of the novel in time, confirms the industrial crisis sweeping over the country, brings us through Bonnemort into contact with life in the mines. The person of the old man reveals the effect of forty-five years spent underground. His short stature, big head, powerful neck, square hands, simian arms, his flat, livid features blotched with blue, his game legs, his dreadful cough and black spittle,[6] all testify to the unhealthy life he has led. Bonnemort represents the worker who has been brutalized and stupefied by a lifetime in the mines. He deserves retirement and a little ease, but here he is, clinging to a surface job which he is barely able to accomplish in order to get a few more francs pension. His family history, related before the leaping flames, sums up a hundred and six years of hard, dangerous labour in which five members of the family had "left their skins."

We also learn in this chapter something about the Montsou Company. While not as wealthy as its neighbour, the Compagnie d'Anzin, it is still rich and powerful with nineteen active pits and several others for drainage and ventilation. Its general manager, we are told, is a M. Hennebeau, a paid employee. And when Étienne Lantier asks who owns the mine, the old man can only make a kind of impotent gesture and say: "God knows . . . People . . ." "And he pointed to some vague unknown distant spot [. . .] His voice had taken on a kind of religious awe, as though he were speaking of some inaccessible tabernacle, where dwelt unseen the gorged and crouching deity whom they all appeased with their flesh but whom no one had ever beheld." Like the mine itself this remote god is voracious.

At the end of the first chapter, the exposition is not, of course, complete. But the atmosphere has been created, two of the human protagonists introduced and others mentioned, the non-human protagonists—the insatiable, devouring mine and the distant capitalistic ogre—have been evoked, the storm image presented. An epic struggle of men against forces more powerful than they lies just ahead.

These colours and images seem to us naturally suggested by the subject which Zola has chosen to treat. To compare the mine with hell is an obvious comparison. To personify capitalism as an ogre or to present it as a remote deity to which men are sacrificed was not in 1885, thirty odd years after the *Communist Manifesto*, particularly startling. But natural as they may be, the colours and images of this opening chapter are appropriate and effective, and they continue throughout the book, both in its action and its descriptive passages.[7] Much of the action takes place underground [8] where black is, logically, the surrounding colour. White, except when the miners are seeking to escape from their subterranean condition, rarely is synonymous with the pleasant or the brilliant, but rather with the sickly, the wan, or the weak. The storm theme, as Mr Walker has eloquently stated, reappears in the imagery of the "human flood thundering across the plain in Part V" and the "catastrophic, apocalyptic descriptions of the inundated mines in Part VII." The voracious monster evoked in the first chapter swallows its daily ration of men as Étienne later watches them disappear into its gluttonous jaws and is in turn absorbed. The remote deity, against whom the workers are pitted, never ceases to be all-present though invisible. The hell conjured up in the opening chapter is confirmed by the underground scene where the gallery being exploited by Maheu's squad is explicitly stated (ch. 3, Part I) as being "in hell." The concept recurs with greater force in the first chapter of Part V. Here the proximity to the Jean-Bart mine of Le Tartaret creates hellish conditions indeed, and the name itself is, of course, suggestive of the classical lower-world region, Tartarus, as far below Hades as Heaven is above the earth. The classical comparison is doubtless commonplace. Indeed, the resemblance of a mining region to phenomena of ancient mythology had already been indicated in one of Zola's principal source-books. Simonin's *La Vie souterraine*.[9] We doubt whether Zola in coining a name like Le Tartaret meant to imply, as Mr Walker thinks, that just as the Cyclops were released by Jupiter from Tartarus to take part in his war against Cronus, so the colliers emerge from the depths to battle against the remote deity, capitalism. We cannot see, as he does, any widespread or significant "application of Christian, Celtic, and Greco-Roman mythology" in *Germinal*. Moreover, nothing in Zola's "notes de travail" indicates such an intention on his part. But we agree that the images of storm and struggle strewn throughout the book, sometimes classical, sometimes not, help markedly to lift the text above the drab and dreary scene which Zola chose to depict and to give the subject greater distinction. The images are not incompatible with his concept of the naturalistic novel. As a naturalist, he lets reality carry its own meaning, and uses imagery, not to explain action, but to confer greater stature on reality. His images are, therefore, appropriate and effective. It is not necessary to clothe them with supernatural significance.

The fourth chapter of Part I is devoted to an account of Étienne's first day in the mine. Here we see the men at work. The chapter (which we do not intend to analyze *in toto*) is skilfully constructed from Zola's personal observation at Anzin and from his reading. Take, for example, the description of "le travail à col tordu." At Anzin, in spite of the strike, a few men were apparently working and Zola reports in his notes that the miner "lies on his side and attacks the vein obliquely." "I saw one," he adds, "completely naked, his skin black with coal-dust." [10] And in Simonin's book he found a picture bearing the legend: "Le travail à col tordu" which showed a miner working in this uncomfortable position.[11] We find in this chapter of *Germinal* a thoroughly naturalistic description of coal mining under similarly difficult conditions. "In order to get at the coal," says Zola, "they had to lie on one side with twisted neck, arms above their heads, and wield their short-handled picks slantways." In the French original, the correct technical word, *rivelaine*, is used (as we saw in an earlier chapter) for the type of pick in question. In this cramped posture, in the midst of intolerable heat, these men hacked away without exchanging a word. "All that could be heard," writes Zola, now utilizing his imagination together with his information, "was their irregular tapping, which sounded distant and muffled, for in this dead air sounds raised no echo but took on a harsh sonority. The darkness was mysterious in its blackness (il semblait que les ténèbres fussent d'un noir inconnu) [. . .] Ghostly forms moved about and an occasional gleam let one glimpse the curve of a man's hip, a sinewy arm, a fierce looking face daubed with dirt as if for a crime (barbouillée comme pour un crime). Now and then blocks of coal shimmered as they came loose [. . .] then all went black again, the picks tapped on dully, and the only other sounds were panting breath, groans of discomfort and fatigue in the heavy air and dripping water." The scene is interpreted as well as described,—a good example of naturalistic art.

Further details on the terrible task of getting out the coal follow on these initial passages. But a considerable part of the chapter is devoted to Étienne and Catherine,—to their work which requires less experience and skill than demanded of the hewers (*les haveurs*) but arduous indeed, and to their personalities, of which Zola gives us various traits during the luncheon break. Here it is that he links the novel with the Rougon-Macquart series when Étienne tells of his mother, a laundress in the *rue de la Goutte d'or*, and admits the effect alcohol has on him. Here it is, too, that after first finding the girl unattractive, Étienne begins to perceive her charm. And here, too, Zola gives important details on Catherine: her frank friendliness, her fundamental decency, her intellectual limitations. In the last moments of this scene we have also the beginning of the rivalry between Étienne and Chaval over the girl when this brutish miner, seizing her by the shoulders, plants a kiss on her mouth, just before Étienne can do so. The whole scene is an effective one, adding to the reader's knowledge and understanding of this pair, and laying the groundwork for later action.

But at the end Zola returns to the collective scene, and the final, eloquent paragraph renews in us a strong impression of the incredible labour required of these men and girls to earn a modest day's wage. "In this desperate fight for such hard-earned gain," writes Zola, "everything else faded into insignificance." Suffering and fatigue pile up, but "like moles burrowing under the weight of earth, without a breath of air in their burning lungs, they went on wielding their picks without pause" (Eux, au fond de leur trou de taupe, sous le poids de la terre, n'ayant plus de souffle dans leurs poitrines embrasées, tapaient toujours). What reader can fail to be moved by this vision of hardships so grimly endured? The vocabulary, the whole arrangement is not only calculated to tell the truth, to reproduce reality, but also to arouse compassion, to inspire pity, and to win the reader's sympathy. It succeeds.

Another chapter worthy of analysis is the last one of Part VI relating the clash between the miners and the soldiers summoned to guard the pits. In contrast to the opening pages of the book, these are full of action, announced by an ominous paragraph at the end of the preceding chapter where a bugle-call orders the soldiers to take up their arms and "in the growing daylight a band of men and women could be seen coming down from the village *(le coron)*, their anger apparent in every gesture."

Logical, clear construction with the narrative marching implacably to its inevitable conclusion of death is an important method used by Zola in this chapter which is also particularly notable for its skilful mixture of truth and invention. The first device is dramatic. The events unfold with chronological exactitude, creating automatically their formidable impact. The second relies on a technique which Zola uses here with special skill: the weaving of fact and fiction into a single, integral pattern.

The novelist assembles gradually most of the miners and mining women whom we have met, and gives to each a rôle consonant with his or her character. La Maheude, for example, is there and her mood of angry exaltation which has been growing throughout the strike reaches its foreordained climax when she urges her husband to violence. Catherine plays a somewhat unexpected rôle which Zola takes pains to motivate. But La Mouquette and her brother arrive and act as we might predict. Zacharie exhibits his usual indifference, Souvarine his customary aloofness. And so it goes.

The assembled strikers are increased by Zola in a rapid build-up from thirty-five to four hundred, then more than five hundred, with new waves still arriving to swell the flood. Against them stand but sixty soldiers. Only their guns keep the mob at bay.

The action falls into several fairly distinct parts. There is a kind of prologue in which the corpse of Trompette is brought to the surface while the author, with his habitual love of animals, relates the creature's friendship with Bataille and the latter's despair when his younger friend sickened and died. The episode creates a grim, lugubrious note. Meanwhile the original thirty-five miners have been joined by others, and soon the platoon of soldiers is confronted by a mob far outnumbering them. During this first stage, Étienne typically tries to win over the captain in charge. Zola is here utilizing an idea that he had found in Laveleye's *Le Socialisme contemporain*: that the supreme peril for the established order would be the conversion of the army to socialism.[12] Failing in this attempt, Étienne ceases to hold back his comrades, who rush ever closer to the troop, shouting insults and threats. Some of the actual words and gestures were found by Zola in the newspaper accounts of the violence that occurred during the strikes at La Ricamarie and Aubin in 1869. When the strikers yell: "Vivent les soldats! au puits l'officier," this is but a slight modification of the cry at La Ricamarie: "Au puits, les officiers! Vivent les

du linge. Trois fois déjà, la recrue avait reçu des éra-
flures; sa main droite saignait, une brûlure l'agaçait
au genou droit, est-ce qu'on allait
se laisser embêter longtemps? Près de lui le vieux
chevronné se mordait les lèvres, dans un dernier effort de patience,
lorsqu'une pierre ricocha et vint le frapper au ventre:
ses joues tannées verdirent, son arme trembla, s'al-
longea, au bout de ses bras maigres. À deux reprises,
le capitaine fut sur le point de commander le feu.
Une angoisse l'étranglait, une lutte intermi-
nable où quelques secondes heurta en lui des idées, des de-
voirs, toutes ses croyances d'homme et de soldat. La grêle des briques redoublait, et il ouvrait la
bouche, il allait crier: Feu! lorsque les fusils par-
tirent d'eux-mêmes, trois coups d'abord, puis cinq,
puis un roulement de peloton, puis un tout seul,
longtemps après, dans le grand silence.

    Ce fut une stupeur: ils avaient tiré, la foule
béante recula immobile, sans le croire encore. Mais des cris
déchirants s'élevèrent, tandis que le clairon sonnait
la cessation du feu. Et il y eut une panique folle,
un galop de bétail mitraillé, une fuite éper-
due dans la boue.

    Bébert et Lydie étaient tombés l'un sur l'au-
tre, aux trois premiers coups, la petite frappée à
la face, le petit troué au dessous de l'épaule gauche.

A PAGE OF THE MANUSCRIPT

(Photostat by the Bibliothéque Nationale)

militaires." [13] And when they shout: "A bas les pantalons
rouges!" they are repeating verbatim what the strikers at
Aubin cried out in 1869.[14] The captain's order to his men to
present bayonets is modelled on the action of the military
officers at La Ricamarie.[15] But, with his good sense of novelistic
needs and of dramatic composition, Zola does not rely exclusively on source material. When one hears the shrill voice of
Lydie say: "En voilà des andouilles de lignards" ("Just look at
those silly old sausages of soldiers"), the cry is doubtless in the
spirit of La Ricamarie, but the vocabulary is Zola's own. The
intervention of Richomme is also original. It introduces a
moment of hope, quickly dashed by the tactless, if courageous,
appearance of Négrel. The rôle of La Brûlé, while suggested
in part by the newspaper accounts all of which emphasized the
wrath of the mining women, is explained even more by the
traits of character that Zola attributed to her.

A new part of the action now begins. Before the growing
and ever threatening mob, the captain, like his prototype at
La Ricamarie, orders the guns to be loaded in the hope of
cowing the crowd. Here again, while employing some of the
actual words and gestures from the 1869 strikes—such as the
reference to the Crimean campaign [16]—, Zola has used his own
imagination, for La Mouquette's famous gesture had no
counterpart at La Ricamarie or Aubin. It brings this section
of the narrative to a colourful climax.

The final section begins with the captain's decision to take
a few prisoners. It leads to what Zola—again utilizing details
from the strikes of 1869—calls the "bataille à coups de pierre,"
appropriately begun (as was seen in an earlier section of this
study) by La Brûlé, and this battle in turn culminates in the
spontaneous discharge of the guns by the exasperated soldiers.
Here, Zola skilfully combines fact and fiction. At La Ricamarie
the soldiers had likewise fired spontaneously, before the
captain could utter the command. At Aubin the clash had
resulted in fourteen dead and twenty-odd wounded. In
Germinal the number is the same. But, of course, the persons
killed are of Zola's choice and invention. He selects Maheu to

be the victim of the last shot, which in the Aubin strike killed one of the company's guards, a man greatly esteemed, as Maheu is highly regarded by his comrades and, before the strike, by the company's officials. He introduces the noble act of La Mouquette who saves Catherine at the cost of her own life. At the end, he reminds us of the corpse of Trompette lying in eloquent juxtaposition to the human corpses, and he brings to this lugubrious scene abbé Ranvier, the socialist priest, who calls down God's wrath on the assassins and the fire of heaven on the bourgeois guilty of massacring the wretched workers of the earth.

The chapter is notable as well for its skilful manipulation of the crowd. All critics from Jules Lemaître to F. W. J. Hemmings and Angus Wilson have admired Zola's ability with mob scenes. In these pages, as elsewhere in the book, Zola displays great powers of epic narration and description. The dramatic night meeting of three thousand men and women in the nearby forest with its admirable chiaroscuro effects under the rising moon (in Part IV), the march of the miners and their women singing the Marseillaise and demanding bread (in Part V), and now this conflict between the strikers and the troops,—these are unforgettable scenes in which Zola has proved his genius. Dr Hemmings explains his success by his intuitive recognition of the truth that "people in the aggregate are more ferocious, and yet more cowardly, than each separate component of the group." [17] Without the contagion of mass emotion would Maigrat in that earlier scene have received his extraordinary treatment? Without the circumstance of mass action would a man like Toussaint Maheu have pressed his bared breast against the fixed bayonets of the soldiers?

The chapter is very different from the opening pages of the novel. It is narrative rather than expository. It utilizes specific, documentary data in combination with invented material. The former, which Zola could conceivably have imagined but which he was doubtless glad to find, lends authenticity to the total composition, for it has the ring of truth. The struggle forecast in the initial chapter comes to a great climax here. With it come compassion and pity for these human beings caught in a conflict which they seem powerless to avoid.[18]

B.   A STRIKING EXAMPLE OF THE DESCRIPTIVE IN "GERMINAL"

There is more than the epic in *Germinal*. Indeed, the chapters just analyzed are richly evocative, with generous use of the pictorial. Zola paints with a firm hand, now giving a wide sweep to his brush, now concentrating on a detail. This descriptive technique supports the expository, the symbolic, the narrative, and, when it exists, the epic. Chapter 2 of Part III in a sense reverses this procedure. Devoted to the Montsou fair-day ("le jour de la ducasse de Montsou"), these pages are predominantly descriptive and pictorial, supported by a minimum of narrative. The chapter deserves special examination.

When Flaubert wrote *Mme Bovary*, one of his aims was to depict provincial customs, as the subtitle, *Mœurs de province*, proclaims. He, therefore, included a description of the rustic wedding which linked Emma and Charles to a common fate, and composed that wonderful tableau of an agricultural fair during which Rodolphe Boulanger begins his campaign of seduction. Now Zola did not give any comparable subtitle to *Germinal*, but the representation of life in the mining area is nevertheless part of his purpose. That is evident in his evocation of the Maheus' home and the Grégoires' way of life. The chapter on the Montsou fair-day is a *tableau de mœurs* in which, at the same time, the mining characters of the novel reappear and some action occurs, for it is in these pages that the marriage of Zacharie and Philomène is arranged and, as a consequence, the decision that Étienne will become a boarder in the Maheu household is taken. Nor does Zola forget the coming conflict, for Étienne talks up his project of a "caisse de prévoyance," convincing Maheu and Chaval of its desirability.

A holiday spirit and atmosphere reign throughout the chapter. The mining village (*le coron*), obviously all agog over the fair, rises later than usual—though still early—, hurries through preparations for the noon repast at which rabbit and beef make their rare appearance, sends its men strolling afterwards to Montsou, where drinks and games vie with the open-air bazaars for their attention and their pocketbooks. A game of ninepins at the Avantage is won by Levaque while La Mouquette watches in the fruitless hope of persuading Étienne to join her. Later, the men make the rounds of the beer parlors, Levaque and others succumbing to the lure of Le Volcan with its cheap prostitutes. A cockfight and a finch contest are a brief but colourful attraction for many. A fist fight between a nailmaker and Zacharie, offended by the man's pinching Catherine's thigh, is averted only by Chaval's intervention. The afternoon wears on, and all drift toward the cabaret and dance-hall of the Bon-Joyeux.

This scene at the Bon-Joyeux is the climax of the chapter and gives an idea of Zola's pictorial powers and possibly his limitations. The dance-hall—suggested, incidentally, by one that Zola saw at Anzin [19]—is represented as a huge room with a wooden floor in the centre only, the rest being laid with brick. It was "adorned with two chains of paper flowers crossing from one corner of the ceiling to the other and caught up in the middle by a wreath of the same flowers." On the walls were "gilt shields bearing saints' names: Saint Éloi, patron of iron workers, Saint Crispin, patron of cobblers, Sainte Barbe, patroness of miners, and, in fact, the calendar of all the trades." The ceiling was low,—so low that "the three musicians on their platform no bigger than a pulpit were almost squeezed against it."

The dominant quality of the scene depicted is the physical, the grossly physical,—beginning with the owner of the Bon-Joyeux, widow Désir, "round as a barrel," with her six lovers, "one for each weekday" and "all six together on Sundays." Rivers of beer have been consumed in this establishment and heaven knows how many kegs will be broached and emptied before this fair-day is ended. On the dance-floor the couples swirl to the music. As Zola puts it: "the three musicians played like mad, and nothing could be seen but the movement of hips and bosoms in a confusion of waving arms" ("les trois musiciens faisaient rage, on ne voyait plus, dans la salle, que le remuement des hanches et des gorges, au milieu d'une confusion de bras"). But when the lamps were brought in, then "everything was suddenly lit up: red faces, hair coming down and sticking to the skin, skirts flying, wafting a strong odour of couples all a-sweat" ("brusquement tout s'éclaira, les faces rouges, les cheveux dépeignés, collés à la peau, les jupes volantes, balayant l'odeur forte des couples en sueur"). La Mouquette, "round and fat like a bladder of lard, was gyrating in the arms of a tall, thin trammer" ("ronde et grasse comme une vessie de saindoux, tournait violemment aux bras d'un grand moulineur maigre.") While there is a touch of caricature in this little glimpse of the fat girl and her skinny partner, the main impression is still the grossly physical,—combined with the rapidity of the motion.

Zola now creates a brief interlude with the arrival of Maheu's wife and children, the Levaque woman accompanied by Bouteloup and Philomène's two infants. But the dancing goes on: "a quadrille was ending in a cloud of reddish dust, the walls were splitting, a cornet was giving vent to shrill whistlings like a railway engine in distress, and when the dancers stopped, they were steaming like horses" ("une fin de quadrille noyait le bal dans une poussière rousse; les murs craquaient, un piston poussait des coups de sifflet aigus, pareil à une locomotive en détresse; et, quand les danseurs s'arrêtèrent, ils fumaient comme des chevaux"). Here again, the predominant element is the physical, the grossly physical, for there is no suggestion of grace or charm in the picture. Nor does a polka which follows change the impression.

When Zacharie, Mouquet, and Levaque finally arrive, they bring with them the fumes of strong drink and worse. And the evening wears on, with a continual swilling down of beer, drunken laughter, exposed flesh, sweating dancers, and noisy music. At the end, the miners return to their homes, while some of the young men and girls wander off into the wheat field. But the last sentence of the chapter reminds us of the social conflict, for Étienne, conversing with Chaval, cries out that "only one thing warms his heart: the idea that they will one day sweep away the bourgeois."

The picture drawn by Zola is partly static, partly active. Thanks to a good choice of verbs and several effective similes,[20] it is animated and lively. But colours are lacking. We are not told whether the chains of paper flowers decorating the hall are pink or red or green or yellow. The only bit of colour in the ornamentation is the gilt on the shields around the room. Nothing is said about the dresses of the girls; their faces are red from exertion, but of their costume not a syllable. The contrast between this picture and one like Auguste Renoir's *Bal au moulin de la Galette* [21] is startling, for in Renoir's work colour is all-important, with an infinite variety of shades skilfully blended together. Furthermore, in this painting Renoir brought into central focus, not only a group seated at a table in the right foreground, but two or three couples dancing to the left and rear. Zola, to be sure, shows us a group seated at a table (though not at the edge of the dance-floor which was more or less separate at the Bon-Joyeux), but in depicting the dancing he pays less attention to individual couples than the painter did. The novelist states that Chaval and Catherine dance together, without, however, showing them in a close-up. The only pair really spotlighted—and how briefly!—is La Mouquette with her anonymous partner. What Zola really gives us is, rather, a vision, almost a blur, of moving, sweating men and girls, swaying in a welter of sound. He adds, of course, one sensual effect that Renoir could hardly render in painting, the odour emanating from these bodies dripping with sweat. Zola is more discreet here in his use of smell than one might expect in view of his sensitivity to it, but it is there.

The comparison with Renoir is perhaps unfair to both men, for their aims were quite different. The painter was depicting an outdoor scene in which light, shade, colour, and human beings were the essentials. His painting gives some impression of movement, but the effect is rather like that produced by stopping a moving-picture (in colour) at a given point. For

Zola, the movement was more important, but above all the collective effect and the social content interested him. Whereas Renoir relied almost exclusively on the visual, Zola was able through the written word, not only to conjure up the visual, but to create motion, sound, and smell. It all leads to an intellectual interpretation that Zola undoubtedly intended, for while there is gaiety in this chapter, while the miners are evidently having a good time, the reader cannot help thinking that even in their pleasures the lot of these human beings is far from enviable. Is this the best that society can do for them? They lead a limited, restricted, almost animalistic existence which none can envy and which all must deplore. From this point of view, the picture of the dance at the Bon-Joyeux, like the whole chapter, is eminently successful. Doubtless it lacks the grandeur or the epic force which we find in certain sections of the novel, but the style and technique adopted by the author are appropriate to his subject and his purpose.

These chapters, whether epic or simply descriptive, reveal Zola's skill as a writer. Doubtless he is not the master of the individual sentence, pre-occupied above all with rhythm, as was Flaubert. Nor has he the poetic, melodious style of a Victor Hugo. There is no music in his lines. The "écriture artiste" of the Goncourts had small appeal for him.[22] His adjectives, in particular, tend to be commonplace. But his limitations are counterbalanced by undeniable qualities. His imagination is essentially epic and he therefore works with broad effects, vast canvases, tremendous clashing forces. Appropriately then, his style is robust, full-bodied, rising at times to great eloquence, well adapted to the subject he has chosen to treat. As he himself wrote: "Je suis pour toutes les audaces, pour toutes les intensités, mais je les veux en bronze, solides et impeccables, autant que franches et colorées."[23] He, therefore, does not seek the exquisite word or the delicate detail. But his pictures and narratives, convincingly reproducing reality, often magnifying it on an epic scale and in an epic vision, are full of intensity and life. The pages we have analyzed testify to these qualities of his work.

CHAPTER VII

CRITICAL OPINION OF "GERMINAL"

After the success of *L'Assommoir*, every novel published by Zola was an event in the literary world of Paris. *Germinal* was certainly no exception. While it was not, for obvious reasons, as sensational as *Nana*, it aroused intense interest and won widespread acclaim. Not that the critcs were unanimous in their praise. Those who were hostile to Zola because they disapproved of naturalism or because they were hopelessly conservative were not converted. Brunetière, for example, could hardly be expected to admire anything emerging from Zola's pen. In fact, he very largely ignored *Germinal*, his only comment appearing incidentally in a discussion of Octave Feuillet's novels in which he implied that characters like Catherine Maheu are hardly worth writing about as they are not sufficiently complex: "leurs actions sont trop simples, et plus simples encore les mobiles qui les leur dictent." [1] Other critics—if we may dignify some of the book reviewers by that name—were equally hostile. The anonymous critic of *La Liberté* (5 March, 1885) not only considered the book inferior to Talmeyr's *Le Grisou*, but maintained that Zola had not even succeeded in portraying the miners correctly, for he had committed the egregious error of making them talk like Parisian workers. Zola took the trouble to answer this particular attack. In an interview in *Le Matin* (7 March, 1885) he said: "Si j'avais écrit mon roman dans le patois du Nord, je doute que personne ait jamais consenti à me lire." *La Liberté* had also complained about the *tutoiement* that Zola attributed to the miners, claiming that in reality they always used *vous*. To this Zola replied that at Anzin the miners had many of the habits of other workers, including the use of the familiar forms ("y compris le tutoiement"). The paper also criticized the great catastrophe caused by Souvarine. Zola's reply was brief: "ce n'est que l'adaptation d'un fait célèbre dans l'histoire des mines: la catastrophe du puits de Marles dans le Pas-de-Calais." Perhaps no favourable criticism could be expected from *La Liberté*, which included

Edouard Drumont among its collaborators. Drumont's notoriety as an anti-semite had not yet been established, but he was already conservative and his reaction to Zola's novels, including *Germinal*, was unfavourable. Not many years later he dismissed the novelist as "coprologique." [2]

In 1885 opinion similar to Drumont's was expressed by the reviewer of *La République Française* (28 February, 1885) who accused Zola of dirtying everything he touched and called *Germinal* "une longue diffamation de la société française." And Jean Morin, in *Le Gaulois* (9 March, 1885), while unbothered by the so-called crudities of the novel, condemned it in a sentence that was partially self-contradictory: "Le livre de M. Zola est lourd, puissant, bien construit, mal écrit; en somme, peu intéressant."

But hostile criticisms unmitigated by any admiration were rare. More common was a mixture of praise and blame. The anonymous reviewer of *Le Télégraphe* (11 March, 1885) summed up his views by saying: "C'est toujours, c'est plus que jamais le mélange bien connu de pages maîtresses, vigoureusement enlevées, et de hors-d'œuvre grivois." Much more thorough in its treatment of the book was Octave Mirbeau's article in *La France* (11 March, 1885), which made some reservations but expressed genuine enthusiasm. Referring to the volumes of the *Rougon-Macquart* already published, Mirbeau wrote: "Il se dégage de toute son œuvre une force, souvent brutale, parfois grossière, mais belle en somme, malgré l'exagération de ses muscles et la fougue emportée de ses gestes." Concerning the new novel, he confessed his impatience with Zola's tendency to over-employ a crude vocabulary, but he considered that the novelist had admirably indicated "par des réalités impitoyables ce qu'il y a d'insalubre et pour ainsi dire de fatal dans les disproportions des destinées humaines," and he concluded his article by urging this man, essentially a poet, to throw overboard his naturalistic methods. "Cet admirable écrivain," he wrote, "qui sait donner de la vie au plus petit et au plus fugitif de ses rêves, est un poète aux larges coups d'ailes qui l'emportent, malgré lui, vers les pures et splendides régions de l'art. Par

quelle déraison veut-il faire croire à la foule qu'il a coupé ses
ailes, et qu'il rampe tristement sur des moignons, dans la boue
du chemin?"

Victor Fournel (in *Le Moniteur universel*, 14 April, 1885) dis-
liked the documentary aspect of *Germinal*, objected to its crudities, admired the mob scenes, and concluded: "De tous les
romans publiés jusqu'à ce jour par l'auteur des *Rougon-Macquart*,
Germinal est peut-être le plus puissant, celui qui renferme le plus
de tableaux vigoureux et qui, à certaines pages, par les procédés
naturels à M. Zola,—l'entassement des traits, la multiplication
des touches, l'outrance froide des peintures,—saisit le mieux,
comme dans le rude engrenage d'une machine, l'esprit du
lecteur. Avec tous ses défauts habituels [. . .] il contient tous les
éléments d'un beau livre, sombre, pessimiste, terrible, mais
d'une force rare."

The socialistic side of the novel inevitably caused some dis-
pleasure. Hippolyte Fournier, the conservative critic of the
conservative paper, *La Patrie* (6 March, 1885) registered that
point of view by saying that in this novel Zola was taking off
the mask and showing the features of a literary Jacobin, "ra-
jeuni par le souffle de ce socialisme nuancé de nihilisme qui
caractérise une névrosiaque fin de siècle." But, from a purely
literary point of view, he considered *Germinal* as "une œuvre
de maître." All the descriptive part of the novel he dubbed
"superbe." He particularly admired the scene of the strangling
of Cécile Grégoire by Bonnemort which he called a "trouvaille
de génie," "à la fois shakespearienne et dantesque." This harm-
less daughter of bourgeois parents and this semi-paralyzed,
quasi-imbecile old man take on, he asserted, "symbolic value."
"Les voilà bien les deux races, l'une la privilégiée, et l'autre la
martyre." And Fournier added: "Lorsque, dans un effort
suprême [. . .] il [Bonnemort] serre de ses doigts noueux le cou
blanc de Cécile [. . .] c'est, écrit avec la puissance de Zola,
l'apologue de la revanche prise et de la mission de destruction
accomplie." Fournier was correct in this judgment, for, as we
have seen,[3] Zola wished in this scene to show clearly "cette
résultante des Maheu contre les Grégoire."

L'Événement did well by Zola, publishing two articles, a review by Edmond Deschaumes (2 March, 1885) and a longer more general discussion by Louis Desprez (8 May, 1885). The former had some misgivings, to be sure. "Jamais Zola ne s'est montré d'une sensualité aussi violente, aussi brutale," he wrote. One wonders whether he had ever read *Nana*. And he also felt that *Germinal* was less a novel than a social study. But he had great praise for Zola's narrative of the strike which he called a "tableau saisissant, d'une intensité cruelle." The clash with the soldiers seemed to him "une maîtresse page." The description of the catastrophe after Souvarine's sabotage he deemed admirable. "De page en page," he wrote, "Zola nous déroule de fortes et superbes études, qui n'ont que le malheur d'être trop sincères et trop rudes et de traduire trop textuellement la réalité." At the same time he could not help concluding that Zola had written "un beau livre, mais un livre de douleur et d'amertume, qui ne laisse aucun espoir que celui de la vengeance, de la satisfaction des haines et de l'asservissement des appétits."

Louis Desprez devoted the first part of his article to Balzac, whom he describes as an intellectual. The pleasure one derives from his work is that of the intelligence. In contrast, Zola seems to him essentially a "sensitif." He makes his reader see and feel. "Sa vraie gloire ce sera d'avoir été le grand poète de la chair jouissante et souffrante, d'avoir poussé le cri de misère le plus terrible peut-être que l'humanité ait encore entendu." *Germinal* is the most "feverish" of his books. Part V in particular aroused Desprez's admiration: "Il y a là des pages d'une couleur fauve, bien nouvelle dans la série des *Rougon*, et d'un effet splendide; je veux parler de la cinquième partie, où l'on sent la griserie sauvage d'un peuple en tumulte, où les femmes exaspérées, débridées, semblent des hyènes."

If *L'Événement* did well by Zola, *Le Figaro* did even better. On 4 March Philippe Gille wrote: "M. Zola a pris encore cette fois la nature brute et terrible pour modèle et avec quelle vigueur de tons, quelle magistrale force de couleur il nous a peint des scènes de la vie cruelle!" Quoting from the scene at

the bottom of the mine when Chaval's corpse floats close to
Catherine and Étienne, he says: "je ne connais pas dans l'*Enfer*
de pages plus effroyablement dramatiques que celles que je
viens de citer et [. . .] si Dante les avait écrites, elles seraient
depuis longtemps classiques dans notre pays." [4]

Ten days later, under the pseudonym of Quidam, Anatole
Claveau gave his reaction in *Le Figaro* to Zola's latest novel.
Disliking naturalistic literature and, therefore, certain aspects
of *Germinal*, he nevertheless pronounced it "un livre puissant,
un livre superbe!" "Il est certain," he adds, "que l'auteur a
senti, à un moment donné, passer en lui l'âme des masses
populaires, et qu'il lui a suffi de la toucher au point juste, en
certaines pages de son roman, pour en tirer les plus grandioses
et les plus terribles effets. Vous trouverez là une émeute de
mineurs qui vous donne vraiment la chair de poule, une mêlée
féroce, où les femmes débridées mêlent une note infâme et qui
produit sur nous autant d'impression, par exemple, que l'*Assassinat de l'évêque de Liège* d'Eugène Delacroix."

Some of Claveau's reservations about the novel led Zola to
send him a personal letter, part of which Claveau printed in
Le Figaro on 27 April, 1885. "Pourquoi," wrote Zola, "re-
trancher de la vie, par convenance, le grand *instinct génésique*,
qui est la vie même? Vous mettez l'homme dans le cerveau, je
le mets dans tous les organes. Je puis me tromper, mais il n'est
pas juste de voir une vilenie de charlatan où il y a une conviction
de philosophe. Et j'ajoute que dans la peinture des classes d'en
bas, je croirais mon tableau faux et incomplet, si je n'indiquais
pas toutes les conséquences du milieu d'ignorance et de misère."
Zola's sincerity is beyond dispute.

Meanwhile on the 4th of April *Le Figaro* had published a
letter from Henry Duhamel criticizing *Germinal* on purely
technical grounds. Women no longer work in the mines, he
maintained, and since the strike in question seems obviously to
be that of 1884 rather than a conflict of the Second Empire, it is
incorrect to put them underground. Zola's description of the
mining village with its odious promiscuities he also believes
erroneous. Duhamel states that in reality they are located "en

plein champ," that they are "bien aérées," and that they present "un aspect tout à fait frappant de propreté, de confortable, et quelquefois d'élégance." Zola lost no time in replying to this attack. The complete text of his letter was published in *Le Figaro* the very next day and the curious reader will find it in Zola's *Correspondance* (Bernouard edition, pp. 638–639). He argued correctly—that the action of his novel took place during the Second Empire, that the strike is not that of 1884, but rather a composite of the strikes that occurred toward the end of the Empire, "particularly those of Aubin and La Rica-marie." As for other accusations, specially that of immorality, he wrote: "Hélas! j'ai atténué [. . .] Pourquoi veut-on que je calomnie les misérables? Je n'ai eu qu'un désir, les montrer tels que notre société les fait et soulever une telle pitié, un tel cri de justice, que la France cesse enfin de se laisser dévorer par l'ambi-tion d'une poignée de politiciens, pour s'occuper de la santé et de la richesse de ses enfants." All in all, *Le Figaro* gave Zola a lot of publicity and a considerable measure of support.

Marcel Fouquier, writing in *La France* (23 March, 1885), commented on the contrast between Zola's theories and his work. The theories demand scientific exactitude, but the work reveals the presence of a romantic poet. Like others, Fouquier admired greatly the scenes of mass action which he called epic, and his general conclusion was that the novel is "belle, im-posante, saine."

One of the most favourable reviews came from the paper that had published *Germinal* in serial form. Paul Ginisty (*Gil Blas*, 1 March, 1885; also *L'Année littéraire*, 1885, pp. 47–49) saluted Zola's extraordinary industry as well as his literary skill. Con-cerning the characters he wrote: "quel prodigieux relief il leur a donné, de quelle vie intense, dans sa réalité violente, il les a fait vivre." The landscapes seem to him no less admirable: "Et quels paysages aussi! Quelle puissance d'évocation dans ces tableaux des mille aspects de la mine, cette dévorante d'hom-mes." The only reservation, rather timidly made, concerns the description of Maigrat's mutilation which he obviously thinks too audacious. But he views the novel as essentially noble, proclaiming, as it does, the right to life and liberty, to sunlight, and to repose after a lifetime of labour.

A somewhat belated opinion came from the pen of Gustave Geffroy in *La Justice* (14 July, 1885). Everything in the book, he declared, takes on life: "On voit tout tressaillir, s'animer, lutter, aimer, haïr." As a result: "La matérialité prend ainsi une existence et une grandeur qui seront difficilement dépassées." And Geffroy concludes with a paragraph on the poet in Zola: "N'est-ce pas assez de ces hallucinations devant la matière, de ces créations d'objets vivants, de ces violentes interprétations des inconsciences naturelles, de ces cadences qui parcourent tout un volume, de ces retours de rythmes,—n'est-ce pas assez pour montrer en Émile Zola le poète qu'on se refuse généralement à voir, le poète panthéiste qui sait superbement augmenter et idéaliser les choses."

Other newspapers either ignored *Germinal* or paid it but a brief tribute. Albert Dubrujeaud, writing in the *Echo de Paris* (3 March, 1885) had a lot to say about Zola's earlier novels and almost nothing about the latest. But he did go so far as to state that Zola had finally learned how to write and to recommend *Germinal* to his readers. The book reviewer of *Le Siècle* (18 April, 1885) called the novel "le sombre poème de la mine," and Eugène Asse, in a discussion of various new novels,[5] saw in *Germinal* "le poème épique de la grève." Louis Bougier in *Le National* (8 March, 1885) expressed his admiration mingled with some curiosity about the possible influence of Turgenev on the composition of the novel.[6] *Le XIXe Siècle* (10 March, 1885) permitted Francisque Sarcey to begin a discussion of *La Joie de vivre* and *Germinal* which for some reason was never concluded. But Sarcey committed himself (at the end of the first article) to the extent of saying that *Germinal* was an admirable study.[7] Later he said of Zola's novels in general: "Zola procède par masses, le développement, chez lui, se répand en nappes immenses [. . .] Zola vaut par l'ensemble." [8]—a criticism that contains a good deal of truth.

The foregoing pages indicate that newspaper reaction was, in general, favourable with comparatively little outright hostility and with much genuine enthusiasm. The same can be said of weekly and monthly publications. Except for the very incidental comment of Brunetière, already mentioned, *La Revue des Deux Mondes* ignored the book. *Le Journal des Débats* (17 March, 1885), through the pen of André Mori, reproached Zola for the "sensualité obsédante" of the novel, called attention to the discrepancy between his theories and his performance ("chez M. Zola, le souci du vrai passe presque toujours après la recherche du grandiose"), but greatly admired the scenes of mass action. Léon Allard in *La Vie moderne* (14 March, 1885) gave unstinted praise to the novel, clearly showing that he had been profoundly moved by it. He concluded: "Un livre comme *Germinal* assurerait à lui seul la gloire d'un auteur; celle de M. Émile Zola, depuis si longtemps et si solidement établie, grandit encore avec cette belle œuvre." In *Les Annales politiques et littéraires* (8 March, 1885), Adolphe Brisson, while obviously shocked by the "crudités salées" he found in the book, gave it nevertheless high praise: "Ce que nous ne pouvons citer, ce qui lui donne sa haute valeur, c'est la vigueur des peintures et le parfum de réalité terrible qui s'en exhale." Édouard Rod's only adverse criticism (in the *Revue contemporaine*, 25 March, 1885) was the inclusion of Mme Hennebeau's adultery which he viewed as out of place in this epic history of a strike.[9] Otherwise he admired the book, emphasizing its humanitarian aspect: "à chaque page se dresse ainsi la terrible question des injustices sociales: pourquoi ceux-ci et pas ceux-là? [. . .] pourquoi tant de douleurs massées en un coin de la terre?"

The large majority of the reviewers and critics listed so far in this chapter have left no reputation that impresses today's historian of literature. But Jules Lemaître stands in a different category, for his opinions still command respect. He gave voice to them in a substantial article in the *Revue politique et littéraire*.[10] Zola, he says, is not really a naturalistic novelist in the meaning he gives to the word "naturalistic"; his pictures are too "outrées" and "systématiques" for that. Zola is, rather, an epic poet and a pessimistic poet (un poète épique et un poète pessimiste"). As for *Germinal*, Lemaître sums up this "épopée de douleur, de faim, de luxure et de mort" as follows:

> Un troupeau de misérables, soulevé par la faim et par l'instinct, attiré par un rêve grossier, mû par des forces fatales et allant, avec des bouillonnements et des remous, se briser contre une force supérieure: voilà le drame. Les hommes apparaissant, semblables à des flots, sur une mer de ténèbres et d'inconscience: voilà la vision philosophique, très simple, dans laquelle ce drame se résout. M. Zola laisse aux psychologues le soin d'écrire la monographie de chacun de ces flots, d'en faire un centre et comme un microcosme. Il n'a que l'imagination des vastes ensembles matériels et des infinis détails extérieurs. Mais je me demande si personne l'a jamais eue à ce degré.

Lemaître goes on to assert that whereas the old epic poets sought to deify their characters, Zola animalizes his. The epic machinery—what the French call "le merveilleux"—of the *Rougon-Macquart*, is the Paradou of *La Faute de l'abbé Mouret*, the dram-shop of *L'Assommoir*, the department store of *Au bonheur des dames*, the mine of *Germinal*. His final word is that the famous series is "une épopée pessimiste de l'animalité humaine."

Zola replied at once to Lemaître: "J'accepte très volontiers votre définition: 'une épopée pessimiste de l'animalité humaine,' à la condition pourtant de m'expliquer sur ce mot 'animalité. Vous mettez l'homme dans le cerveau, je le mets dans tous ses organes. Vous isolez l'homme de la nature, je ne le vois pas sans la terre, d'où il sort et où il rentre. [...]" [11] While the reply is a good one, it is a little surprising to see Zola accepting the qualification of "pessimist" for however somber his pictures of reality may be, there is always the underlying hope of improvement. *Germinal* closes on such a hope and in *Le Roman expérimental*, Zola declared that one of the aims of the genre is reform and amelioration. The determinist is not necessarily a fatalist meekly accepting the status quo.[12]

About this same time Paul Bourget spoke with respect of Zola's novel. Calling attention to the social transformation which made great individualists less likely to flourish than in the time of Stendhal—perhaps a debatable proposition—Bourget declared that Zola had observed this fact of society and had depicted it with great power in his novels: *Le Ventre de Paris*, *Au Bonheur des dames*, *Germinal* where the principal character is no longer an individual but a section of a city, a department store, a mine.[13]

While Zola must have been, on the whole, pleased by Lemaître's article and Bourget's comments, both of which paid him the tribute of taking his work seriously, certain letters he received doubtless gratified him fully as much. Huysmans, for example, wrote him at length, praising the "prodigieuse carcasse de ce livre écrit avec une poigne de fer," and commenting specially on Zola's use of black. He admired the "descente dans les puits, au milieu du noir dont vous êtes seul parvenu à faire une couleur, qui révèle une puissance de rendu vraiment unique à l'heure actuelle." And he confessed himself moved by Catherine, whom he described as "vraiment charmante de résignation et d'innocente impudeur." [14] In another letter he called the novel "un sacré beau livre," and added: "Si jamais la théorie des milieux a donné de magnifiques résultats c'est bien dans ce livre où la mine est gigantesque et vous étreint comme un cauchemar." [15]

A letter from Ferdinand Fabre called the book "superbe," and a note from Richepin praised it as "admirable et absolument beau." [16] From Palermo, Maupassant wrote that he found *Germinal* the most powerful of all Zola's novels. "Vous avez remué là-dedans," he continued, "une telle masse d'humanité attendrissante et bestiale, fouillé tant de misère et de bêtise pitoyable, fait grouiller une telle foule terrible et désolante au milieu d'un décor admirable que jamais livre assurément n'a contenu tant de vie et de mouvement, une pareille somme de peuple." [17] Then, more laconically, Camille Pissarro wrote the author that the book was "beau, grand et terrible," certainly the work of "un grand cœur." [18] While the novel was still *en feuilleton*, Claude Monet in a brief note dubbed it admirable, superb.[19]

Since these were private letters, not destined for publication, the writers' opinions should possibly be discounted, but it would be churlish to deny them all sincerity.

Outside of France, comment on *Germinal* was relatively scarce. The British and Americans [20] were both too dominated by Victorianism to appreciate Zola's novels, even as good a one as *Germinal*. *Blackwood's Magazine*, in May 1887 and September 1888 ran two articles on "French Contemporary Novelists" in which Zola's name was mentioned, *en passant*, but not one of his novels was discussed. In the British Isles the chief exceptions to this indifference or hostility were men like Vizetelly who translated Zola (and was imprisoned for doing so), Sherard, who was to be his biographer, and the Irishman George Moore who wrote Zola before he had finished reading the book to express his admiration. [21] In the United States, most critics were offended by the crudities of the *Rougon-Macquart*. [22] *Nana* and *Pot-Bouille* had outraged them. But even *Germinal* met with their disapproval. The anonymous reviewer of the *Nation* was of the opinion that "not one of the numerous characters— miners or bourgeois—has the faintest notion of virtue, of chastity, of common decency," and he went on to say that "neither in England nor in France could there be found a community so depraved, so utterly God-forsaken as that of M. Zola's miners." [23] On the other hand, Henry James, while not at that time giving his views on *Germinal*, could not help respecting the "solid and serious" aspect of Zola's work in general. [24] In Bohemia, *Les Rougon-Macquart* did not receive the welcome that one might expect. Masaryk viewed its author as a kind of uncouth Romantic. One critic, however, was impressed by *Germinal*. Puchmajer considered it Zola's most interesting work, a powerful and truthful masterpiece. [25] From Germany, in striking contrast to England and the United States, came one of the most eloquent tributes that *Germinal* has ever received. "I do not believe," wrote Karl Bleibtreu, "any man so abandoned by God, so bare of all moral emotion, that he is not gripped and shaken by this immortal work." [26]

By 1902, enough progress away from Victorianism had been

made in the English-speaking countries so that William Dean
Howells did not hesitate to praise Zola's novels [27] without,
however, singling out Germinal for any special commendation.
Soon after, Henry James penned his well-known tribute to
Zola.[28] Admiring the labour and persistance of the builder of
Les Rougon-Macquart, he selected L'Assommoir, Germinal, and
La Débâcle as being the greatest of the series. In Germinal (as in
L'Assommoir) he felt "almost insupportably the sense of life."
He felt it in the "historic chapter of the strike [. . .], another of
those illustrative episodes, viewed as great passages to be
"rendered"; for which our author established altogether a new
measure and standard of handling, a new energy and veracity,
something since which the old trivialities and poverties of
treatment of such aspects have become incompatible, for the
novelist, with either rudimentary intelligence or rudimentary
self-respect." In England, too, progress occurred. The British
authorized Édouard Rod to review Zola's work, which he did
in the Contemporary Review.[29]

Since Zola's death, the reputation of Germinal has steadily
grown. A few critics still prefer L'Assommoir or La Terre, but a
large number give first place to Germinal. An ultra-conservative,
like Baron Seillière, may try to dismiss it as "une œuvre d'agi-
tateur communiste," [30] but others recognize its pre-eminence.
Barbusse's enthusiasm should perhaps be discounted for he was
as prejudiced in the other direction as Seillière in his. But we
feel that there is much truth in his statement that "les livres de
Zola, et notamment ce Germinal, ont chu comme des bolides
au milieu des livres fades ou apprêtés mettant en scène le
travailleur moderne." [31] Louis Cazamian declared that Zola's
art has "eminent virtues" and his description "of the inner life
of a coal-mine (Germinal) [has] not been surpassed." Cazamian
added that Zola is "far from an indifferent writer: he has
pathos, graphic power, and eloquence." [32] A propos of Germinal, Jean Guéhenno has admired Zola's style, saying: "Qui
ose parler du mauvais style de Zola? Quel esthète? Quel
étranger au monde? [. . .] cette première impression que j'eus
de lui [Zola] à la lecture de Germinal m'a révélé les principes de

son œuvre, cette puissance du tempérament et cette ampleur de la respiration qui font la grandeur du cœur, cet entêtement aussi et cette volonté admirable qui peuvent seuls faire les longs poèmes." [33] Guéhenno was not alone in admiring Zola's style, for Jules Romains had already stated that in his view "Zola, comme écrivain et comme artiste est grand." [34] In England, Angus Wilson defended Zola against the dogmatic Marxist critic, George Lukács, who saw in the author of the *Rougon-Macquart* a "naïve liberal," one of those men "whose talents and human qualities destined them for the greatest things, but who have been prevented by capitalism from accomplishing their destiny and finding themselves in a truly realistic art." [35] Wilson views *Germinal* as "one of the greatest novels of the masses," adding that "it declares and shouts the decay of the bourgeois system from within, and shows the *actual* power of the workers as opposed to any sentimentally conceded 'rights.' " [36] Returning to France, Armand Lanoux considers *Germinal* to be "le premier grand roman sur la classe ouvrière qui soit basé sur une analyse vraie au lieu d'un seul élan sentimental." The book has, of course, its sentimental side and appeal, but, says Lanoux, its "infrastructure politique" is realistic.[37] In his biography of Zola, while condemning the "écriture grossière, vocabulaire pauvre, syntaxe négligée" of *Germinal*, the same critic states that the novelist "excelle dans la description du malheur de ceux qu'il aime et devient magistral dans les déferlements catastrophiques." [38] He quotes Albert Thibaudet's opinion that Zola's style is "grossièrement épique," and he might well have included Thibaudet's opinion that Zola is "un très grand primaire," explaining that he is not using the word in any malicious or pejorative sense but rather "dans son sens solide et sain, efficient et positif." [39]

The fiftieth anniversary of Zola's death brought forth a good many comments on Zola and his work. The Bibliothèque Nationale organized an exhibition of manuscripts, letters, first editions, pictures, etc. in his honour. Some of the important studies which are included in our Bibliography appeared appropriately in 1952 or 1953. The left-wing periodical *Europe* devoted a special issue (Nov.-Dec. 1952) to the author of *Les Rougon-Macquart* and the defender of Dreyfus. The principal tribute to *Germinal*, which the editors viewed as Zola's greatest novel, was unfortunately missing because of the imprisonment of André Stil who had been chosen to write it, but the comments of Françoise d'Eaubonnes, Raymond Escholier, and Jean Rousselot testify to the enduring appeal that *Germinal* makes to men and women of good will. Not long after 1952, the French universities surrendered to the movement of opinion and placed *Germinal* on the programme of the Agrégation. This was doubtless not equivalent to posthumous election to the Academy, but it was certainly an important recognition of literary worth and interest.

Perhaps we may terminate this survey by quoting from a writer whom the advance guard reveres: André Gide. The author of *La Symphonie pastorale*, who appears in most ways remote from Zola, confided to his *Journal* that *Germinal*, which he was reading for the third or fourth time, seemed to him "plus admirable que jamais." [40] He listed it among his favourite ten novels written in the French language,[41] and stated categorically that its author deserved to be placed very high,—"en tant qu'artiste et sans aucun souci de 'tendance.'" [42]

CONCLUSION

IN scope and stature Zola's two novels on the working class, *L'Assommoir* and *Germinal*, outstrip all the previous narratives of *Les Rougon-Macquart*. *La Fortune des Rougon* came close to achieving comparable impressiveness in the account of provincial revolts against the *coup d'état* of 1851. *Son Excellence Eugène Rougon* might have possessed considerable grandeur had not Zola left himself become enmeshed in the net of petty machine politics and governmental corruption. *Nana*, to be sure, attempts to depict a "société en décomposition," to use Professor Robert's phrase, but it has always seemed to the present writer that Zola did not succeed in making Nana's principal victim, Count Muffat, a sufficiently credible character, and that in general the group chosen for portrayal is not a convincing microcosm of French society. In the other novels there are interesting moments, personages, or settings; there are passages where Zola's imagination soars and permits him to see things or types "en grand." But either his personal experience was inadequate or his technique still too faulty to sustain a high level of novelistic creation throughout the book. *La Curée* and *Eugène Rougon* are good examples of the former. Zola's contact with the world of speculation was entirely at second hand, through documentation; his political experience was limited to a very brief period of service in 1871 as secretary to Glais-Bizoin, a member of the government of National Defense, and as a reporter for *La Cloche* in 1871 and 1872. On the other hand, *Le Ventre de Paris*, in spite of great merits, is an example of faulty technique. It contains an admirable picture of the Paris markets, full of colour and odour. It also presents the fat (*gras*) little *commerçants* of the foodshops, represented by Lisa Quenu with her indifference to anything but her own comfort and prosperity, and her cruelty to anyone, like her brother-in-law Florent, who seems to threaten her status. These, as Mr Angus Wilson well says, "are the themes on three levels which combine and intertwine to make up that impressionistic picture, part social, part moral, part sensuous, which was to be the pattern of Zola's great works." But, as Mr Wilson admits, Zola's technique fell down. The political plot is in one sense overly involved; in another, inadequately pursued and developed. Other elements "lead nowhere." However original and interesting, *Le Ventre de Paris* simply does not rank among the greatest of *Les Rougon-Macquart*. Nor do the other novels published before 1885 enter the highest rank. There is power in *La Conquête de Plassans*, fascination in *La Faute de l'abbé Mouret*, valuable social history in *Au bonheur des dames*, interesting pages in all. But they nevertheless reveal defects of technique or inadequacies of experienced insight.

For most critics *L'Assommoir* is Zola's first authentic masterpiece. While its central action is the limited rise and the complete fall of Gervaise Macquart, the surrounding material—the life and movement of this drab working-class quarter—imparts to her story social significance. For she is not just one woman. She is a symbol of heredity, with the sins of the fathers descending on the children, and of suffering, the product of ignorance and poverty. The book possesses a sustained realism accompanied by deep compassion which places it well above the previous novels of the series.

Germinal does this and more, for not only does it depict social suffering, not only does it reveal the existence and effect of ignorance and poverty, it discloses some of the economic forces operating within a nation, and above all it narrates in all its intensity and bitterness a social conflict. It combines the compassion of *L'Assommoir* with a penetrating glance into the structure of French society and pays some heed to the causes of the workers' lot. The suffering of the miners is shown to be the result of a system rather than the deliberate work of individuals. The guilt is collective. What is more, the unrelieved pessimism of *L'Assommoir* gives way in *Germinal* to an ultimate expression of optimism. There are those who hold that the title is not meant to convey anything hopeful, merely the emergence of social upheaval. But the final pages with their vision of a springtime drenched with sunshine surely suggest a promise of a better life for those who labour on (or under) the earth.

They cannot be overlooked in any interpretation of the novel.

We have discussed in a previous chapter the epic qualities of this book and in another analyzed its characters. We need not repeat what was said there. It is perhaps sufficient to state in conclusion that as a compassionate narrative of suffering and struggle, *Germinal* has rarely, if ever, been surpassed.

NOTES

NOTES

CHAPTER I

Page

3. 1. Bibliothèque Nationale, Nouvelles acquisitions françaises, MS. 10345, f. 23.

3. 2. *Ibid.*, f. 129. The bracketed words were written by Zola in the interlines. The list of 17 novels may well have been drawn up in 1871.

3. 3. *Émile Zola's Letters to J. Van Santen Kolff*, edited by R. J. Niess, *Washington University Studies*, May, 1940; Letter XXXII, 6 October, 1889.

4. 4. Ch. Seignobos, *Le Déclin de l'Empire*, p. 37, vol. 7 of *Histoire de France contemporaine*, ed. by E. Lavisse, Hachette, 1921.

4. 5. G. Weill, *Histoire du mouvement social en France 1852–1910*, Alcan, 1911, pp. 73–74.

4. 6. P. Louis, *Histoire de la classe ouvrière en France*, Libr. des sciences politiques et sociales, 1927, p. 169.

5. 7. *Ibid.*

5. 8. The 10-hour day for women was not established by law until 1892. In mines, however, the 10-hour day was introduced voluntarily at a fairly early date.

5. 9. Weill, *op. cit.*, p. 255.

5. 10. "Différences entre Balzac et moi," MS. 10345, f. 14–15. See also Le Blond's edition (Bernouard) of *La Fortune des Rougon*, pp. 356–357.

6. 11. Huysmans' *Les Sœurs Vatard* came after *L'Assommoir* and was influenced by Zola rather than the reverse. V. Cherbuliez' *Olivier Maugant*, which includes a strike, appeared too late to have influenced the genesis of *Germinal*. The same is true of C. Lemonnier's *Happe-chair*, which he dedicated to Zola.

7. 12. F. W. J. Hemmings & R. J. Niess, *Émile Zola. Salons*, Droz, 1959, p. 249.

7. 13. C. Mauclair, "Les Peintres du travail en France," *La Revue des revues*, 1902 (vol. XLIII).

7. 14. MS. 10308, f. 439. There is also a note in the dossier of *Germinal* from a M. Rodney (or Rocher) dated 18 February, 1884 telling Zola where he can get information on various strikes.

8. 15. MS. 24520, f. 143. This letter is dated simply: "Paris, lundi 18." But a glance at the calendar for the year 1884 shows that the third Monday of February was the 18th day of that month. In view of this fact and of Zola's literary activity in 1884, it seems reasonable to conclude that the correct date of Hennique's note is 18 February, 1884.

Page

8. 16. MS. 10308, f. 308.

8. 17. E. Vuillemin, *La Grève d'Anzin de février-mars-avril 1884*, Lille, Danel, 1884. See also I. M. Frandon, *Autour de "Germinal"*. *La mine et les mineurs*, Droz, 1955, p. 124, *n. 296.*

8. 18. Zola received authorization from M. de Forcade to visit the Anzin mines (see MS. 10308, f. 434, dated 25 February, 1884). At Anzin, he saw a local manager. In an interview which the novelist granted in 1887 to Maurice Harel (*Le Parti national*, 22 August), he told of getting permission from M. Guerry (*sic*) who turned him over to Mercier, described in the terms we have quoted. As for M. Dubus, his name appears on the verso of f. 435 (MS. 10308), where one reads simply: "M. Dubus, ingénieur à la fosse Renard, Denain (Nord)." This is probably the source of Le Blond's statement which may well be correct.—The name of the local manager is given in various newspapers of 1884 as Gary (cf. *L'Événement*, 25 February, 1884).

9. 19. R. H. Sherard, *Émile Zola*, London, 1893, p. 204.

9. 20. MS. 10308, f. 208–303. These notes contain references to the *Ébauche*. See, for example, f. 270, 271.

9. 21. MS. 10307, f. 1–7. Professor Van Tieghem has published this plan in his *Introduction à l'étude d'Émile Zola*, Centre de documentation universitaire, 1954, pp. 108–115, but unfortunately there are some serious errors and omissions in his text.

9. 22. *A Structural Study of Zola's "Germinal,"* Yale University, 1956, p. 89. Cf. also the *Ébauche*, MS. 10307, f. 494/91: "et dans une partie que j'ajouterai" etc. Mr. Walker has reproduced in his study the text of the *plan par parties*.

9. 23. With one exception: chapter 2 of Part I has only one outline. —In the bound manuscript volume, preserved in the Bibliothèque Nationale, the plan written first *follows* the plan composed second. In this study, whenever we refer to the first plan, we shall always mean the plan written first, not the one appearing first in the dossier.

9. 24. Cf. G. Robert, *Émile Zola. Principes et caractères généraux de son œuvre*, Paris, Les Belles Lettres, 1952, pp. 57–58. Spellings of proper names are a good clue. For example, the crippled boy is called Jenlain in the *Ébauche* (MS. 10307, f. 453/51), in the *Personnages* (MS. 10308, f. 2 and 29), and in the first set of chapter plans (for example, MS. 10307, f. 27, 91, and 309–311). The spelling Jeanlin appears in the second set (for example, MS. 10307, f. 23, 87, and 304–305).

9. 25. There is some evidence that at least a few of the portraits were composed before the first set of chapter plans. In the earlier plan

Page

for ch. 2 of Part II (MS. 10307, f. 75) Zola writes: "Portrait de la
Maheude à consulter absolument (éb. 24). Dans les deux chapitres
suivants aussi." This *feuillet* does not link very well with the
preceding one, so perhaps we should not draw definite conclusions
from it. We find more evidence elsewhere, for example, in the
first plan for ch. 1, Part IV (MS. 10307, f. 155): "Enfin voir les
portraits des personnages, et les employer utilement ici." This
certainly does not look like a later addition to the plan, for it is
not located at the end of the *feuillet*, nor is it written in the
interlinea. Cf. also f. 183 (*first*, *i.e.* earlier plan of ch. 4, Part IV)
where Zola writes: "voir si je dois réserver quelques personnages
pour la forêt, Chaval y est-il? Voir le portrait." Again, we do
not find these words at the end of a *feuillet* or in the interlinea. If
we look at the portrait of Chaval (MS. 10308, f. 52–53), we
discover that it is not at all helpful concerning this particular
point; but it is interesting to note that the portrait closes with the
words: "Devient porion à la fin et se montre très dur." The first
plan for the last chapter of the book says: "Chaval porion, leur
commandant" (MS. 10307, f. 394), while the second (f. 386–391)
naturally omits him, for between the first and second set of plans
Zola had decided to have him killed by Étienne in the flooded mine.

On the other hand, the spelling of Souvarine's name with an
"a" in the portrait devoted to him (MS. 10308, f. 81) suggests
that this portrait was penned after the first set of chapter plans,
though presumably before the second.

The naming of the "petit soldat" as Jules in the portrait of
Étienne (MS. 10308, f. 7) may indicate that this portrait, too, was
composed after the first set of chapter plans, for the lad is nameless
in the earlier plan for both chapters 1 and 6 of Part VI (MS. 10307,
f. 284, and 309–311); in this same portrait of Étienne the name
of Catherine's brother is spelled Jenlain as it is throughout all
the first set of chapter plans.

9.   26. *Correspondance*, ed Bernouard, v. 1, p. 611.

9.   27. *Ibid.*, p. 613.

10. 28. This committee, established by the vote of 2 February, 1884, held
hearings in February and March. It listened, among others, to
delegates from the Anzin strikers, including one deposition by
Émile Basly. There is no proof, however, that Zola read the
procès-verbal of these hearings. But there is in the dossier of
Germinal a report of the speech delivered by Giard on 6 March
1884 (MS. 10308, f. 413).

10. 29. Gustave Geffroy wrote to Zola on 13 November, 1885: "J'ai fait
part à Clémenceau de votre désir de lire son rapport sur la grève

Page

d'Anzin: il vous l'a immédiatement fait envoyer." (MS. 24519, f. 295). This is confirmed by Mlle Frandon, *op. cit.*, p. 126, *n.* 369.

10.   30. *Correspondance*, ed. Bernouard, v. 1, p. 614.

10.   31. *Ibid.*, p. 618.

11.   32. The "notice" published by the *Gil Blas* was probably written by Zola himself. It has been reproduced by P. Lambert in his edition of Huysmans' letters to Zola: *J. K. Huysmans. Lettres inédites à Émile Zola*, Droz, 1953, p. 112.

11.   33. *Correspondance*, ed. Bernouard, v. 1, p. 627. Another bit of evidence is found in Zola's "notes de travail." His second outline for ch. 3 of Part VII includes eight pages of technical notes (f. 340–347, MS. 10307) which interrupt the outline that he began on f. 335, resumed on f. 348, and completed on f. 353. On the back of f. 341 we find: "Médan, 24 novembre 1884"; on the back of f. 345: "Médan, 25 nov 84. Vous êtes bien aimable mon cher confrère." Obviously the technical notes on the recto could not have been written earlier than the dates on the verso, for the pages are clearly discarded, unfinished letters which Zola was economically using up.

11.   34. *Correspondance*, ed. Bernouard, v. 1, p. 631.

11.   35. *Ibid.*, p. 632.

12.   36. Letter to J. Van Santen Kolff, 6 October, 1889: "Et c'est un jour, par hasard, que le mot: Germinal, m'est venu aux lèvres. Je n'en voulais pas d'abord, le trouvant trop mystique, trop symbolique; mais il représentait ce que je cherchais, un avril révolutionnaire, une envolée de la société caduque dans le printemps. Et peu à peu, je m'y suis habitué, si bien que je n'ai jamais pu en trouver un autre. S'il reste obscur pour certains lecteurs, il est devenu pour moi comme un coup de soleil qui éclaire toute l'œuvre." (R. J. Niess, *op. cit.*, p. 33).

In the interview in *Le Figaro*, 18 September, 1884, mentioned above, the title was interpreted as follows: "Dans l'esprit de M. Zola, *Germinal* est cette première végétation que produisent les graines. Ici les graines sont les idées de liberté, d'égalité qu'on a semées dans le peuple." It is impossible to say at exactly what date Zola determined on the title. He refers to it about midway in the *Ébauche* (MS. 10307, f. 449/47), so that he had evidently chosen it by then. It is mentioned in *Le Cri du peuple*, 2 March 1884.

37. While this book was in press, Professor Salvan's publication, "Vingt messages inédits de Zola à Céard," *Les Cahiers naturalistes*, n°. 19, 1961, appeared. On p. 143 he discusses the date of Zola's departure for Anzin, and is inclined to accept Feb. 23 which I have therefore adopted (*supra*, p. 8).

CHAPTER II

Page

16. 1. See the preceding section on the "Genesis of *Germinal.*" Also Van Tieghem, p. 4, and Moreau, pp. 14–15.

17. 2. Professor Robert indicates the almost certain existence of cuts or omissions on f. 420, 453, 470, and 492. See his *Émile Zola. Principes et caractères généraux de son œuvre*, Paris, Les Belles Lettres, 1952, pp. 187–188, note 6. To Robert's list I should also add f. 444/42–445/43. Since Zola himself numbered the pages of his *Ébauche* (from 1–96), any such cuts or omissions would seem to be his responsibility, not that of some later person.

17. 3. f. 418/17.

18. 4. f. 426/25. It is to be noted that this idea is in the section of the *Ébauche* written before the trip to Anzin and presumably before Zola had done much of his documentation.

19. 5. See preceding chapter and MS. 10308, f. 219(11).

20. 6. "Concerning the sources of *Germinal,*" *Romanic Review*, Oct. 1958, p. 171.

20. 7. This *éboulement* was reported in the Paris press. See *L'Événement*, 21 April, 1884.

22. 8. G. Robert *op. cit.*, p. 188, note 12; p. 123.

22. 9. See above, p. 18 and footnote 4.

22. 10. Ph. Van Tieghem, *op. cit.*, pp. 79–80.

22. 11. See, below, chapter III on the sources of *Germinal*.

24. 12. *Op. cit.*, p. 82.

CHAPTER III

Page

25.   1. See above, p. 7–8. References to characters in the novel are found
in some of the notes he took from technical works he consulted
as well as in *Mes notes sur Anzin*. On the other hand, allusions
in the part of the *Ébauche* written before the trip to Anzin, such
as "le vieux puits" and " la mine qui brûle près du vieux puits,"
suggest that he may already have read some of Simonin's book.

25.   2. Ph. Van Tieghem, *Introduction à l'étude d'Émile Zola. "Germinal"*,
Centre de documentation universitaire, 1954, p. 8.

25.   3. See above, p. 7. Maurice Le Blond listed them with others on
p. 548 of his edition. See my article "Concerning the Sources of
Germinal," *Romanic Review*, Oct. 1958, p. 168.

25.   4. MS. 10308, f. 427–428. The name is illegible.

25.   5. Interview in *Le Matin*, 7 March, 1885. As published, the interview
stated that the *Vocabulaire* was by Bormange, doubtless a typo-
graphical error or a mistake made by the reporter.—One should
note that Zola used the *second* edition (1883) of Laveleye's book,
not the first (1881). The second edition contained a long introduction which provided Zola with much material. Notes taken
by Zola from Laveleye's book are found in f. 342–355, MS.
10308; from Simonin in f. 385–396, MS. 10308, and from Testut
in f. 365–369, MS. 10308. But Zola must have had in his study
copies of these three books which he could consult directly.

26.   6. Attention was first called to Zola's use of Simonin by Le Blond
(though he gave the wrong title) and to Laveleye and Leroy-
Beaulieu in my edition of *Germinal* (Scribner, 1951). Professor
Robert confirmed this the following year in his *Émile Zola.
Principes et caractères généraux de son œuvre*. Frandon's valuable
booklet, *Autour de "Germinal," La Mine et les mineurs*, 1955, studies
in detail Zola's use of Simonin, Dormoy, and others. Her chapter
on Dormoy is particularly good. Van Tieghem reproduces many
of the "notes de travail" including notes taken by Zola from
Laveleye, Leroy-Beaulieu, Simonin, Dormoy (incomplete), and
Georges Stell (pseudonym for V. B. Flour de Saint-Genis),
author of *Les Cahiers de doléances des mineurs français*, 1883. Van
Tieghem also calls attention to Zola's possible use of the Encyclopédie Roret. Roret's name appears in the "notes de travail"
but litte or nothing from this source went into the novel. Van
Tieghem fails to indicate that Zola often supplemented his notes
by referring directly to the text of the source books. Cf. also
"Concerning the Sources of *Germinal*," *Romanic Review*, Oct.
1958. See, below, note 58.

Page

26. 7. MS. 10308, f. 208–303. Reproduced by Van Tieghem (though with some omissions and errors) *op. cit.*, pp. 15–38.

26. 8. F. Loquet, "La Documentation géographique dans *Germinal*," *Revue des sciences humaines*, juillet-septembre, 1955.

26. 9. "Mes notes sur Anzin," MS. 10308, f. 209 (1) – 210 (2), 226 (18).

26. 10. *Ibid.*, f. 296 (89).

26. 11. *Ibid.*, f. 212 (4).

27. 12. *Ibid.*, f. 211 (3).

27. 13. *Ibid.*

27. 14. *Germinal*, pp. 32–33, ed. Bernouard or pp. 25–26, ed. Charpentier-Fasquelle.

27. 15. MS. 10308, f. 244 (36)–246 (38): "La machine, 400 chevaux, superbe, trois étages dans l'escalier de bois pour aller en haut. La bielle énorme montant et descendant. La mise en train par une manœuvre à la vapeur, le fil qui descend sur un tableau, le puits en raccourci, avec les hauteurs des différents arrêts marqués. Les deux bobines colossales où les deux câbles de fer plats s'en roulent en sens contraires. Le massif énorme de maçonnerie en briques sur lequel repose la machine. Pas un ébranlement. Quand les bobines se dévident à toute vitesse, le spectacle, avec la bille (*sic*). On peut suivre les câbles à 25 mètres jetés au travers de la nef, montant en haut sur les mollettes et redescendant dans le puits. La charpente de fer et de tôle de fer qui soutient les mollettes, une charpente de cathédrale. [. . .] Un signal correspond avec le bas".

27. 16. *Germinal*, ed. Bernouard, p. 10 or ed. Charpentier-Fasquelle, p. 3, and "Mes notes sur Anzin," MS. 10308, f. 261 (53 bis).

28. 17. L. Simonin, *La Vie souterraine*, 1867, pp. 124–125; S. Bormans, *Vocabulaire des houilleurs liégeois*, Liège, 1864.

28. 18. "Mes notes sur Anzin," MS. 10308, f. 227 (19)–242 (34). This text is available in Le Blond's edition (*i.e.* ed. Bernouard) pp. 561–565 and in Van Tieghem, *op. cit.*, pp. 19–22. In the former, Le Blond has omitted one short paragraph of f. 240 (32) and failed to catch three inconsequential errors; otherwise his text is reliable.

28. 19. *Germinal*, ed. Bernouard, pp. 39ff or ed. Charpentier-Fasquelle, pp. 34ff. Cf. also my ch. VI, pp. 109–110.

28. 20. Simonin, *op. cit.*, pp. 134–137,—quoted by Frandon, *op. cit.*, pp. 26–27.—Among other items of interest, mention may be made of the lowering of the horse into the mine. While Zola was aware even before going to Anzin of the presence of horses underground (*Ébauche*, f. 428/27) and found confirmation of that when he got there, the episode of the lowering of the horse was probably suggested by Simonin (see Frandon, *op. cit.*, p. 26).

Page

28. 21. Dormoy, op. cit., p. 63: "Les deux principales difficultés que l'on rencontre dans le creusement des fosses proviennent des infiltrations d'eaux souterraines et de la présence de sables ébouleux et aquifères. Le terrain crétacé supérieur [. . .] est formé de bancs alternatifs de craie, de sable, et d'argile plus ou moins marneuse: c'est dans ces derniers [. . .] que l'on rencontre généralement les venues d'eau les plus considérables appelées *niveaux*." Cf. Frandon, *op. cit.*, pp. 81–82. On p. 117, Dormoy describes the *torrent*.

29. 22. Cf. Mlle Frandon's chapter on Dormoy.

29. 23. Simonin, *op. cit.*, pp. 164–165; Frandon, op. cit., p. 29.

29. 24. See the *Ébauche*, f. 428/27 and especially f. 434/33–435/34.

29. 25. Simonin, *op. cit.*, p. 218 (cf. Frandon, p. 40). And *Germinal*, ed. Bernouard, pp. 523–524 or ed. Charpentier-Fasquelle, v. 2. pp. 239–240.

29. 26. *Germinal*, ed. Bernouard, p. 527 or ed. Charpentier-Fasquelle, v. 2, pp. 243–244. Simonin, *op. cit.*, pp. 218–219, 221–222; quoted by Frandon, pp. 41–43.

Many other similarities could be cited. There is just no doubt that Simonin's pages account for much in Zola's narrative. Even such a detail as Étienne's hair turning white was suggested by *La Vie souterraine*.

30. 27. See *La République en marche*, texte présenté par J. Keyser, Fasquelle, 1956, v. 2. pp. 204 ff.

30. 28. H. Barbusse, *Zola*, Gallimard, 1931, pp. 162–163.

30. 29. MS. 10308, f. 418–424.

30. 30. Leroy-Beaulieu's *La Question ouvrière* gave Zola confirmation of the influence of socialist theory on the working class: "A défaut des images et des souvenirs religieux, les rêveries socialistes viennent hanter le cœur de nos populations ouvrières" (p. 14). Its description of "réunions ouvrières" (p. 16) and its suggestion that the Revolution of '89 had been profitable only to the bourgeoisie, not to the workers, influenced the novelist. And it contained (p. 83) reflections on labour leaders some of which probably went into Zola's portrait of Etienne.

31. 31. *Germinal*, ed. Bernouard, p. 154 or ed. Charpentier-Fasquelle, p. 159; Laveleye, *op. cit.*, p. xxiv.

31. 32. *Germinal*, ed. Bernouard, p. 151 or ed. Charpentier-Fasquelle, p. 156, and Laveleye, *op. cit.*, pp. 237–238. Laveleye quotes in these pages from the *Revolutionary Catechism* drawn up by Bakunin (or possibly Nechayev). See in our chapter on the characters of *Germinal* the section devoted to Souvarine.

31. 33. Laveleye, op. cit., p. 268 and *Germinal*, ed. Bernouard, p. 297 or ed. Charpentier-Fasquelle, p. 320. Zola must have copied directly

Page

from Laveleye's book for in his "notes de travail" all we find is: "Programme des collectivistes. On pourrait le donner à Étienne (268). Lui veut l'instruction. Souvarine hausse les épaules: à quoi bon" (MS. 10308, f. 355).

As a matter of fact, still more of Étienne's speech is taken from Laveleye. The latter also included among collectivist principles: "garantie de l'indépendance individuelle grâce à la possession, par chaque producteur, du surplus de valeur obtenu, par son travail, sur la matière qu'il a travaillée" and "l'assurance, pour chaque membre de la société, de recevoir, aux frais de la collectivité, une instruction intégrale et professionnelle en rapport avec l'ensemble des connaissances de son temps." Zola shortened these a bit and made them a little less technical, but the similarity between these words and Étienne's is still very close.

31. 34. Professor Hemmings, in an article on "Zola, *Le Bien public* and *Le Voltaire*," *Romanic Review*, 1956, p. 107, has called attention to a radical priest created at an early date by Zola. This early priest, however, is a forerunner of Pierre Froment in *Les Trois Villes* rather than of Ranvier.

31. 35. *Ébauche*, f. 407/6.

31. 36. *Germinal*, ed. Bernouard, p. 446 or ed. Charpentier-Fasquelle, v. 2, p. 154.

32. 37. Zola apparently did not make use of the *Rapport Clémenceau* on the Anzin strike. I agree with Mlle Frandon; see above, ch. 1. —It should also be noted that more than once Zola chose not to use certain items from source material. For example at Montceau-les-Mines during the strike of 1882 anti-religious acts occurred. In spite of his anti-clericalism Zola failed to utilize them. The indifference in *Germinal* of the miners to religion and the church is something that he noted in his own trip to Anzin (MS. 10308, f. 295/88).

The strike at Fourchambault in 1870 furnished Zola with the *affiche* posted by the administration of the Montsou company (chapter 1, Part VII of *Germinal*). Zola copied the text almost verbatim from the *Gazette des Tribunaux*, 18–19 April, 1870. See also my article "Concerning the Sources of *Germinal*," *Romanic Review*, Oct. 1958.

33. 38. *Germinal*, ed. Bernouard, p. 175 or ed. Charpentier-Fasquelle, p. 183, and MS. 10308, f. 408.

33. 39. MS. 10308, f. 410 and 413; *Germinal*, ed. Bernouard, p. 196 or ed. Charpentier-Fasquelle, p. 206. (I have quoted directly from the *Journal officiel*, 7 March, 1884, p. 651. The wording of the text in Zola's notes differs slightly, but not essentially).

Page

33. 40. I have not found a lottery in which "le gros lot de 100,000 francs" was won by "ouvriers chapeliers de Marseille" as in *Germinal* (ed. Bernouard p. 419 or ed. Charpentier-Fasquelle, v. 2, p. 124). The nearest is the Franco-Algerian lottery of 1882 in which the grand prize of 500,000 fr. was won by ten factory workers from Marseilles. *La Vérité*, 2 February, 1882, said of them: "il n'en est resté que deux à la fabrique où ils travaillaient; les huit autres l'ont quittée définitivement samedi dernier et se proposent de tenter quelque commerce à leur compte avec le capital que la fortune vient de mettre entre leurs mains." Not long after, a workman (un tâcheron) won 100,000 fr. in the "loterie des artistes dramatiques." *La Vérité* reported (27 April, 1882) that after collecting the money he invested it before returning home. I am not suggesting that either item is the source of Zola's text. They merely indicate that events of this type did occur and show that some reality probably lay behind the statement in *Germinal*.

33. 41. For further evidence see farther on in chapter 5 my discussion of Souvarine's past.

34. 42. Cf. Frandon, *op. cit.*, p. 97 and *Germinal*, ed. Bernouard, p. 112, 175 or ed. Charpentier-Fasquelle, p. 114, 183.

34. 43. Cf. Frandon, *op. cit.*, pp. 98–99. But also see "Mes notes sur Anzin," MS. 10308, f. 221 (13)–222 (14): "Les filles très débauchées ne se marient qu'au 2e ou 3e enfant. Vont dans les blés, dans les coins noirs (le long du canal)."

34. 44. Frandon, *op. cit.*, p. 95.

34. 45. MS. 10308, f. 330: "Les houillères sont obligées de produire beaucoup pour baisser leur prix de revient." F. 331: "Malheur au faible qui ne peut produire (*Voilà ma petite mine.*)"(Cf. Frandon, p. 119, note 167. Amédée Burat was the author of numerous works and reports on the mining industry. He died in 1883.

34. 46. Leroy-Beaulieu, *op. cit.*, pp. 59–62.

34. 47. Y. Guyot, *La Science économique*, 1881. See in particular the chapter entitled "Crises commerciales." Cf. Frandon, *op. cit.*, pp. 59–62.

34. 48. *Germinal*, ed. Bernouard, p. 88 or ed. Charpentier-Fasquelle, p. 87.

36. 49. Frandon, *op. cit.*, pp. 54–55.

36. 50. *Ébauche*, f. 442/40–443/41.

36. 51. Unless la mère Brûlé was influenced by Talmeyr's Ghilaine. It seems unlikely, for while la mère Brûlé is violent, she is not technically crazy. The only similarity is age.

37. 52. I have discussed this question more fully in "Concerning the Sources of *Germinal*," *Romanic Review*, Oct. 1958. See also, above, note 45 and see below, note 58.

Page

37. 53. "Le *Germinal* d'Yves Guyot," *Revue d'histoire littéraire de la France,* 1954.

37. 54. Frandon, *op. cit.*, p. 68.

38. 55. *Ibid.*, pp. 72–75.

38. 56. *Ibid.*, p. 76.

39. 57. See Loquet, *loc. cit.*

39. 58. A word of comment on M. Tersen's not uninteresting article entitled "Sources et sens de *Germinal*" (*La Pensée*, janv.-fév., 1961), is perhaps desirable. Written from a sociological-historical point of view, it advances certain conjectures difficult to accept, for example: (1) that the strike in *Germinal* was inspired not only by that of Anzin (1884) and those of La Ricamarie and Aubin (plus a detail or two from Fourchambault and Montceau-les-Mines), but also by the "grève dite des Quatre sous, en mai 1833"; (2) that the clash between miners and soldiers was suggested not only by the events at La Ricamarie and Aubin, but also by "la fusillade des mineurs sous Louis-Philippe." M. Tersen gives no real proof in support of these statements.

Throughout his article M. Tersen seems unaware of the certain influence of the books by Laveleye, Leroy-Beaulieu, and Testut —to say nothing of Simonin and Dormoy—on the composition of the novel.

A word, too, on Mr. Zakarian's unpublished doctoral dissertation, "A Study of the Sources of *Germinal*, based upon an examination of Zola's manuscripts, notes, and their sources" (Northwestern University, 1960). This title did not come to my attention until after my own study was written and accepted for publication.

CHAPTER IV

Page

40. 1. See, above, Chapter I, notes 24 and 25, and below notes 13 and 17,

40. 2. Words followed by an asterisk and enclosed in brackets were written by Zola in the interlinea.

41. 3. The earlier plan is found in MS. 10307, f. 12–16, the later in f. 8–11. In both, Zola notes that he must include some fact that will date the action.

41. 4. MS. 10307, f. 12: "Étienne seul, sur la route de Marchiennes à Montsou [. . .] la nuit noire [. . .] le vent glacial qui souffle dans la plaine rase." And on f. 13: "Comme distribution de la description, il ne faut d'abord qu'une masse presque informe, une vision fantastique de la fosse aperçue dans la nuit."

41. 5. *Ibid.*, f. 13.

41. 6. *Ibid.*, f. 13–14. The words followed by an asterisk and enclosed in brackets were written by Zola in the interlinea.

41. 7. *Ibid.*, f. 13–14.

42. 8. In the novel: huit jours.

42. 9. MS. 10307, f. 9.

42. 10. *Ibid.*, f. 12: "Il [*i.e.* Étienne] aura mangé son dernier morceau de pain à Marchiennes et il y aura dormi dans un coin de forge. L'avenir vide devant lui, pas un morceau de pain, pas de place, renvoyé de partout, et la crise qui sévit, que va-t-il faire."

42. 11. *Ibid.*, f. 10.

42. 12. *Ibid.*, f. 11.

43. 13. With regard to the intervening chapters a few points may be noted. There is only one detailed plan for ch. 2 of Part I. Since, in this outline, the 11-year-old boy's name is spelled Jenlain it appears to have been penned at the time when Zola was doing the first set.—Ch. 3 of Part I calls for some comment. Here the *Plan par parties* indicates that Zola planned two chapters instead of one, the first being devoted to the "arrivée des ouvriers au puits" with a description of the buildings and the hiring of Étienne, the second to the "descente." The earlier detailed plan throws these proposed chapters into one. The later plan has Étienne descend into the mine in the same *berline* with Catherine instead of with La Mouquette as in the earlier one,—a superior arrangement which permits a bit of humour to enter the chapter.

In Part II, the earlier detailed plans for chapters 4 and 5 show that le père Caffiaux was still in the *dramatis personae* (see f. 93 and 100, MS. 10307). In fact there is reference to him in the later plan (f. 97–98) for chapter 5.

A number of items in the planning of Part III are of interest.

Page

The *Plan par parties* shows that originally Étienne was to become
a lodger at the Maheus' in ch. 1 and that the chapter on the
ducasse was to be the third chapter of this part.

In the second chapter of Part IV, the later detailed plan describes
Maheu's speech as "son discours du paysan du Danube."

Two points in the planning of ch. 3 are of interest. La Maheude's careless exposure of her breast leading to Chaval's insult
is included in the later plan, not in the earlier one. But it is
mentioned in the preliminary portrait in the *Personnages*. Then
the end of the chapter is much better forecast in the later plan
than in the earlier one.

43. 14. MS. 10307, f. 4. See note 2.

43. 15. MS. 10307, f. 209.—There are, of course, other points touched
on by Zola in his detailed plans. He notes on f. 207 apropos of
Étienne's speech: "Prendre le programme dans Laveleye" (See,
above, my chapter on the sources). In both plans Souvarine is
scheduled to be present. In the later plan Zola shows concern
about the arrangement of his cast, grouping them effectively,
and adding: "Poser chaque personnage, avec son attitude, et
préparer l'effet sur lui." (f. 205).

44. 16. In the first four chapters of this part, a few points may be noted.
Chapter 2 in the *Plan par parties* has an even more succinct outline
than usual: "Un travail au fond qui me donne la mine. Catherine
et Antoine au fond. Trouver la scène. Jusqu'aux câbles coupés.
Ils remontent par les échelles." While the earlier detailed plan for
this chapter suggests the terrible heat in which Catherine has to
work, it places her in a different working group from Chaval's
and does not specifically mention her collapse. The later plan
places Catherine and Chaval in the same squad, with even a
moment of tenderness after her collapse (see my discussion of
Chaval, p. 91). It emphasizes much more than the earlier plan
the escape via the ladders: "Donner surtout la sensation des cent
deux échelles" (f. 231).

The plans for chapter 4 show some hesitation. One item in the
Plan par parties: "Ingénieur rencontré" was abandoned by Zola;
another: "Terreur du pays" was postponed. The earlier outline
is shorter than usual and consequently far less detailed on the
headlong race from one mine to another than the later plan will
be. The singing of the Marseillaise and the cry: "Vive la sociale!
mort aux bourgeois" with which this outline ends were finally
reserved for chapters 5 and 6.

44. 17. In the preliminary portrait of Négrel in the *Personnages* (MS.
10308, f. 66) Zola wrote: "Lui donner pourtant un moment de

Page

peur, la vue de la révolution sociale de plus tard qui passe, pendant qu'il est caché quelque part avec sa tante. Cette scène est excellente, il faut cette vision pour compléter le livre, voir où l'on la placera." The last words suggest that this portrait was penned *before* the first (*i.e.* earlier) chapter plan. See notes 7 and 8 in the next chapter (V, B).

44. 18. MS. 10307, f. 158. This is part of the earlier outline for ch. 1 of Part IV.

45. 19. "Je voudrais aussi avoir la mort de Maigrat. Mais je voudrais qu'il se tuât lui-même et que les violences n'eussent lieu que sur son cadavre." Another indication that the *feuillet* may not have been written at the same time as f. 260–263 is a paragraph like the following: "Paul et sa tante partis de bonne heure. Hennebeau monte chez son neveu pour reprendre un livre, un plan, et l'objet aperçu dans les draps tombés à terre. La chambre n'est pas encore faite—cette chambre où sa femme monte retrouver le jeune homme.—Hennebeau devrait empêcher cela. Il faut en parler à sa femme. A arranger." In any case, it suggests that Zola was still groping for his definitive arrangement.

45. 20. On f. 262 of the earlier plan he writes: "Montrer que le bonheur humain ne sera pas encore dans la solution sociale," and in the later plan (f. 259) he is even more explicit: "Faire entendre que lorsque la justice régnera, le bonheur humain n'y gagnera rien, à cause du malheur des passions." Cf. the *Ébauche*, f. 441/39–442/40, 460/57.

45. 21. This plan is contained in f. 271–275; the later one in f. 265–270, 276. The *feuillet* numbered 276 is clearly misplaced in the dossier; it belongs with the outline beginning on f. 265 and is evidently the last *feuillet* of that outline.

46. 22. MS. 10307, f. 268. And cf note 2.

46. 23 Ms. 10307, f. 6–7.

47. 24. *Ibid.*, f. 278. "Là, je voudrais un mot de la terreur de Montsou, et l'effet d'un prône par l'abbé maigre aux yeux de braise rouge que l'abbé Joire promenait comme son successeur. Il tombe sur la bourgeoisie libérale à propos de l'émeute, regarde ça comme sa punition (Laveleye 167)." Zola also envisaged a meeting between him et Étienne (f. 280–281) which he abandoned when he came to write the chapter.

47. 25. *Ibid.*, f. 292: "Une scène centrale, des enfants demandant du pain chez les Maheu. Un malade, le désespoir farouche du père, attitude de la mère." The later plan specifies almost at once f. (287) that Alzire is the sick child.

47. 26. *Ibid.*, f. 287: "Là je voudrais l'épisode des querelles et la surprise de la Pierronne. Les cancans des femmes qui poussent les hommes les uns sur les autres." F. 288: "Et Lydie vendant sa mère [. . .] Dansaert est là, il a fait le coron avec deux gendarmes [. . .], et il les a renvoyés à la nuit pour rester seul avec Pierronne."— F. 291: "Alzire de plus en plus mal."

In the later plan Zola decides to introduce abbé Ranvier (f. 289). He was not mentioned in the earlier one.

47. 27. *Ibid.*, f. 291. "Et enfin Pologne qu'on lui a fait manger, son dégoût, deux larmes."

47. 28. *Ibid.*, f. 325.

47. 29. *Ibid.*, f. 317. Cf. *La Gazette des Tribunaux*, 6 August, 1869.—A minor point worth reporting about this chapter is that abbé Ranvier, not mentioned in the earlier plan, appears in the second "au moment des coups de feu" (f. 318). In the book he will appear at the very end of the chapter.

48. 30. By the time he composed the first set of chapter plans, Zola had settled on six chapters, instead of seven, and had transferred much of the material of the sixth paragraph of the *Plan par parties* to the fourth chapter and the balance to the fifth.

48. 31. The *Plan par parties* indicated that Souvarine's act of sabotage was to occur in this chapter. That was dropped in the first detailed plan.—One curious item in this earlier plan was to suggest that Deneulin's oldest son, the army officer, might return "pour le donner comme amant à madame Hennebeau." Concerning Chaval it says: "Chaval nommé peut-être (est-il déja porion? non)."

48. 32. MS. 10307, f. 333: "La collision qui le décide, la seule façon d'attaquer le capital."

48. 33. *Ibid.*: "J'ai envie de faire partir Souvorine (*sic*) dans la nuit, sans regarder derrière lui, même sachant que du monde descendra, ayant lu les affiches."

48. 34. *Ibid.*, f. 330: "Dehors ils rencontrent Souvarine debout [. . .] Où allez-vous? Et quand il le sait, son mépris pour Étienne qui se soumet. Il veut l'arrêter, puis le laisse aller à la mort. Pas d'ami, pas d'amour."

48. 35. For example, on f. 351 Zola writes: "Et Négrel descendant seul (ou avec Dansaert)." There is no statement about Dansaert's cowardice as there will be in the novel where he is described as "ivre d'épouvante" and where in consequence Négrel descends alone to inspect the damage.

48. 36. MS. 10307, f. 367.

49. 37. *Ibid.*, f. 364. See my article, "Marriage or Murder: Zola's Hesitations concerning Cécile Grégoire," *French Studies*, Jan. 1961.

Page

49. 38. *Ibid.*, f. 385.—In this outline Zola even thought of including the charitable visit of the Grégoires to the Maheus: "Est-ce là que les Grégoire vont porter des souliers au vieux Maheu, Bonnemort [. . .]" (f. 385).

49. 39. *Ibid.*, f. 370–371. Cf. note 2.

49. 40. *Ibid.*, f. 394–395. But Zola adds: "Je ne voudrais pas finir sur Étienne partant, comme il est arrivé au premier chapitre."

50. 41. This may also be a reminiscence of f. 471/68 of the *Ébauche.*—The "claques" which she administered to Étienne in this chapter were not actually mentioned in the preliminary plans for the chapter. They are indicated farther on, at the beginning of the second plan for ch. 6 (f. 265) where Zola writes that Étienne is "dégrisé par les claques de Catherine."

50. 42. MS. 10307, f. 333: "J'ai envie de faire partir Souvorine (*sic*) dans la nuit, sans regarder derrière lui [. . .] Il va dans l'inconnu, portant ailleurs la destruction, sans qu'il soit jamais question de lui."

50. 43. *Ibid.*, f. 392 and 395.

51. 44. In the *Ébauche*, f. 466/63 and in the portrait of Étienne in the *Personnages* there are suggestions that may have provided the initial spark for this paragraph, but they are very slight.

51. 45. MS. 10305, f. 335. Cf. "The Newspapers of *Germinal*: their Identity and Significance," *Modern Language Review*, Jan. 1960.

51. 46. MS. 10307, f. 308.

52. 47. *Ibid.*, f. 171. As before, the words followed by an asterisk and enclosed in brackets were written by Zola in the interlinea.

CHAPTER V

A. THE PRINCIPAL PROTAGONISTS: THE MAHEU FAMILY

Page

55. 1. Quite apart from the fact that Étienne existed in *L'Assommoir*, the first reference to him in the *Ébauche* (f. 415/14)—where Zola uses the expression "mon Étienne"—seems to indicate that the author already had him in mind for a rôle in this novel.

55. 2. Cf. notes 24–25 in our section entitled "The Genesis of *Germinal*."

55. 3. Van Tieghem, *op. cit.*, p. 76.

57. 4. *Ébauche*, f. 427/26.

57. 5. *Ibid.*, f. 453/51.

57. 6. *Ibid.*, f. 479/76.

57. 7. MS. 10308, f. 13–16.

57. 8. *Ibid.*, f. 14–16: "Au demeurant, d'un esprit juste et raisonnable [...] Bon ouvrier, fait sa besogne en conscience. Ne se fâche que devant une injustice et peut alors devenir terrible. Le vieux flamand qui bout, la brutalité qui éclate [...] Estimé, aimé de ses camarades, parce qu'il est très bon ouvrier. C'est lui qu'on charge de porter la parole parce qu'il est honorable." Zola probably omitted the word "sang" between "vieux" and "flamand."

58. 9. *Ébauche*, f. 426/25.

58. 10. *Ibid.*, f. 428/27.

58. 11. *Ibid.*, f. 427/26.

58. 12. *Ibid.*, f. 453/51.

58. 13. *Ibid.*, f. 426/25.

58. 14. MS. 10308, f. 17.

58. 15. *Ibid.*, f. 213 (5).

58. 16. She is called Flora in the *Personnages* and in the first set of chapter plans.

59. 17. Y. Guyot, *Scènes de l'enfer social. La famille Pichot*, p. 135.

59. 18. MS. 10308, f. 212/4.

59. 19. *Ébauche*, f. 454/52.

59. 20. *Ibid.*, f. 414/13, 442/40. For the spelling of his name see above, note 2.

59. 21. *Ibid.*, f. 442/40.

59. 22. *Ibid.*, f. 443/41. See also my article, "Concerning the Sources of *Germinal*," *Romanic Review*, Oct. 1958, pp. 175–6.

60. 23. *Ibid.*, f. 446/44.

60. 24. *Ibid.*

60. 25. *Ébauche*, f. 442/40.

60. 26. *Ibid.*, 414/13.

Page

60.   27. *Ibid.*, f. 415/14.
60.   28. *Ibid.*, f. 417/16.
60.   29. *Ibid.*, f. 424/23–425/24.
60.   30. She was still sixteen in the text published in the *Gil Blas.*
60.   31. *Ébauche*, f. 425/24.
60.   32. For example, p. 54, ed. Bernouard.
60.   33. *Ébauche*, f. 433/32.
61.   34. *Ibid.*, f. 437/36.
61.   35. G. Robert, *op. cit.*, p. 142.
61.   36. *Ébauche*, f. 472/69.
62.   37. *Ibid.*, f. 449/47.
62.   38. *Ibid.*, f. 464/61–465/62.
62.   39. *Ibid.*, f. 485/82.
62.   40. *Ibid.*, f. 497/94.
62.   41. MS. 10308, f. 21–23. This portrait was originally that of Caffiaux. It still reveals some confusion between the two men, for instead of writing a new one for Bonnemort, Zola merely made a few corrections and additions.
63.   42. MS 10306, f 558: "Lui-même ignorait, s'il voulait l'étrangler ou la secourir. Il semblait ivre" etc. Cf. *Germinal*, ed. Bernouard, p. 377, line 40 or ed. Charpentier-Fasquelle: v. 2, p. 80, line 2.

ÉTIENNE LANTIER

63.   1. Bibl. Nat. Nouvelles acquisitions françaises, MS. 10345, f. 3.
63.   2. Quoted by Le Blond, *La Fortune des Rougon* (*Œuvres complètes. Émile Zola*), ed. Bernouard, p. 361.
64.   3. *L'Assommoir*, ch. VIII, p. 254, ed. Bernouard.
64.   4. *Ibid.*, p. 441 (ch. XIII).
64.   5. MS. 10308, f. 7.
65.   6. *Une campagne*, ed. Bernouard, article on Daudet, p. 313.
65.   7. *Numa Roumestan*, Charpentier, p. 15. Daudet identifies his character as Buisson in his *Souvenirs d'un homme de lettres*, pp. 48–49.
65.   8. *Ébauche*, f. 417/16.
65.   9. *Ibid.*, f. 481/78.
65.   10. *Ibid.*, Cf. the hero of *La Bête humaine.*
66.   11. MS. 10308, f. 10. The words in brackets are in the interlinea.
66.   12. MS. 10307, f. 385. See, above, ch. IV, p. 49.
66.   13. *Ébauche*, f. 415/14.
66.   14. MS. 10308, f. 9.
66.   15. *Ibid.*
66.   16. See our discussion of Catherine Maheu.

Page

67.   17. *Ébauche*, f. 416/15.
67.   18. *Ibid.*, f. 450/48.
67.   19. *Ibid.*, f. 451/49.
67.   20. *Ibid.*, f. 440/39.
68.   21. G. Robert, *op. cit.*, p. 121.
68.   22. See my article, "The Newspapers of *Germinal*: their Identity and Significance," *The Modern Language Review*, Jan. 1960.—And see, above chapter III, p. 33, and note 38.
69.   23. *Ébauche*, f. 493/90.
69.   24. I. M. Frandon, *op. cit.*, pp. 123–124, note 296.
69.   25. MS. 10307, f. 178.
69.   26. *Ibid.*, f. 207. Cf. also f. 216: "Montrer Étienne acceptant les idées de Souvorine."
69.   27. *Ibid.*, f. 295.
70.   28. M. K. Kleman, *Émil' Zola, sbornik statey*, Leningrad, 1934, pp. 166, 188.
71.   29. F. W. J. Hemmings, *Émile Zola*, p. 190.
71.   30. See above, p. 68.

SOUVARINE

72.   1. Not to be confused with his cousin Peter.
72.   2. That Zola knew him is clear from certain letters of Turgenev to Zola preserved in the Bibliothèque Nationale. They are in vol. xv of the *Correspondance Émile Zola*, MS. 24524.
73.   3. *Le Figaro*, 21 March, 1881; republished in *Une campagne*.
73.   4. M. K. Kleman, *Emil' Zola, sbornik statey*, Leningrad, 1934, p. 178.
73.   5. *Ibid.*, p. 170.
73.   6. MS. 24524, f. 223, verso.
73.   7. See the *Ébauche* (MS. 10307, f. 434/33.)
74.   8. We find it spelled that way in the *Ébauche* and in all or nearly all of Zola's *first* set of chapter plans. See, for example, MS. 10307, f. 109–111. The original spelling with an "o" is confirmed by Van Tieghem, *op. cit.*, p. 75.
74.   9. The list of *Personnages* (MS. 10308, f. 2) shows the actual change. Zola has clearly corrected the spelling there.
74.   10. Quoted by Kleman, *op. cit.*, pp. 176–177.
75.   11. If an individual, alive in 1884, is sought as a model, then, of course, Bakunin is automatically eliminated.
75.   12. MS. 10308, f. 81–84, and p. 213 of this book.
75.   13. MS. 10307, f. 106, 111.
75.   14. P. Aubery, "Quelques sources du thème de l'action directe dans *Germinal*," *Symposium*, Vol. XIII, 1 (1959), p. 66. Prof. Aubery

Page

quotes from Kropotkin: "Notre action doit être la révolte permanente, par la parole, par l'écrit, par le poignard, le fusil, la dynamite." He then cites Souvarine in *Germinal* (ed. Bernouard, p. 256), but this text has a different source which will be identified farther on.

75.   15. See G. Woodcock and I. Avakumovic, *The Anarchist Prince*, London, Boardman, 1950, pp. 96, 112.

76.   16. *Germinal*, ed. Bernouard, p. 256.

76.   17. MS. 10308, f. 84.

77.   18. "La Source historique d'une scène de *Germinal*," *Revue d'histoire littéraire de la France*, janv.-mars, 1960.

77.   19. See G. Robert, *Émile Zola. Principes et caractères généraux de son œuvre*, Les Belles Lettres, 1952, p. 189, *n.* 18 and 19, and my own article "Concerning the Sources of *Germinal*," *Romanic Review*, Oct. 1958. See also P. Van Tieghem, *op. cit.*, pp. 57–63. Note that Zola used the second edition (1883) of Laveleye with the long introduction, rather than the first edition of 1881.

77.   20. Laveleye, *op. cit.*, pp. 235: "Le brigand est le vrai héros, le vengeur populaire, l'ennemi irréconciliable de l'État, le véritable révolutionnaire en action, sans phrases et sans rhétorique puisée dans les livres." On page 236 Laveleye quotes from Bakunin: "N'admettant aucune autre activité que celle de la destruction, nous déclarons que les formes dans lesquelles doit s'exprimer cette activité peuvent être extrêmement variées: poison, poignard, nœud coulant. [. . .]" What is needed first is "une série d'attentats et d'entreprises audacieuses insensées même, épouvantant les puissants et réveillant le peuple [. . .]" This is the source apparently unknown to Prof. Aubery. Cf. note 14.

79.   21. A. Yarmolinsky, *Road to Revolution*, London, 1957, p. 239.

79.   22. MS. 10307, f. 296–297. Italics mine.

79.   23. See above, note 2.

80.   24. MS. 1471 (Bibliothèque Méjanes, Aix-en-Provence), f. 132. I am indebted to my former colleague, Professor Murray Sachs, for this information. (Note also that the manuscript number does not coincide with that given in the Bernouard edition.)

80.   25. *Ébauche*, f. 417/16.

80.   26. *Ibid.*, f. 434/33.

80.   27. *Ibid.*, f. 489/86.

81.   28. *Ibid.*, f. 496/93. Note that just before the last section of the *Ebauche*, on f. 489/86–490/87, Zola thought momentarily of letting Souvarine die in an act of self-sacrifice. He doubtless rejected this because of its incompatibility with a revolutionary attitude.

Page

81. 29. MS. 10305, f. 365: "Souvarine, assis près du bureau, la débarrassa et posa le plateau sur un coin de la table. Pluchart put continuer; mais ce n'était qu'un remerciement, il se dit très touché," etc. (Cf. ed. Bernouard, p. 259, line 37 or ed. Charpentier-Fasquelle, p. 276, line 26.)

MS. 10305, f. 367: "ce discours de cafard; tandis que Souvarine regardait, peu à peu échauffé, une flamme au fond de ses yeux clairs," (Cf. ed. Bernouard, p. 261, line 7 or ed. Charpentier-Fasquelle p. 278, line 9.)

MS. 10305, f. 373: "Et Souvarine, exalté, tapa lui aussi des deux poings sur la table afin d'aider Pluchart à obtenir le silence. Sous ce redoublement," etc. (Cf. ed. Bernouard, p. 262, line 40 or Charpentier-Fasquelle, p. 280, line 13.)

At the end of the chapter Souvarine is still present in the manuscript version where he is said to be "amusé de la défaite de Rasseneur" (f. 376).

81. 30. MS. 10305, f. 433-434: "Près de lui, Souvarine avait applaudi ses propres idées, à mesure qu'il les reconnaissait, content des progrès anarchiques du camarade, assez satisfait du programme," etc.

81. 31. MS. 10306, f. 547-548: "Quand il eut reconnu Souvarine, Étienne entra [. . .]—En voilà du tapage inutile! reprit Souvarine à demi-voix, en allumant une nouvelle cigarette. Je savais bien que vous vous éreinteriez sans rien faire de bon . . . Un seul tonneau de poudre, dans la maison, en face, ça valait mieux. [. . .] —Ce qui me [i.e. Étienne] gêne, ce sont les lâches qui, les bras croisés, nous regardent risquer notre peau . . . Et je dis cela aussi pour toi, Souvarine, car à la fin tu m'embêtes à parler sans cesse de tout démolir, sans jamais donner une chiquenaude à une mouche. [. . .]"

82. 32. MS. 10306, f. 588-589. Cf. ed. Bernouard, p. 398, line 1, or ed. Charpentier-Fasquelle, v. 2, p. 101, line 13.

82. 33. MS. 10306, f. 620 and 660. The latter reads as follows: "Il [i.e. Souvarine] était justement de service, il venait là jeter un coup d'œil, quand il pouvait quitter la machine quelques secondes. L'air calme, muet, avec l'idée fixe clouée au fond de ses yeux clairs, il n'avait pas lâché un seul jour sa barre de mise en train, depuis le commencement de la grève." Cf. ed. Bernouard p. 442, line 13 or ed. Charpentier-Fasquelle, v. 2, p. 149, line 21.

82. 34. MS 10306, f. 706, Cf. ed. Bernouard, p. 472, line 16 or ed. Charpentier-Fasquelle, v. 2, p. 171, line 30.

83. 35. *Le Révolté*, du 10 ou 23 mai 1885.

RASSENEUR

Page

83.   1. See my discussion of Étienne, footnote 22; also, above, p. 33.
83.   2. MS. 10308, f. 219 (11).
83.   3. MS. 10307, f. 456/53–457/54.
83.   4. Some of Basly's traits and activities were transferred to Étienne. See above, p. 69. Note also that the preliminary portrait of Rasseneur in the *Personnages* (MS. 10308, f. 85–86) must have been written *after* the last section of the *Ébauche*.
83.   5. MS. 10308, f. 88.
84.   6. *L'Illustration*, 19 April, 1884, article entitled "La Grève d'Anzin."

THE GRÉGOIRE FAMILY, HENNEBEAU, & DENEULIN

84.   1. *Ébauche*, f. 460/57–461/58.
84.   2. *Ibid.*, f. 498/95–499/96.
84.   3. MS. 10308, f. 67–73. This portrait was probably composed after the first set of chapter plans was penned.
85.   4. "Marriage or Murder: Zola's Hesitations concerning Cécile Grégoire," *French Studies*, Jan. 1961.
85.   5. Hemmings, *op. cit.*, p. 191.
86.   6. MS. 10307, f. 364.
86.   7. *Germinal*, ed. Bernouard, p. 223.
87.   8. *Ébauche*, f. 403/2, 458/55–459/56.
87.   9. *Ibid.*, f. 405/4, 418/17.
87. 10. *Ibid.*, f. 442/40.
87. 11. MS. 10308, f. 58–60.
87. 12. *Correspondance*, 27 March, 1885.
87. 13. MS. 10307, f. 158. He is listed under much the same description on f. 5 of MS 10308 where Zola adds: "en arrière sans qu'on le nomme." See also note 7. Again on f. 95, MS. 10308, Zola writes: "Des actionnaires que je ne nommerai pas, un grand seigneur, grand propriétaire, ministre, jetant l'argent. Fortune royale."
88. 14. *Ébauche*, f. 460/57.
88. 15. MS. 10308, f. 61.
88. 16. *Ébauche*, f. 461/58.
88. 17. MS. 10308, f. 2. The name, though listed, is crossed out.
88. 18. See, above, chapter IV, p. 48. "Et là, je les finirai: d'une part, le mariage de Paul, conclu ou non; d'autre part Hennebeau devant sa femme et un nouvel amant peut-être, le fils aîné de Deneulin, un officier arrivé d'Afrique.—A voir." (MS. 10307, f. 367).

NÉGREL, CHAVAL, LA MOUQUETTE, *et al*

Page

89.   1. We recall that there is some confusion about his identity. See chapter I, p. 8 and note.

89.   2. P. Moreau, *"Germinal" d'Émile Zola. Épopée et roman*, Centre de documentation universitaire, 1954, p. 15.

89.   3. MS. 10307, f. 441/39.

89   4. Frandon, *op. cit.*, pp. 46–47. It must also be recalled that the engineer named by Zola in the interview in *Le Parti national* was described by him as being a man of great courage. But we persist in thinking that it is more likely that the source of this trait was furnished by the engineer of whom Simonin wrote.

90.   5. MS. 10307, f. 460/57.

90.   6. *Ibid.*, f. 44. He is described here as "courageux par nécessité."

90.   7. MS. 10308, f. 64–66. See note 17, preceding chapter.

90.   8. MS. 10307, f. 250–251; 257, 260. On Négrel's projected marriage with Cécile Grégoire, see, above, my discussion of the Grégoire family and my article in *French Studies*, Jan., 1961.

90.   9. *Ébauche*, f. 437/36. It seems unlikely that the inspector who took advantage of girls and wanted to possess Catherine (f. 425/24) was a precursor of Chaval.

90.   10. *Ibid.*, f. 438/37.

90.   11. f. 456/53.

90.   12. f. 467/64.—*Germinal*, ed. Bernouard, p. 244–245 or ed. Charpentier-Fasquelle, p. 260.

90.   13. f. 468/65.

90.   14. f. 471/68.

91.   15. f. 472/69–473/70.

91.   16. f. 476/73. Van Tieghem has misread the text of the *Ébauche* which surely reads "discret", not "déshonorant."

91.   17. Ms. 10307, f. 356.

91.   18. MS. 10308, f. 52.

91.   19. *Ibid.*

91.   20. MS. 10307, f. 229.

91.   21. Bernouard edition, p. 55; italics mine.

92.   22. Ph. D. Walker, *A Structural Study of Zola's "Germinal"*, Yale University dissertation (unpublished), p. 258.

92.   23. f. 467/64. But the very last section of the *Ébauche* says: "La Mouquette l'adore."

92.   24. MS. 10308, f. 50.

92.   25. MS. 10307, f. 193: "Voir ce que deviennent les trois Mouque. La Mouquette très bien, faisant vivre son père des sous qu'elle tire des hommes (?)." The question mark shows that Zola was uncertain, and in the second plan for this chapter he changed his mind: "comment elle vit [. . .] elle s'est mise blanchisseuse." (f. 186).

93.   26. *Ibid.*, f. 257.

93.   27. MS. 10305, f. 443, and *Germinal*, ed. Bernouard, p. 304, line 22.

94.   28. This characterization is in the preliminary portrait of Suzanne Pierron, MS. 10308, f. 42.

94.   29. MS. 10308, f. 46.—In this portrait, Zola gives her age as 50, but she appears older in the novel, where her exact age is not mentioned. Was her name possibly suggested by the "sentier creux du Brûlé" at La Ricamarie? or by Dormoy, p. 175?

96.   30. *Ébauche*, f. 416/15.

96.   31. f. 426/25.

97.   32. MS. 10307, f. 76. On the possible influence of Guyot's novel, see our ch. 3.

97.   33. *Ibid.*, f. 274.

97.   34. *Ibid.*, f. 276. See, above, chapter IV, p. 45 and note 21.

97.   35. Zola's two old men (*Ébauche*, f. 485/82) become ultimately Bonnemort and Mouque, but the latter is made the "palefrenier." Cf. *Ébauche*, f. 491/88 and 499/96. The "raccommodeur" whom Zola intended to call "le père Caffiaux" survived into the chapter plans, even into the second set. See, for example, ch. 5 Part II (MS 10307, f. 97–98): "Puis Étienne, le long du canal arrive à Réquillart. Poser le vieux Caffiaux, resté seul vivant dans Réquillart [...] Montrer les trois vieux (Mouque les a rejoints) assis sur d'anciennes berlines au rebut et causant au milieu des amours."

97.   36. *Ébauche*, f. 455/52.

97.   37. "Mes notes sur Anzin", MS 10308, f. 291 (84)

97.   38. MS. 10308, f. 39.

97.   39. *Ébauche*, f. 455/52.

98.   40. MS. 10308, f. 44–45.

98.   41. Saint-Louis is the name of one of the mines Zola saw at Anzin.

98.   42. MS. 10308, f. 57.—Zola also used a portion of this description for le père Quandieu in ch. 4 of Part V.

98.   43. Named Marsoulan in the last section of the *Ébauche*, in the first set of chapter plans, in the *Personnages*, and even in the second plan for ch. 6 of Part I.

98.   44. "Mes notes sur Anzin," MS. 10308, f. 218/10–219/11: "Le médecin de la Cie à l'homme qui se plaint: 'C'est ta femme qui t'a esquinté,' à la femme: 'Vous prenez trop de café'." Cf. also MS.10308, f. 91.

99.   45. MS. 10305, f. 101 shows the change.

99.   46. See above, p. 47.

Page

99.   47. See second plan for ch. 1, Part III, MS. 10307, f. 105: "Mouque avec Bataille qui se prend de tendresse pour Merveille, dans l'écurie."

99.   48. MS. 10307, f. 428/27 and 490/87–491/88. See also above, p. 19.

99.   49. MS. 10308, f. 93.

100. 50. M. Turnell, "Introduction", *Germinie* (English translation of *Germinie Lacerteux*) N.Y. Grove Press, p. x.—Mr. Turnell has done rather better by Zola in his more recent publication, *The Art of French Fiction*, N.Y. New Directions, 1959

101. 51. Turnell, "Introduction," p. viii.

101. 52. *Correspondance*, letter to Henry Céard, 22 March, 1885.

CHAPTER VI

Page

104.   1. *Correspondance.* Letter to H. Céard, 22 March, 1885.

104.   2. G. Robert, *op. cit.*, chapters V and VI; F. W. J. Hemmings, *op. cit.*, *passim;* M. Girard, "L'Univers de *Germinal,*" *La Revue des sciences humaines,* 1953; F. Doucet, *L'Esthétique de Zola et son application à la critique,* Nizet & Bastard, 1923; A. Lanoux, *Bonjour Monsieur Zola,* Amiot-Dumont, 1954, pp. 191–201; —, "Style chez Zola," *L'Éducation nationale,* 16 oct. 1952; —, "Où en est Zola? En marge de *Germinal,*" *Hommes et mondes,* août, 1952; J. H. Matthews, *Les Deux Zola,* Droz, 1957, pp. 39–40, 47, and *passim;*—, "L'Impressionnisme chez Zola: *Le Ventre de Paris,*" *Le Français moderne,* juillet 1961; Ph. D. Walker, "Prophetic Myths in Zola." *PMLA,* Sept., 1959; —, *A Structural Study of Zola's "Germinal".* (an unpublished doctoral dissertation), Yale University, 1956.

105.   3. Translations of *Germinal* in this section are based on Mr L. W. Tancock's version (in The Penguin Classics), but I have modified his text whenever I thought it necessary or desirable. In my analysis of the first chapter I have used only English because I felt that the use of one language only would in this case be stylistically preferable. The original French can, of course, be easily located by any reader.

105.   4. Red is important throughout the novel, as M. Girard states later in his article, and as Mr Walker has also clearly established, for he has made an exact count of the number of repetitions (see his dissertation, p. 498).

105.   5. *Ébauche,* f. 420/19 and 451/49.

107.   6. Lanoux, in his essay "Où en est Zola?", complains that Zola repeats too often the *crachat noir* of Bonnemort. But Zola's repetition is obviously deliberate, as Lanoux notes in his biography, p. 197, and in my opinion effective.

108.   7. For example, the image of the "unknown god" for capitalism recurs in chapters 2 and 7 of Part IV, and again in the final chapter of the book.

108.   8. M. Girard notes, *loc. cit.*, p. 63 that out of forty chapters, only ten "se situent à la lumière du jour." The other thirty are not all underground; many occur at night.

109.   9. L. Simonin, *La Vie souterraine,* 1867. See, for example, pp. 46–47, where Simonin writes: "les fictions de l'antiquité ont pris un corps: on dirait le pays des Cyclopes."

109. 10. "Mes notes sur Anzin," MS. 10308, f. 238 (30).

110. 11. *Op. cit.*, p. 115, Fig. 37. Cf. Frandon, *op. cit.*, p. 24; Stell, *op. cit.*, p. 31.

Page

112. 12. E. de Laveleye, *Le Socialisme contemporain*, 2e ed., 1883, p. xxxiv.

113. 13. *La Gazette des Tribunaux*, 6 August, 1869.

113. 14. *Ibid.*, 12 November, 1869.

113. 15. *Ibid.*, 6 August, 1869: "Je dus faire charger les fusils en leur présence et simuler plusieurs charges à la baïonnette, mais rien n'y fit. Ils se précipitaient audacieusement sur la pointe des sabres en disant: 'Tuez-nous, si vous voulez'." This is from testimony by Jt Bouteiller. Then Capt. Gausserand testified: "C'est à cet instant que des pierres ont été lancées sur la troupe et que deux coups de feu ont retenti. [. . .] Je n'ai point commandé le feu, les soldats ont tiré spontanément; mais je déclare que j'aurais été contraint d'en venir à cette extrémité." Zola copied these texts more or less verbatim in his notes (MS. 10308, f. 158–165).

113. 16. See above, p. 32.

114. 17. Hemmings, *op. cit.*, p. 185.

115. 18. In this chapter, one finds here and there a recurrence of the vocabulary of a storm: "le flot toujours montant des mineurs," "la marée montante," "la grêle des briques," "rafale de pierres," "l'ouragan des balles." Should one draw any general conclusions from this? It would be difficult to describe such an action without using some of these expressions.

116. 19. "Mes notes sur Anzin": "Autre cabaret beaucoup plus grand sur la route de Condé. A côté salle de bal, le milieu planchéié. Plafond de 3 mètres au plus, qui semble écraser la salle; petite tribune pour les musiciens dont la tête doit toucher le plafond. Au plafond, deux guirlandes de papier de couleur vont d'un angle à l'autre. Au milieu une couronne de fleurs en papier. Le long des murs, des écussons tricolores, portant le nom des saints et saintes des métiers: Ste Barbe, mineurs; St-Éloi, forgerons, etc., à chercher les autres." MS. 10308, f. 215 (7)–216 (8).

118. 20. Verbs: *s'écrasaient, faisaient rage, balayant, tournait violemment, noyait, craquaient, poussait, fumaient, sifflait, gonflait, cuisait,* etc. Add a couple of verbal nouns: *remuement, assourdissement.* Similes: *une chaire à prêcher, une vessie de saindoux, une locomotive en détresse, comme des chevaux, comme des sacs d'avoine.*

118. 21. While Zola must have seen the picture at the Salon des Impressionnistes in the rue Le Peletier where it was exhibited in 1877, I am not suggesting that he had it in mind in composing this section of his chapter. I am simply using it as a basis for comparison.

119. 22. It is true that Zola quoted Edmond de Goncourt's use of the phrase "écriture artiste" which occurs in the preface to *Les Frères Zemganno*, implying that he himself practiced that style of writing

Page

(See *Le Roman expérimental*, ed. Bernouard, p. 216, 221), but he went on to condemn it, urging the "jeunes romanciers" to abandon it in favour of a "style fort, solide, simple, humain." Mr J. H. Matthews has called attention to this, adding: "Il faut donc reconnaître que seul des écrivains impressionnistes, Zola a vu le danger de la méthode qu'il employait, *sans toutefois renoncer au style impressionniste*" (*Le Français moderne*, "L'Impressionnisme chez Zola: *Le Ventre de Paris*," juillet 1961; italics mine). Now while there is some impressionism in the style of *Germinal* (if we adopt Mr Matthews' definition that "dans le style impressionniste, l'impression précède aussi bien l'identification que l'explication"), I do not see anything comparable to the kind of description found, for example, in chapters XXXV and XXXVI of the Goncourts' *Mme Gervaisais* where the style is extremely *recherché*. The style of *Germinal* may not, perhaps, be "simple," but it can justifiably be called "fort, solide, humain."

119. 23. Quoted by G. Robert, *op. cit.*, p. 124.

CHAPTER VII

Page

120. 1. F. Brunetière, "L'Idéalisme dans le roman," *Revue des Deux Mondes*, 1 May, 1885.
121. 2. E. Drumont, *La Fin d'un monde*, 1889, pp. 93–4.
122. 3. See ch. 4, p. 49.
124. 4. I should perhaps call attention to an unfortunate misprint in the Bernouard edition (p. 571). Le Blond quotes part of Gille's article. In the second paragraph read *reprochées*, not *rapprochées*.
126. 5. *Le Moniteur universel*, 30 March, 1885.
126. 6. See above, ch. 5, p. 71.
126. 7. Sarcey obviously intended to write a second article dealing in detail with *Germinal*. It never appeared in *Le XIXe Siècle*.
126. 8. F. Sarcey, *Souvenirs d'âge mûr*, Paris, Ollendorff, 1892, p. 293.
127. 9. For Zola's reply, see chapter 5, p. 87.
127. 10. 14 March, 1885, and subsequently in *Les Contemporains*, ère série, pp. 249–84.
128. 11. *Correspondance* (ed. Bernouard) pp. 633–4. It will be noted that Zola uses in this letter a sentence that he repeats verbatim in his letter to Claveau. See above, p. 124.
128. 12. *Le Roman expérimental* (ed. Bernouard) p. 28, 31–32.
129. 13. *Études et portraits*, vol. II, "Réflexions sur l'art du roman."
129. 14. MS. 24520, f. 366–367.
129. 15. MS. 24520, f. 364 (12 November, 1885). This letter and the preceding published in *Lettres inédites à Émile Zola* (annotées par P. Lambert), Geneva, Droz, 1953, pp. 113–117.
129. 16. MS. 24518, f. 448–9 (Fabre's letter is dated 6 March, 1885) and MS. 24523, f. 222 (16 April).
129. 17. MS. 24522, f. 69–70.
129. 18. MS. 24523, f. 52.
129. 19. MS. 24522, f. 220. Letter dated 24 February, 1885.
130. 20. On American criticism, see A. J. Salvan, *Zola aux États-Unis*, Brown Univ. Studies, vol. VIII, Providence, R.I., 1943.
130. 21. MS. 24522, f. 380.
130. 22. Cf. Salvan, *op. cit.*
130. 23. *The Nation*, 2 April, 1885, p. 286.
130. 24. H. James, "The Art of Fiction," *Longman's Magazine*, Sept. 1884, p. 521.
130. 25. Girard, M. & Hermies, V. d', "Émile Zola devant la critique tchèque," *Revue des études slaves*, 1950.
130. 26. Quoted by W. H. Root, *German Criticism of Zola, 1875 to 1893*, Columbia Univ. Press, 1931, p. 54.
131. 27. *North American Review*, 1902, vol. 175, pp. 587–596.

Page

131. 28. See *Notes on Novelists*, 1914, reprinted from the *Atlantic Monthly*, August 1903.

131. 29. E. Rod, "The Place of Émile Zola in Literature," *Contemporary Review*, Nov. 1902. The article deals with Zola's work in general not with any one specific novel.

131. 30. E. Seillière, *Émile Zola*, Grasset, 1923, pp. 281–2.

131. 31. H. Barbusse, *Zola*, Gallimard, 1932, p. 182.

131. 32. L. Cazamian, *A History of French Literature*, Oxford, 1955, pp.360–362.

132. 33. *Le Figaro littéraire*, 9 October, 1954, "Zola, l'homme du vrai."

132. 34. J. Romains, *Zola et son exemple*, Flammarion, 1935, pp. 20–21.

132. 35. G. Lukács, *Studies in European Realism*, London, 1950, p. 95.

132. 36. A. Wilson, *Émile Zola. An Introductory Study of his Novels*, N.Y. Wm. Morrow, 1952, pp. 114–116. It is a pleasure to be able to quote Mr Wilson with approval. Much of his little book is written from a Freudian point of view which we find difficult always to accept.

132. 37. A. Lanoux, "Où en est Zola. En marge de *Germinal*," *Hommes et mondes* (7e année), août, 1952, p. 551.

132. 38. A. Lanoux, *Bonjour Monsieur Zola*, Amiot-Dumont, 1954, pp. 197–8.

132. 39. A. Thibaudet, "Réflexions. Sur Zola," *Nouvelle Revue Francaise*, 1935 (vol. 45) pp. 906–912.

133. 40. *Journal*, Ed. de la Pléiade, p. 1143.

133. 41. A. Gide, *Incidences*, Gallimard 1924, pp. 155–156.

133. 42. *Journal*, Ed. de la Pléiade, p. 1220.

PART II

Ébauche
=

Le roman est le soulèvement des salariés, le coup d'épaule donné à la société, qui craque un instant : en un mot la lutte du capital et du travail. C'est là qu'est l'importance du livre, je le veux prédisant l'avenir, posant la question qui sera la question la plus importante du XXe siècle.

Donc, pour établir cette lutte, qui est mon nœud, il faut que je montre d'une part le travail, les houilleurs dans la mine, et de l'autre le capital, la direction le patron, enfin ce qui est à la tête. Mais deux cas se présentent : prendrai-je un patron qui personnifie en lui-même le capital, ce qui rendrait la lutte plus directe et peut être plus dramatique ? ou prendrai-je

THE FIRST PAGE OF ZOLA'S *ÉBAUCHE*
(*Photostat by the Bibliothéque Nationale*)

SECTION I. ÉBAUCHE*

(MS. 10307)

(402/1) Le roman est le soulèvement des salariés, le coup d'épaule donné à la société, qui craque un instant: en un mot la lutte du capital et du travail. C'est là qu'est l'importance du livre, je le veux prédisant l'avenir, posant la question la plus importante du vingtième siècle.

Donc, pour établir cette lutte, qui est mon nœud, il faut que je montre d'une part le travail, les houilleurs dans la mine, et de l'autre le capital, la direction, le patron, enfin ce qui est à la tête. Mais deux cas se présentent: prendrai-je un patron qui personnifie en lui-même le capital, ce qui rendrait la lutte plus directe et peut-être plus dramatique? Ou prendrai-je (403/2) une société anonyme, des actionnaires, enfin le mode (*sic*) de la grande industrie, la mine dirigée par un directeur appointé avec tout un personnel, et ayant derrière lui l'action-naire oisif, le vrai capital? Cela serait certainement plus actuel, plus large, et poserait le débat comme il se présente toujours dans la grande industrie. Je crois qu'il vaudra mieux prendre ce dernier cas.

Alors, j'aurais d'une part les ouvriers et de l'autre la direc-tion, puis derrière les actionnaires, avec des conseils d'admini-stration, etc. (tout un mécanisme à étudier). Mais après avoir posé ce mécanisme discrètement, je pense que je laisserai de côté les actionnaires, les comités, etc., pour en faire une sorte de tabernacle reculé, de dieu vivant et mangeant les ouvriers dans l'ombre: l'effet (404/3) à tirer sera plus grand, et je n'aurai pas à compliquer mon livre par des détails d'admini-

---

* Zola numbered his *Ébauche* from 1 to 96. We indicate this pagination by the number which follows the pagination of the manuscript, 402–499.

Words placed between brackets are words that Zola wrote in the inter-linea.

We do not reproduce inconsequential errors such as missing accents, or a singular for a plural. Those of any consequence or a reading about which there is doubt we indicate by (*sic*).

stration peu intéressants. Il suffit de montrer la décision prise
qui amène la grève et d'indiquer les décisions suivantes qui
pourront être nécessaires. Le conseil a décidé que . . ., le conseil
exige que . . .; et c'est comme un oracle qui parle, une force
inconnue et terrible qui plane et écrase toute une population
de houilleurs.

La lutte visible reste par conséquent entre les houilleurs et
le directeur, avec son personnel. Là il faut que j'entre dans
quelque détail. Je montrerai le Directeur chez lui, dans sa
maison, dans son jardin, j'opposerai son intérieur, sa vie, ses
plaisirs, son con- (405/4) fort à mes ouvriers, à un intérieur,
une vie, une misère d'ouvrier. D'autre part, il faut que je lui
donne une famille; il est marié, lui 50 ans, la femme 45,
2 filles, l'une de 20 ans, l'autre de 16. Intérieur à peindre (après
notes prises). Un mariage doit être réglé pour la fille, ou autre
chose: un drame peut-être, une fille séduite, etc., de façon à
dramatiser ce côté de l'action et obtenir un dénouement à la
fin. J'aimerais assez une fille qui se donne, la plus jeune peut-
être; et l'amant tué à la fin, ou autre chose.—Du reste, quelle
que soit cette action, j'ai toujours le tableau de cette famille
perdue au milieu (406/5) de la révolte, lorsque la grève éclate.
Peur, drame, maison attaquée, dangers courus, défense, mort
peut-être. La poussée ouvrière est terrible, ce que deviennent
les femmes; et le siège de la maison peut-être; jusqu'à l'arrivée
des troupes.—Il faudra faire sans doute de mon Directeur un
homme de discipline, dur, correct, *représentant l'argent, in-
carnant l'argent*, sans qu'il soit mauvais pourtant. L'action chez
le Directeur se déroule donc, en même temps que chez les
ouvriers, et dénouements qui se déduisent.

Il faut que je fasse attention à ceci. Dans la grève, si je veux
montrer les pertes communes, souffrance des ouvriers et ruine
du capital (407/6) je suis assez mal placé pour le faire avec une
vaste et puissante compagnie anonyme. Il faudrait donc que
j'aie à côté un autre puits, une petite concession, dont le patron
direct serait ruiné par la grève ou plutôt achevé. Cela me
permettrait aussi de montrer la grève s'étendant, les grévistes
mettant le pays en interdit, débauchant les ouvriers des autres

puits. Et même il faudrait que je fasse entendre dans le pays le
retentissement d'autres ruines pendant la grève, ou à la suite:
banquiers, commerçants de la ville voisine (étudier les ruines
que les grèves peuvent entraîner, surtout lorsqu'une grève se
déclare, comme presque toujours, au moment d'une (408/7)
crise industrielle.—Montrer par contre un cabaret qui fait ses
affaires.)

J'ai donc deux exploitations: la grande mine par société
anonyme, et la petite mine par un patron responsable, moins
riche et facile à ruiner. C'est chez celui-ci que je montrerai
la misère allant de compagnie avec celle des ouvriers, la lutte
de l'argent et du travail. Il tient le coup, car il ne peut augmenter le salaire, sans y rester. Mais il souffre, la maison morte,
les machines qui chôment, la mélancolie de tout cela, à
étudier. Et, dès lors, je me demande si ce n'est pas ce patron-là
que je dois mettre au premier plan, en (409/8) laissant dans le
fond la grande mine par société anonyme qui jouerait le rôle
de dieu muet et impitoyable. J'aurais sans doute plus d'humanité avec le patron, qui défend sa peau, sa vie, celle de sa
famille, tandis que le Directeur ne défend rien, sait bien que la
Compagnie est riche, et qu'elle supportera le désastre, et
qu'elle le maintiendra à sa place, d'autant plus qu'il se montrera
ferme. Il y aurait lieu alors de reporter le drame chez le patron.
Cela est à voir. C'est de la grande compagnie que serait partie
la grève, ce qui me permettrait peut-être de la faire éclater
presque tout de suite. Transe du patron qu'elle ne gagne son
puits, et elle le gagne, étude de cette (410/9) première lutte,
ce qui me donne le travail du puits pendant un certain temps,
tandis que la grève s'étend à côté. La grande mine reste alors
le décor, le fond, le drame se passe dans la petite mine. J'y
perds de la grandeur, dans la mine même, dans l'installation;
c'est à voir. Puis, quelle serait la conclusion logique? Le grand
capital, la société anonyme, assez forte pour résister, et en-
traînant dans la ruine les patrons qui n'ont pas les reins solides:
cela serait bon, montrerait où l'on va, à la royauté triomphante
de l'argent, des gros capitaux, sur le travail, sur l'effort même
des patrons. Comme fin logique, mon patron est ruiné, se

trouve absorbé par la grande mine, où il devient employé; et
ses (411/10) ouvriers, pour lesquels il était bon, se trouvent
soumis à la règle de fer. Cela me plaît, cela est bon. Mais
il ne faut pas que la grande mine soit un simple décor, il faut
qu'elle ait dans le plan une importance au moins égale, et
même un peu plus grande que la petite mine. C'est une affaire
de disposition dans le plan.

Je passe aux ouvriers. D'abord, voici la grande marche:
les ouvriers réduits à un excès de misère, se révoltent, se mettent
en grève, lorsque la compagnie, compromise elle-même par
une crise industrielle, veut encore baisser les salaires. Alors, la
révolte, peinture de la misère qui augmente, sauvagerie (412/11)
de la lutte. Et enfin la défaite par la faim, les ouvriers capitulant
et se remettant au travail. Mais finir par la sensation farouche
de cette défaite, bien indiquer qu'ils plient devant la force des
choses, mais qu'ils rêvent de vengeance. Les menaces de l'avenir, dernière page du livre. La secousse donnée à la société
qui a craqué, et faire prévoir d'autres secousses jusqu'à l'effon-
drement final.

Je reprends. Pour peindre la misère croissante, il faut donc
que je montre avant tout les ouvriers au travail. (Une scène
dans la mine, une scène dans un intérieur d'ouvrier. Une scène
chez le directeur, une scène chez le patron. La grève éclate
dans la grande mine, scène. (413/12) La peur du patron que
la grève ne gagne son puits, nouvelle scène dans la mine,
détails du travail. La grève éclate aussi là. Nouvelle scène chez
le patron, nouvelle scène chez l'ouvrier. La lutte d'entêtement
réciproque. La répression, troupe amenée, bataille. Et la
défaite des ouvriers, le travail reprenant dans les deux mines,
la grande absorbant la petite, menace de l'avenir.

Voilà la carcasse en grand. Seulement, il faut mettre là-
dedans des personnages et les faire agir.

Je puis avoir deux familles d'ouvriers. Prenons-en une
d'abord, qui m'a l'air typique. Durand a 45 ans, sa femme en
a 40. Depuis son mariage, elle ne travaille plus à la mine. Ils
ont deux (414/13) enfants, une fille de 18 ans, et un garçon
de 8 ans, dont ils vivaient. Mais la fille se met à part avec un

galant, concubinage, et le petit est estropié. Voilà la famille qui va crever de faim. La femme peut se remettre à la mine et toute la misère qui commence.

Je puis débuter peut-être par le travail au fond de la mine, et un accident qui estropie le petit. Lamentation de la mère. Puis, le soir, la fille que j'ai montrée avec son galant se sauve. Et la misère noire. Ce serait le premier chapitre, dans lequel je voudrais mettre aussi la première menace de la grève, montrer la figure qui conduira la grève. Il faudrait que les Durand aient un autre grand fils qui s'est marié, après avoir concubiné, et qui ne leur donne rien. Au dénouement, je verrai (415/14) volontiers la femme veuve se remettre au travail dans la mine; son homme est mort, on le lui a tué, et elle dirait le dernier mot, mot de vengeance et de menace. Mourante de faim, ayant à nourrir toute seule le petit estropié. Son mari tué par la troupe, dans une action héroique: tous les caractères sont à trouver. Mais ce dessin-là (*sic*) pour la famille reste très bon. Il faudrait à côté d'elle, l'autre famille de l'autre mine, un homme restant et lui donnant à la fin la réplique, dans son mot de vengeance.—J'aimerai assez que mon Étienne soit l'amoureux de la fille Catherine.*

Alors, je les ferai travailler dans la petite mine, ce qui me donnera celle-ci. Catherine peut être allée l'y rejoindre, ou (416/15) peut aussi l'avoir renvoyée de la grande, où les femmes ne travaillent plus. Il me faut arranger Étienne pour qu'il travaille au fond; je le préférerais mécanicien, mais je l'arrangerai pour que je puisse obtenir ses amours avec Catherine au fond. Cela me donne des épisodes, un chef veut prendre Catherine et la bataille (peut-être un meurtre). Quand la grande mine est en grève, les Durand peuvent venir injurier Étienne qui travaille toujours, l'argent de la fille. Enfin, il faut que Catherine meure, mais je me défie de Miette, je ne veux pas en faire une guerrière; c'est la mère Durand qui sera dans les pétroleuses. Souffrance de Catherine, dans son amour pour Étienne, la faim, étude de la grève, le chef lui offrant (417/16)

* Zola first wrote: Louise. But he crossed it out and wrote Catherine instead.

peut-être de l'argent, à étudier. Et trouver une mort, un accident peut-être, [morte de misère *excellent*, morte de la mine] mais pas un coup de feu, pas une mort dans la bataille.

Un ami à Étienne. Un nihiliste, un petit russe, mécanicien, un russe réfugié, et les conversations du soir.

Ne pas oublier que j'ai fait d'Étienne dans la famille un maniaque de l'assassinat. *Il faut que je termine* en indiquant cela. Les idées anarchistes développées en lui, et la mort de Catherine déterminant quelque chose (il faut absolument qu'il agisse, et sur la famille du patron, ou du directeur. S'il tuait une des filles, monomanie du meurtre, en la poussant dans le vieux puits). Ce vieux (418/17) puits me servira pendant toute la grève. On ira s'y réunir, les ouvriers pour s'entendre. On s'y cachera, Catherine et Étienne pour quelque chose (un premier meurtre d'Étienne?) Le petit estropié y descendra. Enfin, si Étienne y pousse la fille du directeur, il pourra y descendre pour la voir. Et finir tout de même dans la mine.

Je puis tout avoir, en réglant les familles du patron et du directeur. C'est le patron qui doit avoir une ou deux filles. Il est veuf. C'est le directeur qui est marié et qui a un fils. Un mariage est en train entre ce fils et une des deux filles du patron.* Ajouter des tantes; des servantes, s'il en est besoin, pour (419/18) avoir un effroi de femmes pendant la grève. Le fils dont on a tué la fiancée se console aisément: trouver.— Les caractères des femmes devant la misère des ouvriers, la charité. Tout à trouver et à équilibrer.

Le membre de l'Internationale qui vient soutenir la grève. Je crois que je ne pourrai avoir Paris, les réunions publiques, que je garderai dans ce cas pour le roman sur la commune. Du reste, c'est à voir. Étienne pourrait aller faire un voyage à Paris et assister à une réunion, il faudrait répéter la réunion. Cela prendrait de la place et détruirait l'unité. A voir.

Naturellement, j'ajouterai plusieurs (420/19) groupes d'ouvriers, pour avoir toutes les spécialités, les rouleurs, les boiseurs,

---

* This word is illegible in the original; we have supplied what seems to us the most logical.

les enfants, les femmes, et cela distribué dans tous les caractères typiques.

Ne pas oublier le médecin.

Le prêtre, avec le rôle de la religion.

Note à prendre sur les lieux.

Pour obtenir un gros effet, il faut que les oppositions soient nettes et poussées au summum de l'intensité possible. Donc d'abord, toutes les misères, toutes les fatalités qui pèsent sur le houilleur. Cela par des faits, sans plaidoyer. Il faut le montrer écrasé, mangeant mal, victime de l'ignorance, souffrant dans ses enfants, au fond d'un véritable enfer; et sans persécution, pourtant, sans méchanceté (421/20) voulue des patrons, uniquement écrasé par la situation sociale elle-même. Au contraire, faire les patrons humains jusqu'à leurs intérêts; ne pas tomber dans la revendication bête. L'ouvrier victime des faits, du capital, de la concurrence, des crises du marché (donc comme cadre de cette première partie, une crise industrielle à étudier). Puis, lorsque la grève éclate, explosion d'autant plus violente que la misère, la souffrance a été plus grande; et là aussi pousser au dernier degré possible de la violence. Les ouvriers lâchés vont jusqu'au crime: il faut que le lecteur bourgeois ait un frisson de terreur. Maison attaquée à coups de pierres, siège en règle; personnes tuées, éventrées, sauvagerie abominable.

(422/21) La bête exaspérée et lâchée, le pauvre contre le riche, la faim contre la satiété. Les hommes contre le repas du directeur, les femmes contre le luxe et la toilette de la directrice (combat pour l'assiette au beurre). Les deux maisons opposées, celle des Durand et celle du directeur. Enfin, après l'émeute, la réaction aussi violente, l'armée qui arrive et qui fusille, une terreur régnant sur la contrée, des morts, des blessés. La force restant maîtresse, après les ouvriers aplatis et muets de rage.

Donc tout cela logique, partant de petits faits, de la misère et de la souffrance première, dont la cause est générale, remonte à l'inconnu social, au dieu capital, accroupi dans (423/22) son

temple, comme une bête grasse et repue, monstrueuse d'assou-
vissement; tout cela n'étant pas voulu par les chefs que je
mets en scène, provenant de l'état de chose supérieur et déterminé par le temps; tout cela s'enchaînant ensuite, se déduisant
par grands mouvements humains, et arrivant aux catastrophes,
aux abominations que je raconterai.—Tel est le drame social
dans sa vérité, dans sa généralité.

Il est bien entendu que mon directeur, que mon ingénieur
en chef, que tout mon personnel supérieur des mines ne veulent
pas écraser l'ouvrier, ont même de bons sentiments, tout en
se trompant par nature, et qu'ils ne sont que les rou—(424/23)
ages d'une machine montée, qu'ils ne peuvent détruire eux-
mêmes, étant chargés de la conduire. Cela me donne leurs
caractères différents selon qu'ils sont plus ou moins conscients.

La misère de mes ouvriers est donc grande. J'aimerais assez
que ma Catherine meure enceinte, par suite du travail et de
la misère. Elle mourrait dans les bras d'Étienne, mais à la fin,
car je veux la garder pendant tout le livre. Son caractère reste
à fixer; ne pas répéter un autre de mes personnages; en faire
peut-être une petite fille chétive et ardente, au lieu de la forte
fille que je voyais. Cela serait plus vrai et plus touchant. Jolie,
mais écrasée par le travail (425/24) et l'hérédité. Frêle avec une
grande énergie, nerveuse, poussant les chariots les plus lourds.
Créature de faiblesse et de courage, avec des idées religieuses,
plutôt superstitieuses. Étienne serait donc attiré par ce charme
et cette faiblesse. J'aurai dans la mine une autre fille, une amie
de Catherine, grosse fille débordante, aux seins énormes, et
qui se livrerait, qui se trousserait devant les étrangers, mal
embouchée, pervertissant Catherine par ses gros mots.—Avec
ça une vieille femme, et une petite fille de douze ans.—Je puis
avoir dans la mine un supérieur, un inspecteur (voir le titre)
qui abusera des filles, qui voudra prendre Catherine, laquelle
se donnera alors à Étienne. La grosse fille elle-même ne voudra
pas de cet inspecteur et le poursuivra d'inspecteur (*sic*). Plus
(426/25) tard dans le sac de la maison, ce sera cet inspecteur
qu'on tuera, et la bande hurlante des femmes pourra lui
arracher les parties génitales. Mais avoir des victimes innocentes

aussi, car c'est là l'effet.—Même je pourrais faire que ce ne soit pas l'inspecteur coupable qui soit tué, mais son frère ou même un inconnu.

J'arrive aux Durand. Il faut que la femme soit toute une création originale et vivante. Je la vois petite, carrée, (figure à prendre sur les lieux), blême. Elle est au début d'esprit équilibré, prudente, de conseil sage, luttant contre la misère; et peu à peu je la montrerai impuissante, s'enrageant elle aussi, arrivant au cri final de désespoir et de négation. Pas parfaitc, lui donner un vice qui emporte un peu d'argent. (427/26) Coquette peut-être, [elle sait lire] (voir sur les lieux). L'homme ignorant, brutal, n'est pas mauvais au fond; et lui obéit assez. La politique n'entre pas dans son crâne, il se bat à la fin comme une bête traquée. Boit, mais sans trop d'excés. Du reste, figure de second plan, je ferai tomber toute la clarté sur la mère. Elle a été épousée après la naissance de son premier enfant; ce que le travail et cette vie ont fait d'elle; dure pour ses enfants, égoïste, mangeant tout pour elle, voulant que les enfants travaillent, comme elle travaille elle-même; voilà le défaut, dans sa prudence et sa sagesse, ce qui ne va pas mal ensemble. —Il est logique que le caractère de mes personnages découle de leur travail, de leur misère: c'est une preuve de plus au dossier. Cette mère est mau- (428/27) vaise parce qu'elle a été élevée là-dedans. N'est pas de mauvais conseil, parce qu'elle est égoïste, et veut jouir en femme qui a été malheureuse. Sa colère contre ses enfants, quand ils ne peuvent plus travailler, ou qu'ils portent l'argent ailleurs. L'aisance qui s'en va. Elle boit sans se griser (A arranger avec les mœurs des mineurs).

Dans la première partie destinée à peindre le travail des mineurs et leur misère, il faut que je mette un accident. Dans la première partie ou ailleurs. J'aimerais bien l'éboulement du puits avec tout coulant à l'abîme. Il resterait quelques ouvriers au fond, avec des chevaux, (Les chevaux ayant rompu leur licol et galopant dans les galeries [poursuivis par l'eau]). Alors le sauvetage. On pense (429/28) que les ouvriers ont dû se réfugier dans une galerie montante et la galerie qu'on perce en partant de la grande mine. Et là le coup de grisou tuant les sauveteurs. On recommence. Ce serait d'un gros effet. Mais où mettre cela? Au milieu, je crois, avant ou après la bataille de la grève, de façon à opposer les violences barbares des mineurs à leur dévouement pour sauver leurs camarades. Je ne garderai, au commencement, dans ce cas, que le petit accident d'où l'enfant sort estropié, un éboulement partiel au fond, ou autre chose. Cela me donne tout mon commencement, le travail au fond, ce qui menace l'ouvrier, l'eau (creux avec réservoir, la flamme, etc.) puis l'intérieur de l'ouvrier et la fille ne rentrant pas, Étienne, etc. Il (430/29) faudrait que tout cela eût lieu dans la petite mine. Le père vient chercher sa fille et trouve son fils estropié (Catherine ne doit rien savoir, et n'arriver que le lendemain, pour ne pas la faire mauvaise).

Peut-être la catastrophe ne devrait-elle arriver qu'à la fin, après la grève. Les morts sont encore par terre lorsque le puits s'éboule. Le directeur a fait venir des Belges qui sont au fond du puits avec l'inspecteur, le terrible. Et tout le monde se met au travail, pour les sauver. Étienne pourrait y être aussi, vaincu, venant chercher de l'argent, pour sauver Catherine. Les deux hommes restant seuls, le duel au fond. Étienne tuant l'inspecteur comme défense personnelle; et le dernier fils de Durand tué par (431/30) le grisou en allant au secours. Puis Étienne sauvé et trouvant Catherine morte. Tous les ouvriers se remettant au travail, après avoir refusé encore, et Étienne remis, travaillant à une galerie près de l'endroit que le grisou a allumé, soixante degrés de chaleur.

Le mal est que cela enlève la belle simplicité du dénouement. Tous les ouvriers vaincus venant reprendre le travail et baissant la tête comme des lâches. Toi aussi, toi aussi.—J'ai une femme, j'ai une mère, j'ai des enfants. Et l'on entend les pics sonner contre le charbon.

Je puis encore mettre la catastrophe (432/31) juste avant la grève, et faire naître celle-ci justement du coup porté à la compagnie qui veut se rattraper. Non, cela est exceptionnel, cela ne vaut rien, non plus. La seule place où je puis la mettre est à la fin, et là, encore, elle gêne. Il faudra voir. Au lendemain de la grève quand des morts sont étendus, quelques ouvriers vont descendre dans le puits, et c'est là qu'on injurie Étienne qui y va. Il cède pour se sauver, il a peur, (car la compagnie a dit qu'elle fermerait les yeux sur tous ceux qui reprendraient le travail). Mme Durand peut se trouver là, après la mort de son homme et l'injurier elle aussi. Alors l'accident avec tous les détails me redonnant la mine du commen- (433/32) cement. Et à la fin, après qu'Étienne est remis, tous redescendant dans la mine. Encore des camarades qu'on nous a pris, et le triomphe du capital même blessé. La terreur! doivent-ils être riches pour supporter tout cela. Si cela se passait dans la petite mine au lendemain de l'achat par la grande compagnie. L'avantage serait de donner un rôle à Étienne. Et si j'enfermais Catherine avec lui, sous l'éboulement. Je finirais ainsi mes deux personnages, ce qui serait très bon. Cela arrangerait tout comme intérêt peut-être. Les voilà ensemble, l'agonie de Catherine. Elle meurt de la mine. D'autres ouvriers avec eux, l'inspecteur peut-être, un duel (?). Voir si elle doit (434/33) être enceinte. Je dois garder l'inspecteur terrible pour commander encore à la fin, redevenir insolent, les écraser plus férocement. Il n'est peut-être pas mauvais de montrer ainsi les ouvriers se remettant au travail, non seulement écrasés par le capital triomphant mais encore dans des conditions de besogne plus abominables, sous des menaces plus affreuses. La mine depuis que le charbon brûle, est devenue d'un séjour plus malsain et plus périlleux. Finir sur cet écrasement, sur cette aggravation de peine.

Il reste à voir comment Étienne descend au fond. On pourrait inventer tout un drame: l'ami d'Étienne, Nicolas, le nihiliste, celui qui veut faire tout sauter, peut à la fin de la grève, aller préparer le puits, scier des douves, déplacer des planches, par un prodige de courage, de façon (435/34) à préparer l'accident. Comme personne n'y descend, il attaque seulement le capital. Tout doit crouler. Le soir il apprend bien que l'administration fermera les yeux sur tous ceux qui se rendront le lendemain au travail. Et il reste farouche, tant pis. Il va voir Étienne et Catherine, la soirée. Étienne ne disant pas qu'il ira, honteux; mais c'est décidé. Le lendemain, douleur de Nicolas quand il apprend que son ami et d'autres sont sous terre. Il travaille, mais ne pas le faire tuer (?). Ne doit-il pas vivre pour représenter l'éternelle menace contre le capital, contre la société! Cela devient plus possible, parce que cela entre dans un drame logique. L'inspecteur s'est sauvé et s'est aperçu des (436/35) poutres sciées, il accuse donc les ouvriers, mais pas ouvertement, je ne veux pas de procès. La compagnie terrifiée étouffe l'affaire. L'état de guerre à la fin, même derrière l'écrasement obéissant des ouvriers.

Il faudra absolument au milieu des scènes se passant dans la mine, puisque j'en ai au commencement et à la fin.

Étudier le personnage de Catherine de façon à le faire central et intéressant. Il faut qu'il emplisse le livre, si je veux obtenir beaucoup d'intérêt. Ne pas le faire passif, idyllique, trouver une lutte humaine, quelque chose de poignant en elle.

(437/36) Ce personnage de Catherine est donc à chercher dans une lutte. Ne pas la faire pourtant au-dessus de sa condition, et lui donner un drame de sa classe. Je ne la vois pas bien encore, je n'ai pas de mouvement dans sa figure; il faudrait que je lui fasse avoir deux hommes peut-être, un brutal qui la dominerait et Étienne qui l'aimerait ensuite. Je lui donnerai à elle une tendresse pour Étienne presque inconsciente, et près de se livrer : bonne étude à faire. Alors Étienne et Catherine, à la fin, dans la mine auraient comme leur nuit de noces. Une scène où elle pleure, à la fille grosse : "Je ne l'aime pas." Que t'es bête, lâche-le. Et tout le livre pour l'amour d'Étienne.

D'autant plus que cela arrange les puits. Au début j'ai maintenant toute la famille Durand dans le puits (438/37) de la grande mine. Durand y travaille ainsi que sa fille, son petit et Étienne. Étienne peut loger chez les Durand ou être leur voisin. On rapporte le petit estropié (un accident à arranger) [amour dans la mine avec Étienne]. Puis Catherine disparaît avec l'homme. Misère des Durand, l'intérieur, le travail dangereux et mal payé. Le directeur de l'usine (sic). La grève qui éclate. Premier tableau. Puis apparaît la petite mine où l'homme travaille avec la fille. Il peut même n'être allé dans cette mine qu'après avoir pris Catherine. Trouver une scène dans la mine, le petit frère estropié va de l'une à l'autre. Alors la grève se déploie, tous les épisodes, le patron ruiné, la direction de la grande mine attaquée, la troupe, l'épisode du petit soldat, les coups de fusil. Un soir (439/38) qu'Étienne est allé voir Catherine (il a pu rester l'ami de l'amant), il l'a trouvée dans une misère affreuse, peinture, tous les houilleurs crevant de faim [scène dehors, pourqu'ils ne puissent se mettre ensemble, neige, froid, Catherine ne pouvant le recevoir chez une amie où elle va coucher]. Étienne lui annonce que son père est mort, on le lui cache. Elle dit : "J'irai à la mine demain," et il répond : "Je vous accompagnerai." Retour à la grande mine, toute la fin. Cela me semble bon. Catherine, là-dedans, est plus victime du milieu : elle cède à la force, en en aimant un autre, et elle lutte ensuite, terrifiée par la peur, prête à se livrer sans morale. Peut-être même la ferais-je se livrer comme une femme mariée : mais cela me retirerait la nuit des noces dans la mine. J'aimerais mieux qu'elle fût un instant sur le point de se livrer dans le livre et qu'elle n'en eût pas le temps.

(440/39) Pour ça, il faut faire Étienne très jeune. Seulement je n'ai pas la fin de l'homme Antoine par exemple. Il me faudrait sa situation aussi. Il se soûle, il la bat. Je le voudrais un peu chef, et il la plante là, après la grève, tandis que lui rentre en faveur, ou autre chose. C'est un maître mineur (?) qui a eu déjà la grosse fille. Enfin après bien de la misère, il la plante là, juste avant qu'Étienne vienne le soir, la veille de la catastrophe. Et à la fin c'est lui qui commande Étienne et Mme Durand. (Le personnage est à arranger).

Étienne peut être mécanicien, et diriger dans le fond une petite machine à vapeur, dans les grandes galeries. Catherine serait une yercheuse (sic), roulant la houille dans les galeries basses. Ce livre est l'éducation de révolte du jeune homme, il assiste à toutes les injustices sociales et s'en aigrit (441/39) beaucoup. Il se prépare pour plus tard à la commune. D'autant plus que son cœur en saigne avec Catherine (Peut-être pourrait-il au lieu d'une locomotive conduire en bas un ventilateur ou autre chose). Je le fais d'une éducation un peu supérieure aux houilleurs, pour les réflexions.

Maintenant reste la partie supérieure, les personnages bourgeois, représentant le capital. Ils doivent fatalement tenir une
place assez grande. Mais je tâcherai que leur drame soit le plus
simple possible. Il est à trouver d'ailleurs. Outre le patron de la
petite mine, et le directeur de la grande, il me faut un ingénieur.
Je pourrais faire que cet ingénieur couche avec la femme du
directeur. En un mot, le joli serait de montrer la classe dirige-
ante, le capital, pourri, (442/40) donnant le mauvais exemple.
Outre l'adultère, je pourrais montrer le directeur ayant un vice,
et ajouter un mariage malpropre entre un fils du directeur et la
fille du patron, une dot volée à la compagnie ou gagnée sur les
ouvriers. Mais tout cela bonhomme, et ne sentant pas la haine
démocratique. Du reste, toute cette partie est à organiser, quand
j'aurai les notes nécessaires.

Le petit estropié doit jouer un rôle. Je lui ferai couper une
jambe, et rester avec un côté de la poitrine défoncée, ce qui le
rend presque bossu, et arrête net sa croissance. Je lui donne tous
les vices, voleur, paillard, gourmand : le total dégénéré de tous
les vices des houillères. Je voudrais bien lui donner son drame
personnel, un petit ménage peut-être, une fillette de douze ans
(443/41) comme lui, qu'il aurait enlevée et qu'il tiendrait dans
l'ancien puits, où ils iraient du moins coucher ensemble. Pendant la grève il volerait à la direction, et ferait là-bas au fond,
des repas à crever, poulets et du vin, ivre-mort tous les soirs.
Étienne qui se douterait de quelque chose, le suivrait et le sur-
prendait au fond. Des échelles à moitié pourries pour descendre,
et la mine déserte, s'étendant à l'infini. Pourque cela ne ressemble pas à Marjolin et à Cadine, donner à l'enfant pour
maîtresse une femme d'âge, mendiante, à moitié folle, quarante
ans, devenue muette à la suite d'un coup de grisou, qui lui a
brisé la mâchoire. Elle mendie dans les rues. Elle peut être tuée
par la troupe, et le petit la nuit la traînant et la jetant dans
(444/42) le puits. ''J'aime mieux qu'elle soit là, ils n'ont pas
besoin de l'emporter.''

Réflexions d'Étienne dans cet enfer, et l'idée du meurtre
s'emparant de lui à la fin. Ébranlement nerveux, pouvant
traîner plus tard à la monomanie du meurtre.—Le puits ancien

pourrait servir aussi pour se cacher, quand les soldats veulent faire des arrestations. Voir à l'employer peut-être pour le nihiliste.

★   ★   ★

Dans les scènes à avoir : au cabaret, une réunion électorale près de la mine. Les femmes chez les fournisseurs. Et la caisse de secours, etc.

La mine qui brûle près du vieux puits.

Le roman aura lieu l'hiver, la misère devant être plus grande, une neige, dans ce pays noir. Description. L'herbe verte, à la mine qui brûle.

(445/43) Il ne faut pas qu'il ait plus de dix ans.

Pour éviter la ressemblance avec l'épisode de Marjolin et de Cadine, il faut absolument que je mette mon petit estropié seul au fond de la mine. Il pourrait y vivre en égoïste, ayant chaud en hiver, par des froids terribles, près de la mine qui brûle, volant et y apportant de la nourriture, godaillant au fond de cette mine déserte. Et un jour, il pourrait y attirer une petite fille avec laquelle il passerait la nuit. Ce pourrait être ce jour-là qu'Étienne entend des voix et descend. La mine déserte, le vieux puits où les arbres ont poussé.—J'oubliais que je voulais faire de mon enfant un criminel, le crime chez l'enfant. Mon petit estropié (446/44) deviendrait la dégénérescence dernière, chétif, maigre, et victime du travail avec son accident. Il résumerait les vices fatals, le produit du salariat sous terre. Et le crime par hérédité. Il peut tuer un soldat assis, par derrière, avec un couteau que je poserai auparavant, dans le dîner au fond de la mine. Quand il a tué son soldat, et qu'il râle, il le traîne jusqu'au puits, où il le jette vivant encore. Le grand cri. Le petit essuyant ses petites mains sanglantes dans l'herbe. Je le ferai mangé de syphilis, pourrissant la petite qui pourra en crever à la fin.

Le puits pourrait encore servir (447/45) à cacher quelqu'un, pendant la bataille, des ouvriers qui fuient, le nihiliste. Étienne lui-même qui connaît l'endroit et qui y mène des camarades. Quand le petit y jette le soldat, il faut que la deuxième échelle

casse et qu'on ne puisse plus descendre. Pour atteindre la
première échelle, on devra se pendre aux arbres qui ont poussé,
déterminer leurs espèces. Description courte et exacte. Le soldat
tué sera le soldat avec lequel un ouvrier fraternisera, Étienne,
peut-être, pendant la faction de ce soldat, sur un terri au grand
soleil. Le faire connaître (448/46) là, ce soldat, une vieille mère,
une maîtresse grosse au pays, petit paysan très doux, depuis peu
à l'armée. C'est décidément à Étienne qu'il se confiera (la
conversation idyllique) ou Étienne l'entendra se confier à un
jeune mineur du pays. Le meurtre sauvage, le mauvais couteau
cherchant le cœur à travers la tunique, le petit lui a sauté sur le
dos comme un chat sauvage. Ils ont roulé, et le reste.

*   *   *

Je n'ai pas encore mêlé mon Étienne à l'intrigue d'une façon
logique. A la fin de l'*Assommoir* je le dis mécanicien dans un
chemin de fer et envoyant parfois 10 francs à sa mère. Comme
Étienne est né en 46, il pourrait avoir à cette époque 20, on
serait donc en (449/47) 66. Cette est exacte (*sic*). Car à cette
époque Nana, née en 51, a 15 ans environ, ce qui nous donne
aussi 66. Maintenant si je triche un peu, je puis faire que l'argent
envoyé par Étienne à sa mère, l'a été en 64, et qu'il était donc
mécanicien dans un chemin de fer en 64. Il faudrait que lui fis
(*sic*) quitter en 65 et entrer alors à la mine. C'est là le point
important. Il aurait dix-neuf à vingt ans pendant tout Germinal
qui doit se passer rapidement, en 65, l'année qui a suivi la loi de
64 sur les coalitions. Le mieux serait de le faire renvoyer d'un
chemin de fer pour insubordination. Impossible de rentrer dans
un chemin de fer de la région. Quant à entrer dans une usine, il
ne peut y arriver, une crise industrielle désolant le pays.—C'est
alors qu'un soir, sur la grande route de Marchiennes, il rencontre mon mineur, qui le voyant accablé de fatigue lui apprend
qu'on cherche des rouleurs, des (450/48) hercheurs. Et il le
mène lui-même au porion, un brave homme qui l'engage.
Voilà donc Étienne dans la mine. D'abord, il couche dans un
garni de mon village, ou même dans une écurie. Puis comme il
semble bien se conduire, et qu'il travaille dur, et qu'il est ques-

tion de le mettre à la veine, il peut devenir le logeur de mon mineur. Ce qu'il y a à organiser, c'est de savoir si Étienne est déjà dans la mine depuis longtemps, lorsque je commence, ou si je l'y fais descendre au début de mon roman. En l'y faisant descendre au début de mon roman, j'aurai la crise industrielle dans tout son vif; elle poursuivrait Étienne dans la mine, après l'avoir traîné sans travail à travers la contrée. Cela serait vraiment bien. Et il ferait là son éducation de socialiste, tout en travaillant. Pas de place de mécanicien (on peut lui en promettre une, mais il ne l'a jamais). (451/49) Il préfère y rester. Si je le mets comme herscheur, je puis ne mettre avec lui que quelques hommes, trois ou quatre mêlés à une troupe de femmes. Et sa honte d'être moins habile que Catherine, qui lui rend en riant des services. Les autres femmes avec lui. Dans ce cas-là, Étienne devient mon lien conducteur pour exposer toute la mine, l'enfer d'en bas. Se méfier du début du Ventre de Paris, mettre Étienne se chauffant à un feu devant les générateurs ou sur le terri, ce qui serait moins bon. Enfin à trouver. Engagement immédiat et descente. Déjà la grève qui gronde. Très belle exposition. Cela me donne aussi tout le personnel. Catherine sera déjà au fond. Mon mineur peut avoir une femme de son marchandage tuée la veille, et il cherche justement une autre personne (on élague peu à peu les femmes), ce qui rend l'embauchement et la descente d'Étienne encore plus raisonnable. Le nihiliste sera un ami qu'Étienne re- (452/50) trouve plus tard à la fosse, aide-machiniste.

Maintenant, le caractère d'Étienne fera le reste. Je veux en faire un révolté, un criminel plus tard. Ne lui donner encore que des colères brusques, la gifle à son supérieur, son renvoi. Ne pas oublier sa vivacité provençale parmi ces gens calmes du Nord. Enfin, il faut le faire sortir de la mine, encore plus révolté qu'il n'y entre, le préparer pour le crime de mon roman sur les chemins de fer, et surtout pour la Commune. Quand il y descend, la révolte doit n'être en lui qu'à l'état latent avec des peurs et des soumissions. Quand il en sort, c'est un soldat de l'anarchie, un adversaire qui raisonne et qui se déclare contre la société telle qu'elle est faite.

(453/51) Ma famille de mineurs doit donc être composée du

mari, dont je fais la moyenne des mineurs, brave homme, paisible, ayant la haine de l'injustice, sachant à peine lire et écrire et se laissant conduire par sa femme. La femme sur laquelle je jette surtout la lumière, raisonnable, un peu bavarde, et aimant le café, mais sans excès, surtout pratique, devenue mère dure par le milieu, etc., et mon analyse est de la montrer s'exaltant peu à peu, et devenant terrible par la faim, et jetant son mari à la bataille, et à la fin ruinée absolument. (Je ne lui donne pas d'amant, mais on peut l'accuser de coucher avec Étienne. Elle a pu refuser au porion qui revient pour la tenter au milieu de la misère, quand les hommes ne sont pas là. Et pourquoi elle refuse encore.) Elle a comme enfants: Catherine (16 ans), un grand fils de 21, puis Jenlain 10 ans, une petite fille bossue de 8 ans, une autre petite fille de 6, un garçon de 4, et cinq sont morts. (454/52) Catherine couche avec sa sœur de 8 ans, bossue très vicieuse déjà, le fils de 21 couche avec Jenlain, la petite fille de 6 avec le garçon de 4, et l'enfant à la mamelle avec le père et la mère. Lorsqu'on prend Étienne, c'est que le fils de 21 s'est marié, après avoir tiré au sort. Il a déjà deux enfants de la maîtresse qu'il épouse, et qui vit chez ses parents. Mariés, ils ont une maison dans un coron. Je me débarrasse de lui ainsi, et je verrai quel rôle à lui faire jouer dans la grève. Pas du tout passionné pour tout ça; l'ouvrier qui s'en moque et qui joue à la crosse pendant que les autres délibèrent. A repris le travail, dès que la faim est venue ou autre chose. A la fin, très dévoué, tué par le coup de grisou, en travaillant pour sauver les victimes de l'action. Catherine y périt, le père a été tué,—la mère reste donc avec Jenlain estropié, sa fille de 8 ans bossue, sa fille de 6 et son garçon de 4, ainsi que l'enfant à la mamelle. Voilà pour ma famille.—L'autre famille de mineurs, dans le (455/52) coron peut être celle dont le fils de 21 épouse une fille. Il y aurait là, la mère qui coucherait [très g . . .*] avec le logeur. La fille qui aurait ses deux enfants, un de 2 ans et un à la mamelle près d'être sevré. C'est une cribleuse. (Cela ne m'empêchera pas de mettre une autre cribleuse souffre-douleur.) Le père très violent, très

---

* The word beginning with "g" is illegible; is it perhaps "gars" or "garce"?

brutal, très exalté pour la politique, une brute d'une cruauté froide plus tard. Un petit garçon, galibot, ami de Jenlain.* Peu d'enfants, ménage relativement heureux.

Il me faut encore un ménage jeune. Le mari 30 ans, la femme 25, deux enfants. Le mari mouchard du chef porion qui couche avec sa femme. Pousse les autres, joue un rôle louche, et à la fin est nommé porion pour services rendus, une traîtrise, à trouver.

Donc, j'ai ainsi trois types de mineurs: mon premier, doux et raisonnable, qui s'affole, que sa femme pousse par esprit de justice; (456/53) mon second, violent acquis déjà à la politique, celui qui pourra retravailler au fond à la fin, et dire le dernier mot avec la femme veuve; enfin le jeune, mouchard et récompensé à la fin. Le frère de Catherine est l'indifférent absolu en matière politique.—Le logeur, amant de la femme du second ménage, est un boweteur, la coupe à terre.

Antoine, l'amant de Catherine, doit être un mineur venu du dehors. Du Pas-de-Calais,** galant et brutal, beau garçon. Séduit Catherine, se conduit mal avec elle, commence par très mal parler de la grève, se fout de tout, va travailler à la petite mine, puis devient traître et précipite les choses. Est nommé plus tard porion, c'est lui qui rudoie Étienne et la veuve. On raconte que c'est Catherine qui le poursuivait. Est nommé porion à la petite mine, où il travaillait avec Catherine.

Mon membre de l'Internationale est un Basli. Ouvrier renvoyé à une grève précédente. S'est établi cabaretier, sa femme tient l'estaminet et, lui s'occupe (457/54) de plus en plus de politique. Se fait nommer secrétaire d'une société de secours mutuelle. Est en rapport avec un chef de section de l'Internationale qui est à Lille. Mène tout, est arrêté, acquitté peut-être. Dans la réunion électorale faire venir l'homme de Lille.

Le chef porion, homme autoritaire, pas méchant, mais se faisant obéir, et jouissant le plus largement possible de sa situation. Figure d'arrière-plan, sans commencement ni fin.—Le

---

* After Jenlain, Zola wrote: et une fillette de 8 ans, herscheuse déjà, bonne amie. He then crossed this out.

** Zola first wrote and crossed out: Un belge peut-être.

porion, ancien ouvrier, très brave homme. Se fait tuer à la fin, en voulant mettre le holà. C'est lui qu'Antoine remplace.

★   ★   ★

Pour que j'aie un type bien net, il faut que mon directeur soit le directeur de la compagnie, ayant plusieurs puits sous lui. Je prends une Compagnie moins étendue et moins riche que la Cie d'Anzin; du reste, je laisse cela dans le vague, car il me faudrait tout un personnel nombreux pour être dans la vérité. Peut-être même me faudra-t-il nommer (458/55) d'une façon abstraite, un secrétaire général, des caissiers, des employés. L'important est de planter mon paysage. Je mets mon directeur dans une construction en brique, une sorte de villa, à mi-route de mon puits et de Marchiennes. Les bureaux sont plus près de Marchiennes, dans de vastes bâtiments.—L'ingenieur habite une petite maison sur la route, à côté du directeur. C'est le sac de la maison personnelle du directeur que je décris, le matin avant son lever, ou le soir (à voir). Le directeur sera* arrivé par un très beau marriage. Sa femme parisienne, blonde.** M9ntre les corons à des amis qui la viennent voir. Le directeur est un salarié, pas méchant homme, autoritaire simplement, défendant sa position, vis-à-vis de sa femme. La fortune est à la femme. La (459/56) femme 45 ans, le directeur 55. Lui, resté dur, a fait son affaire tout seul, a mangé beaucoup de vache enragée, ne pas même le faire passer par les écoles du gouvernement. Plus tard, le beau mariage qui l'a tiré d'affaire et fait nommer directeur, mais la fortune pas à lui, continue à travailler pour vivre. Les cancans abominables sur son compte. La femme, belle sur le retour, grande, forte, encore de belles épaules, espère pousser son mari plus haut, a consenti à vivre dans ce pays de mine, mais regarde cela comme un exil. Reçoit le plus possible, voiture, les bonnes allant au marché, fait tout venir de Paris, etc. Triomphe à la fin de la grève.—Le mari félicité, poussé plus haut, dé-(460/57) coré. Le neveu à son mari, famille pauvre, passé par

---

* After sera, Zola wrote and crossed out: un ancien élève de l'école centrale.

** After blonde, Zola wrote and crossed out: l'air délicat et jolie.

l'école polytechnique, et sorti en assez mauvaise place. Pas passé par l'école des mines. Arrivé à Marchiennes, des bruits le donnent comme amant à sa tante: est-ce vrai? voir s'il faut laisser doute. En tout cas sa tante l'aime jusqu'à lui chercher un mariage riche. Il a vingt-huit ans et elle songe aux deux actionnaires qui ont une fille et qui habitent Marchiennes, de l'autre côté, une des rares propriétés du pays avec des arbres. Elle s'est liée avec ces gens, reçoit, etc. A la fin, elle concluera le mariage.

Mes deux actionnaires, tous les deux vieux. L'homme, soixante-dix ans, la femme soixante environ. Ont (461/58) eu très tard une fille qui a vingt ans. Tous les deux, des figures flamandes, longues, paisibles, froides et bonnes. Il faut montrer en eux la jouissance calme de la vie. Leur histoire, de père en fils n'ont rien fait, ont eu la chance que le petit nombre d'enfants, et des morts ont maintenu l'argent dans la famille; cet argent vient du père. Malheureusement, il a un frère (mon patron) et il avait fallu partager, la fortune réduite de moitié. Ce frère a la bêtise de vouloir traverser, l'achat d'une concession, d'abord tout marche bien, puis cause de ruine, et ruine finale par la grève. Le dieu capital [forme moderne] engloutissant le patronnat. A la fin, le patron employé dans la grande mine.—Mes deux actionnaires ont une fille* (462/59) que j'ai envie de tailler sur leur patron, calme, heureuse, bonne, ignorante de ce qui la nourrit et fait son bonheur. C'est elle que le jeune ingénieur épouserait, ou ce qui serait plus original, ce serait de [la] faire renoncer au mariage, parce que ces mines troublent trop la famille et que l'ingénieur lui a fait peur. (Pourtant il faut que l'ingénieur soit joli; nouvelle formule, école polytechnique, à côté de son oncle, plus noir, plus rude). Éviter le mariage, s'il y a moyen, ce qui serait plus distingué. La tante lui trouvera un autre mariage.—J'ai aussi envie de donner au patron une nombreuse famille. Il est veuf, il a un garçon qui a mal tourné et qui est soldat, un autre très paresseux,** deux

---

* After "fille", Zola wrote and crossed out: pas bien portante, enfant gâtée, pas jolie.
** After "paresseux", Zola wrote and crossed out: reste à sa charge, courant les filles du pays.

filles, très jolies qui lui resteront sur les bras, et un fils encore au collège, cancre abominable. (463/60) A la fin toute cette famille sur le dos et une vie de misère à l'horizon. Il a fallu liquider, dette en arrière, travail de tout ce monde pour payer. Une des filles peut vouloir se faire comédienne (La Clairon). Pas belle, intelligente au possible, faisant causer d'elle dans le pays par ses goûts d'artiste.

Je mets le boulanger et l'épicier dans la même boutique, un boutiquier qui tient de tout. Il habite le petit village; à deux kilomètres. Marchiennes est à deux lieues. C'est un ancien surveillant de la Compagnie qui s'est établi avec la protection de la Compagnie. Il a tué peu à peu le commerce de mon petit village par du crédit plus long et un bon marché apparent (à trouver peut-être dans la coopération). Lorsque la grève éclate, ordre de la Compagnie, refus de crédit absolu. Des scènes. Alors les autres commerçants veulent lutter, mais bientôt pris de peur, et enfin également. (464/61) Refus dans le petit village et refus à Marchiennes où les mineurs sont mal vus. Dans cette donnée-là, il me faudra aussi un boulangeur ou deux et un épicier, nommés et posés.

Le prêtre et le médecin, à peine indiqués, sur un plan très en arrière. Le médecin très occupé, dèpêchant ses visites et ses consultations. Beaucoup trop de malades, si pressé qu'il ne veut jamais croire à la maladie. Le prêtre, bonne cure, vivant bien, ne s'inquiétant de rien.

★   ★   ★

Mon vieil ouvrier serait donc le descendant d'un ouvrier qui a travaillé, dans le temps, au premier puits creusé par la compagnie. J'établis la filiation, le nombre d'ascendants tués à la mine, dans un cadre saisissant. Et après qu'il a passé 52 ans dans la mine, descendu à 8 ans, la compagnie le trouvant valide encore, au lieu de lui faire une pension (465/62) l'emploie au jour, à être charretier, en disant qu'on lui fera une pension quand il ne pourra plus travailler. Son gain, trente sous par jour. La compagnie à court de maisons dans le coron, l'a renvoyé lorsqu'un fils qui le soutenait est mort à la mine, la femme du fils et deux petites filles sont parties avec un amant. Le vieux renvoyé a loué un taudis sur la route, très bon marché. Il vit là, pendant la grève on l'oublie. (D'abord sa rencontre, sa face à face avec la fille des actionnaires). Puis quand on va lui porter des secours après la grève on le trouve chez lui, oublié, mort de faim.

*   *   *

C'est le personnage de Catherine qu'il faut arrêter et mouvementer ainsi que celui d'Étienne. Leurs amours, [le cadre de leurs scènes] leur rôle exact dans la grève.—Puis il faudra distribuer les ouvriers exactement.

Dans la première partie je vois bien Catherine. Elle partage son pain avec Étienne, elle se pose par le chapitre de sa conversation pendant le déjeu- (466/63) ner. Dans la seconde partie, je la vois encore, cédant brusquement à Antoine, par les fatalités du milieu, et partant avec lui à la fin (Étienne peut regretter de ne s'être pas levé la nuit pour aller la retrouver) Mais c'est à partir de la troisième partie que je ne la vois plus. La voilà chez Antoine, dans le village, travaillant dans la petite mine. Sa mère est furieuse car elle a perdu à son départ. Donc fâcherie entre la mère et la fille, Antoine l'accusant d'ailleurs de coucher avec Étienne (et c'est pour cela qu'il l'a emmenée). Dans cette troisième partie, je ne puis guère que ramener Catherine chez sa mère, quand elle sait la famille déjà dans la misère; elle tombe comme sa mère est seule avec Étienne. Les enfants jouent, les grands; quant aux petits, ils dorment. Comment sa mère la reçoit. Étienne si- (467/64) lencieux, (jaloux, n'a pas revu Catherine). Il laisse donc les deux femmes s'expliquer. Catherine apporte un peu d'argent, qu'elle a économisé. Elle le pose; la mère le prendra-t-elle? Et l'arrivée brusque d'Antoine qui l'a suivie; il peut savoir que le père est absent; se moque d'Étienne; serait même enchanté de le trouver. Alors scène terrible, comment il entre, gifle à Catherine. Étienne se dresse, veut tomber sur lui. Mais il n'y a que des menaces [il jure de l'assommer un jour] et en s'en allant Antoine accuse Étienne de coucher avec la mère. Il faudrait

que Catherine rougît devant Étienne, indiquer qu'elle l'aime
tout en se laissant violenter par l'autre. Dans la même partie
je puis faire qu'Étienne s'oublie avec la grosse fille, que tout
le monde a eue: ça ne tire pas à conséquence, elle-même n'y
tient pas, mais enfin ils sont ensemble, elle très gaie. Dans le
chapitre de fantaisie, le chapitre de Jenlain, je ferai voir Étienne
et la grosse fille à Catherine, em- (468/65) barras et pâleur
de celle-ci. Les deux amies peuvent causer, cela dans un cadre.

Dans la quatrième partie, je ne voudrais pas encore la
bataille entre Étienne et Antoine. Je fais d'Antoine le traître.*
La veille dans le bois, il a pu crier contre le patron, dire qu'il
faut arrêter le travail. Le montrer comme obéissant à un
personnage énigmatique que je poserai à côté de mon directeur.
La grève si calme ennuie la direction, elle préférerait des violences, du moins mon personnage énigmatique préférerait cela;
et il pourrait s'être entendu avec Antoine. Dans la forêt,
l'Internationaliste déconseillerait la violence, tandis qu'Antoine
pousserait à l'attaque, à l'arrêt du puits. Cela me donnerait un
chef pour lancer le mouvement de la quatrième partie,
Antoine poussant, puis se dérobant et allant prévenir les
gendarmes; d'autre part, l'Internationaliste voulant arrêter la
bande et se (469/66) trouvant emporté. Plus tard il perdra
lui-même la tête, il conduira les hommes dans la cinquième
partie, tandis qu'Antoine pourra avoir repris du travail.
L'analyse de tout ça me donnera du mouvement. Antoine se
disculpera de ses paroles du bois, dira qu'on l'a mal compris,
qu'il est temps de rentrer; et comme il aura accepté de travailler
avec les étrangers, fureur [on marche contre lui] contre lui.
S'il lâche Catherine dans ces conditions, c'est parce qu'il ne
veut pas l'épouser et qu'un porion ne peut vivre en collage.
Voilà donc tout Antoine trouvé.

Mais c'est Catherine que je n'ai pas. Dans la quatre, Antoine
marche donc contre le petit puits. Catherine qu'il ne prévient
seulement pas, y est descendue. Tout sur elle dans la mine,
un travail qu'elle y fait.

* Here Zola first wrote and crossed out: Il pousse au travail, il dit qu'il
descendra quand même.

(470/67) Non, tout cela est mauvais. Je fais toujours aller Antoine à la forêt, et il s'y montre violent. Sa maîtresse Catherine va toujours travailler, on le lui reproche, ce qui l'exaspère, car il se fait nourrir par elle. On lui dit qu'elle baise au fond du puits, qu'il mange cet argent-là; alors sa colère, et il pousse les autres, malgré l'internationaliste. Le lendemain il veut tout casser. Puis le lendemain, quand Catherine va pour descendre, il est au puits pour l'en empêcher. Mais le patron lui parle et le retourne, en lui promettant beaucoup. Et il descend. Le chapitre du travail au fond. La bande arrive, toute la scène, les ouvriers qui sortent par les échelles lorsqu'on a coupé les câbles, les huées, l'Internationaliste empêchant des violences. Mais son impuissance lorsque paraissent Antoine et Catherine. C'est Antoine qu'on pro- (471/68) mènera et qui de rage, lorsqu'il sera lâché, ira chercher les gendarmes. Comme ça j'évite le côté traître, commun et enfantin. Étienne furieux comme les autres, ne le secourant pas, pouvant même pousser à la persécution. La mère voulant gifler la fille.—Catherine suivra son amant persécuté, en suppliant qu'on le lâche. Je lui voudrais alors une révolte en faveur d'Antoine, des injures adressées par elle à Étienne et à la grosse fille. Vous êtes des lâches, vous couchez ensemble, et toute sa jalousie inavouée éclatant en paroles terribles. Étienne saisi, calmé. La mère, le père.—Puis, à la fin, lorsqu'Antoine est allé chercher les gendarmes, c'est Catherine qui arrive, essoufflée, encore noire, avertir Étienne et les siens pour qu'ils se sauvent.

(472/69) Il me faut maintenant Catherine dans la 5e partie. C'est là qu'elle pourrait s'offrir et que la lutte devrait avoir lieu entre les deux hommes. La scène pourrait commencer dans un cabaret; Étienne y serait seul lorsqu'Antoine et Catherine y entreraient. Non.* Il faudrait amener que Catherine s'offre presque et qu'Étienne ne veuille pas ou du moins que l'un et l'autre soient pris d'une honte et ne fassent rien. Donc, comme je le disais, une querelle entre Antoine et Catherine quelque part. Antoine pourrait être au cabaret, lorsque Cathe-

* Here Zola first wrote and crossed out: Antoine en est à menacer chaque jour Catherine de la planter là.

rine viendrait le chercher et cc qu'il lui dirait—motif de la
querelle entre les deux hommes. Ils sortent, se battent, Étienne
a renversé Antoine, est victorieux lorsqu'Antoine le menace
d'un couteau et l'emporte. Même il pourrait ne pas sortir,
cela aurait lieu dans le cabaret même. J'aimerais mieux ne pas
mettre de couteau pour ne pas escompter (473/70) Jenlain et
le petit soldat. Donc bataille seulement dans un endroit clos,
chercher cela: cabaret ou mieux autre chose si je trouve.
[Mais il y a foule, la bataille vient de ce qu'Antoine va travailler
avec des étrangers et que les autres l'injurient. Vous êtes tous
contre moi. Ça va donc recommencer. Alors Étienne seul.]
La bataille entre les deux hommes devant Catherine paralysée.
Antoine vaincu, jurant de se venger, et criant qu'il laisse
Catherine à Étienne, si celui-là en veut. Ce cri pourrait venir
d'une marque d'intérêt de Catherine pour Étienne. Et Antoine
s'enfuit, enragé. Étienne et Catherine face-à-face. Celui-ci la
supplie de ne pas retourner, mais elle s'entête; après celui-ci
un autre, puis encore un autre; non, elle préfère rester avec le
premier; d'autant plus qu'elle ne peut retourner chez ses
parents. Elle ne parle pas de la grosse fille, mais au fond c'est
un des obstacles. Alors Étienne va l'accompagner. Et leur
promenade dans le noir, ils passent (474/71) auprès du terri où
Catherine s'est abandonnée avec Antoine. La montrer faiblis-
sante, près de céder à Étienne, s'il voulait d'elle, mais quelque
chose les retient, une honte. Catherine rentre, pendant qu'il
rôde autour du logis. Enfin, elle se penche à une fenêtre et dit:
"Il n'est pas rentré, je me couche. Allez-vous-en, ça re-
commencerait." Et c'est en repassant près du terri, où ils
avaient vu le petit soldat, qui leur avait fait peur et qui avait ri,
qu'Étienne assiste au meurtre du petit soldat par Jenlain, et aide
celui-ci à le jeter dans le puits.

A la fin, pendant l'attaque du puits et la collision, il faut que
Catherine rôde comme un corps sans âme, insouciante du
danger et cherchant presque la mort. Jusque là j'ai pu ne pas
(475/72) lui faire prendre parti dans la grève; elle n'est qu'une
femme, n'a pas de passion, souffre les maux du milieu qui
pèsent sur elle. La veille, dans sa conversation avec Étienne, il

a pu lui parler de la grève, de la haine qui gronde contre les soldats, elle ne comprend pas, elle voudrait bien qu'on la laissât travailler tranquille, puisqu'il faudra toujours travailler. Sans toutes ces histoires, elle n'aurait pas été si malheureuse. Mais elle est mise à la porte par Antoine, derrière le dos d'Étienne. "Tu me compromets, va-t-en." On a pu lui promettre de le nommer chef, mais en lui faisant honte. Alors Catherine dehors, n'osant retourner chez sa mère; et la nuit [rôde autour du coron] qu'elle passe. Puis le matin, l'habitude la ramène au puits et là sa mère et son père la retrouvent. L'exaspération. Il m'a mise dehors, tu ne rentreras pas chez moi. Et peu à (476/73) peu la fureur de Catherine qui finit en héroïne, lançant des pierres aux soldats, avec Étienne, etc. Jusqu'à la mort de son père. La grosse fille la sauvant [il y a longtemps que je ne suis plus avec Étienne] et se mettant devant elle: arranger cela. Il ne restera plus qu'à la ramener chez sa mère. Il faut qu'Antoine ait à peu près disparu. "J'aurais dû le tuer hier," dit Étienne rageusement. Voir s'il doit jouer encore là un rôle de traître. Mais je crois qu'il suffirait de le montrer derrière les soldats. Il pourrait venir prévenir de l'attaque du puits ou être pour quelque chose dans la bataille: en tout cas quelque chose de très discret.

Dans la 6e partie j'ai donc maintenant Catherine dans la famille. La mère sombre, depuis la mort du père. Le raccommodeur renvoyé comme trop vieux. La mère dit: "J'étrangle le premier des miens qui retourne au puits."

(477/74) Mais Catherine trop malheureuse, elle n'ose pas manger sous les yeux de sa mère qui la regarde. Elle et Étienne. La scène la nuit, lorsque tous dorment. Catherine se lève et dans le noir va parler bas à Étienne. Il peut la prendre, la serrer désespérément dans ses bras. "Je vais au puits."—"Je t'accompagne" et il se met à la tutoyer. Ils se lèvent et descendent: Qui est là? crie la mère à la dernière marche. Étienne répond: C'est moi, je ne puis dormir, je sors.—Bon, bon! Il faut qu'on ait parlé la veille des affiches de l'administration, promettant l'oubli à tous ceux qui rentrent. Je pourrai toujours garder mon nihiliste, venant au coron, croyant que personne ne descend dans le puits, et préparant son accident. Garder aussi le cabaret de l'Internationaliste où j'ai la femme (478/75) très bonne.— Ce qui est gênant plus tard, c'est Antoine. Je préfère ne plus le montrer là; je ferai dire simplement que la Compagnie l'a nommé porion, au petit puits qu'elle a acheté. Et je le trouverai au petit puits à la fin. Lors des secours portés, il se trouve donc dans le petit puits, et peut-être plus ou moins contre le sauvetage. Voilà donc tous mes personnages.

Maintenant il me faut leur rôle exact dans la grève. L'homme de Lille, j'en ai enfin, ne paraîtra qu'une fois dans la réunion publique. Je puis le montrer une seconde fois dans la 5e partie, dans le cabaret de l'Internationaliste, lorsque l'émeute est décidée. Du reste il ne s'en mêle pas. Il est en paroles pour les moyens révolution- (479/76) naires. Quant à mon internationaliste, je le montre pour l'ordre dans la troisième et quatrième partie. Dans le bois surtout il parle contre Antoine et le lendemain il suit la bande mais pour la calmer plutôt. Il ne se met franchement à la tête du mouvement que lorsque les soldats sont là, dans la 5e partie. Mon premier mineur, brave homme calme, suit sa femme et s'irrite avec elle sous le coup de la misère, de la faim. *C'est là la grande étude centrale* qui doit dominer toutes les autres, une analyse à faire magistrale.—J'ai dit que Catherine restait le type de la femme prise sous la fatalité et ne s'exaspérant qu'à la fin, comme sa mère est la révolte du ventre et de la raison moyenne devant l'injustice trop cruelle.

Étienne est (480/77) aussi très important car il doit rester sinon le centre, du moins le lien du livre, et j'ai à le garder pour m'en servir de nouveau plus tard. Je le montre au début sans place, mis à la porte pour une brutalité. Le voilà déjà mécontent, jeté dans une mine; et je fais là son éducation socialiste. C'est là tout le livre, à son point de vue. Donc, il faut logiquement que la colère monte peu à peu en lui et qu'à la fin il soit un ennemi irréconciliable du capital bourgeois. Dans la première réunion publique il écoute simplement et trouve cela très bien: il applaudit. Éducation socialiste par les théories, il est alors plus avancé que la femme et se dispute avec elle; plus tard elle pourra l'effrayer par une violence plus grande.

Dans le bois, (481/78) il peut être pour la violence avec Antoine.
Et le lendemain, quand il le sent traître, son mépris pour lui,
qui le glace. Il pourrait se mettre à douter de sa propre conduite,
n'agit-il pas pour supprimer un rival; et le faire s'abstenir
tandis que la mère s'exaspère davantage. Il ne faut pas oublier
la dualité chez Étienne, son amour et ses idées sociales. Le
personnage est difficile à cause de cette nuance que je voudrais
très franche, sans tralala, sans romance. Ne pourrais-je mettre
un inconnu terrible chez lui, la névrose de la famille qui un
jour se tournera en folie homicide et j'imaginerai alors qu'un
amour heureux avec Catherine aurait pu l'adoucir, le fixer
peut-être. Une violence de bête fauve qui s'éveille en lui par
moments, un besoin de manger un homme. Cela serait très
bon; quand il tient Antoine, il est sur le point de tirer son cote *
(sic) et de le saigner. "Va-t-en, va-t-en!" (482/79) Et ensuite
quand il voit Jenlain tuer, l'effet que cela lui fait. Pourquoi
as-tu fait cela: "J'en avais envie." Et ce que cela remue en lui.
A la fin il part, soit renvoyé par Antoine, soit sur sa propre
volonté. "Il vaut mieux que je m'en aille, je le saignerai."
Il voit rouge quand il part. Son départ faisant pendant à son
arrivée. Le bruit des pics reprenant sous terre. Son regret
alors exprimé. Si Catherine avait vécu et ne s'était pas mise
avec ce gueux, j'aurais pu être heureux. Donc outre l'éducation socialiste qu'il fait sous terre, l'éclosion en lui de ce besoin
de tuer. En résumé: révolte vague à l'arrivée qui trouve son
programme pendant la réunion publique, violence dans le bois
et mépris le lendemain qui le laisse à l'écart de la bataille;
(483/80) éveil du sang dans sa lutte avec Antoine et devant le
petit soldat; fureur contre les soldats, briques lancées avec folie.
Et à la fin fuite pour éviter le meurtre. Mais cela traversé de
douceur par son amitié, sa tendresse pour Catherine. L'autre
homme en lui, bon et tendre, combat presque continuel.
Jalousie tendre, rêve continu d'une vie heureuse, gâtée con-
tinuellement par le milieu et les circonstances qui le jettent à
toutes les extrémités de sa nature. Tête un peu utopique.
Homme très complexe dans une nature simple.

* Doubtless a slip for couteau.

Maintenant je dois distribuer les autres ouvriers dans la grève. Mon second mineur, celui du ménage à trois est une brute qui gueule, qui est pour le tapage. Peu intelligent, brave homme au fond, ayant le tort de boire. Il sera pour la violence dans le bois, sera un de ceux qui promènera Antoine, attaquera la maison, et sera fait prison- (484/81) nier par les soldats, recevra même une brique. Pendant ce temps, le boweteur qui couche avec sa femme, restera avec elle, parce qu'elle sera grosse et se fera du bon temps. A la fin, naissance du petit et le ménage reprenant comme si de rien n'était, pendant que le mari est en prison.

Mon troisième mineur, celui dont la femme couche avec le chef porion (celle-là n'a jamais descendu dans la mine) est un garçon prudent qui entend ne se mettre mal avec personne. Il a expliqué son cas à la Compagnie, il ne peut faire autrement que les camarades, mais il ne sympathise pas avec eux. Très calme, le chef porion lui a expliqué les choses. Il va à la réunion, trouve cela très bien, va dans le bois où il est pour la tranquillité. Ne va pas au puits, mais rencontre la bande qu'il suit pour voir. A la collision, je le voudrais plus actif, je lui ferais volontiers sauver (485/82) le chef porion très menacé, en le cachant chez lui avec sa femme. La femme peut être avec lui, tandis que je ne ferais jamais sortir la femme du second mineur. A la fin, il sera de ceux qui reprennent le travail, qui sont dans la mine lors de l'accident. Et pendant le sauvetage, je le montrerai très dévoué. Bon ouvrier, calme, flamand, rêvant d'être porion, de faire des économies.

Maintenant je promène les deux vieux, le vieil ouvrier et le raccommodeur, au milieu des événements, fumant, hochant la tête, élevant leurs mains tremblantes, étant les preuves décrépites du mal dont les mineurs souffrent. J'ai tout mon vieil ouvrier, peut-être pourrais-je donner au raccommodeur un petit rôle. On a renvoyé les livrets, il est parmi les congédiés, sous un prétexte, pour éviter la pension. On prétend qu'il a voulu assassiner le directeur pendant l'attaque de la maison, lorsqu'il faisait au contraire le bien. Et à la fin (486/83) le montrer comme un enfant à la charge de sa fille. On a congédié aussi le vieil ouvrier sur un même prétexte.

Le frère de Catherine marié trouve cela très drôle, va avec sa femme par rigolade. Elle peut être gaie et s'amuse. Jusqu'au bois, rien, pas même à la réunion publique, reste dehors à boire. Puis tombe dans la réunion de la forêt, qui l'étonne et l'amuse. Le lendemain va avec sa femme au puits attaqué, s'allume, est de la bande qui poursuit Antoine, est de l'attaque de la maison. Pendant la collision se trouve avec le moulineur, le frère de la grosse fille, et lance des briques par blague lorsque le moulineur est tué. Alors il fuit épouvanté avec sa femme. Paraît le lendemain au coron, dit qu'il travaillera le lendemain, est chassé par sa mère. Se met des travailleurs pour (487/84) sauver sa sœur et se trouve tué par un coup de grisou. La femme reste, elle s'est mise avec un autre.

Jenlain gambille jusqu'à la fin. Sa petite pension disputée à la Compagnie. Il est quelqu'un par cette pension. Il faudrait pourtant finir le petit soldat, le cadavre. Le retrouve-t-on? Non. Jenlain pourrait de temps à autre l'aller voir, s'il l'a déposé dans une galerie. Puis un éboulement qui le cache. C'est fini, on ne le saura jamais. Dans la bataille, tous les enfants galopent. Jenlain et ses deux amis, le garçon du 2e mineur et même la petite de dix ans, herscheuse, celle qu'il invite dans le puits. C'est l'ami de Jenlain qui sera tué.

J'ai oublié la mère de mon troisième mineur. Mère terrible, qui combat, et qui accable son fils de sottise sur sa lâcheté. Elle va partout, le disant cocu, prétendant qu'on la fait sortir quand le chef porion paraît. J'ai bien envie que ce (488/85) chef porion reste le plus possible dans la coulisse. Sans doute, il a possédé la femme et il doit coucher encore avec; mais où, c'est ce qu'on ne peut dire. Laisser cela dans le vague peut-être. En tous cas, la vieille femme, qui est mêlée à toutes les bagarres, qui est celle qui veut arracher la robe de la fille des deux actionnaires, est tuée à la fin, ce qui est, de l'aveu de tous, un soulagement pour tous. Je puis, si cela me donnait quelque chose, faire que le père de mon premier mineur, ait eu autrefois cette vieille pour bonne amie.

Dans le ménage de mon second mineur, le père est en prison, le petit garçon est tué, de sorte que le faux ménage reste avec les deux autres enfants, et l'enfant à la mamelle. Naturellement, le boweteur a repris son travail. L'enfant ne naît qu'après la collision, lorsque le mari n'est (489/86) plus là. Il le trouvera à son retour.

Dans le ménage de mon troisième mineur, la mère est tuée, le ménage reste avec les enfants.

La grosse fille se trouve mêlée aux événements avec les femmes et les enfants. Elle est tuée.

Quant à mon nihiliste, je le fais blond, délicat, avec un sourire pincé, trouvant tout trop doux, et parlant tranquillement, froidement d'extermination. Mais après qu'il aura déterminé l'accident, il me faudra le finir. Je lui ferais volontiers mettre le feu quelque part, en même temps. La situation est celle-ci: tout coule à l'abîme. Son ami est au fond, et il peut être une des premières victimes, se faire attacher pour aller reconnaître et y rester. Cela froidement. N'a pas de femme, les dédaigne, a une histoire de Russie terrible qu'il peut raconter un soir à Étienne étonné. Quand il descend: "Mais c'est la mort.—Je le sais." (490/87) Et son dévouement inutile.

Le chef porion ne doit pas être un mauvais homme, autoritaire simplement, traitant ses hommes en esclaves, mais bon vivant et très coureur, avec une femme âgée et laide, qui le laisse faire. Il est pour la fatalité de ce qui est. Ça a toujours été comme ça, et ça sera toujours comme ça. Vous êtes idiots de vouloir en savoir plus que vos supérieurs. Et il les fouaille, sans rancune d'ailleurs.

Le porion, un ancien ouvrier, qui est de cœur avec eux. Brave et digne homme, conciliant, est tué.

Enfin le cheval. Il y a dix ans qu'il est dans la mine. Très malin, très intelligent. C'est Jenlain et son ami qui le conduisent, l'ami assis devant, Jenlain courant derrière. Je ne puis que le mettre dans la première partie et dans la 6e. Un rappel à la deuxième. Il sera mêlé à l'accident. (491/88) Maintenant je pourrais en avoir un autre qui sera mort et qu'on enlèvera. (Comment) Mon cheval le sentira, le regardera partir. Le rêve de mon cheval, pensant peut-être à ses premières années. Où on l'avait acheté, ce qu'il avait fait d'abord. Et pendant la

grève, le palefrenier seul au fond. Je devrais avoir un palefrenier dans mes personnages. C'est à mettre.—Mettre la
montée d'un cheval mort, mais sans doute pas la descente d'un
cheval vivant. L'écurie lorsque l'eau arrive, et mon cheval qui
s'échappe. Il faut qu'Étienne ou du moins Catherine soit près
du puits, voie l'écurie, s'affole et aille retrouver Étienne.

(492/89) Il serait beau de faire ceci. Prendre Étienne et lui
donner un rôle plus central, en en faisant un des chefs, même le
chef de la grève. Voici dès lors comment je comprendrais le
personnage.

Étienne arrive à vingt ans à Montsou. Il est plus intelligent
que les mineurs, par métier; il a eu une instruction de mécanicien, pas très étendu, mais assez large pourtant. En outre je
peux le mettre en rapport, dès ce moment, avec Marsoulan
qui est un chef de l'Internationale à Lille.—Donc il a allongé
une gifle, on l'a congédié. Livret pas bon. Enfin expliquer
qu'il ne trouve pas de travail à cause de la crise. Rendre
vraisemblable son arrivée à Montsou. Le voilà dans la mine,
peu à peu cette vie souterraine le révolte, il voit les abus, il y a
tout un (493/90) soulèvement en lui. Dès lors il a des aspirations
au-dessus de son travail, il se met en avant, il voit au-delà de
sa classe: travail sourd de l'idée d'avenir chez un ouvrier
intelligent. Mettons qu'on le juge turbulent et qu'on le
congédie. Il vit d'une façon quelconque, et il continue à
réfléchir, il sent le besoin de l'instruction, il apprend en cachette,
sa lutte contre la science, son désespoir de ne pas savoir,
l'utopie qui commence, l'état de demi-savant, plein de trous,
plein d'affirmation et de doute. Ne pas oublier, du reste, de
mettre cela dans le tempérament d'Étienne. Il a été bon ouvrier,
il parle, fait de la propagande et a pris peu à peu une grande
influence sur ses anciens camarades. Le voilà donc chef, ne
déterminant pas la grève, mais l'acceptant, voulant la diriger
d'abord, puis emporté lui- (494/91) même, puis allant au-delà
de ce qu'il a voulu. Et finir par le discrédit où il tombe, les
soupçons qu'on lui adresse, la fin de sa popularité, son écrasement. Cela donnerait l'étude de l'ambition, du combat, de

l'ignorance, de tout le drame qui doit se passer dans un de ces chefs de bagarre. Finir par son départ, sans pour cela faire soumettre les ouvriers, qui renvoient leur triomphe à plus tard.

Le pis est que cela change tout mon plan. J'ai toujours le début, la première journée. A la rigueur, je puis ne pas faire renvoyer Étienne. Il resterait dans la mine et dans une partie que j'ajouterai, je montrerai l'ascendant qu'il prend peu à peu sur ses camarades. D'abord hercheur, puis piqueur, puis accepté chez les Maheu, puis écouté par tous. Dans un chapitre ou deux, j'analyserai ce qui se passe en lui. Je le montrerai travaillant, causant; enfin je préparerai la grève. Dès que la grève (495/92) éclate j'ai son rôle tout indiqué. Son attitude avec Catherine reste la même, je lui donne seulement un rôle plus actif dans la grève. La Mouquette l'adore, et comme je n'en fais pas un rigide, il peut succomber. Dans son emportement, peu à peu, je puis mettre à son insu sa tendresse pour Catherine, sa haine contre Chaval, qui trahit. Il discutera avec lui-même, pourra s'avouer cela un moment. Il gardera aussi sa peur du vin qui le rend fou, son besoin de tuer. Son nouveau rôle ne devient gênant qu'à la fin, et encore on peut l'arranger. On peut imaginer qu'il n'a pas été arrêté, rendre cela vraisemblable. Souvent les chefs ne sont pas arrêtés. Ce sont leurs soldats qui paient pour eux. Le voilà donc libre, rentrant dans le coron, et là je peins ses doutes, sa popularité qui tombe, les ouvriers qui l'accusent de les avoir trahis. Silence froid de Maheude elle-même. (496/93) Tout un petit chapitre sur cela. Alors Étienne plein d'angoisse, ne sait plus s'ils n'ont pas raison; et l'analyse qui le conduit à redescendre dans la mine avec Catherine. Quand on apprend qu'il est au fond, les soupçons s'accroissent, les ouvriers disent qu'il les a poussés pour se faire bien venir. Pourtant les travaux. L'attitude de Souvorine à trouver; et à la fin Étienne obligé de partir, devant la sourde attitude des ouvriers qui promettent que les choses marcheront mieux la prochaine fois, et devant sa peur de jouer du couteau. Si je garde Souvorine à la fin, je puis lui faire dire le dernier mot. Tout détruire. Étienne s'en va, est de son avis. Je montre Étienne s'en allant un soir par la pluie, comme il est arrivé un matin, par la gelée.

Cela supprime Rasseneur tel que je l'avais compris. C'est désormais Étienne qui fait venir Marsoulan, c'est lui qui s'affilie (497/94) à l'Internationale, qui est le secrétaire de la société de secours. Il ne parlera pas à la réunion publique, mais il parlera dans le bois. Comme secrétaire de la société, on peut le payer; et le voilà presque riche. Son après-midi passée à travailler. Rasseneur ne sera plus qu'un cabaretier libre penseur, ancien ouvrier mineur congédié, que sa femme entretient en gagnant beaucoup d'argent, et qui peut devenir l'ennemi politique d'Étienne avec lequel il s'est entendu un certain temps. (Peindre là les divisions qui déchirent le parti ouvrier, voir quelle opinion on peut donner à Rasseneur. Je le vois déjà moins avancé qu'Étienne, demandant simplement des réformes. C'est un possibiliste. Étienne au contraire est un collectiviste autoritaire, Souvorine est un anarchiste.)

*　　　　　*　　　　　*

Je fais de mon vieil ouvrier le père de la Maheude pour avoir toute une famille à opposer à la famille de mes actionnaires. (498/95) Je puis lui garder le nom de Caffiaux ou de Bonnemort. Donc il aura 60 ans et aura 50 ans de fond. Depuis deux ans on l'emploie comme charretier, la nuit. Il dort dans la maison quand les autres sont debout. Il occupe le lit de Zacharie et de Jenlain. Je le fais toujours renvoyer comme révolutionnaire, et je l'ai toujours infirme à la fin. Je puis faire que les Grégoire, à la fin, donnant toujours des aumônes, lui apportent des souliers; mais il est immobile dans son fauteuil, les pieds si déformés qu'il ne pourrait les mettre. Le côté navrant de cette dernière aumône inutile. Toute cette famille dans la maison en deuil, bayant devant ce vieillard fini; le père tué, le fils mort, Jenlain infirme, une enfant boiteuse (sic), les autres sans pain.—Seulement, avec le vieux, père de Constance, il faut que j'arrange la scène où Cécile manque d'être écharpée (499/96) par les femmes. Les Grégoire, ni leur fille ne doivent connaître les Maheu. La Maheu (sic) va chez eux pour la première fois au chapitre I de la seconde partie. Elle a rencontré les Grégoire qui lui ont dit de venir chercher du linge pour les enfants. (Ils ne donnent jamais d'argent parce qu'ils prétendent qu'on le boit, toujours des choses en nature). La Maheu, questionnée, peut donc parler de son père, de ses enfants, etc. (elle mène des enfants, du reste); mais on ne connaît pas le père, et c'est ainsi qu'il peut effrayer Cécile, qu'il prend dans ses bras, pour la sauver, et qui crie; c'est même cela qui fera congédier le vieux.

Je puis garder quand même un raccommodeur, dont je ferai un ami du vieux, pour les montrer parfois ensemble le dimanche.

(f. 6) ÉTIENNE LANTIER.—né en 1846, à Plassans, de Gervaise Macquart et de Lantier. Élection de la mère. Ressemblance physique de la mère, puis du père. Hérédité de l'ivrognerie se tournant en folie homicide. État de crime.

(Passages de l'*Assommoir*) Le lendemain, Gervaise reçut dix francs de son fils Étienne, qui était mécanicien dans un chemin de fer; le petit lui envoyait des pièces de cent sous de temps à autre, sachant qu'il n'y avait pas gras à la maison (p. 548)— (Et auparavant): Goujet lui ayant parlé d'envoyer Étienne à Lille, où son ancien patron, un mécanicien, demandait des apprentis, elle fut séduite par ce projet (p. 314)—Le passage de la p. 548 se trouve après Nana à l'atelier, lorsqu'elle a de 15 à 16 ans; et comme elle est née en 1859, cela met l'envoi des pièces de cent sous en 1866 environ. Je puis donc faire renvoyer Étienne de son chemin de fer tout de suite. *Germinal* com- (f. 7) mencerait en 1866, et Étienne aurait 20 ans. Dater dans le premier chapitre.

Étienne ressemble à sa mère, puis à son père. Je prends le père. Il est donc joli homme, assez petit, brun, [bien rablé, fort sous sa menue apparence] * avec une figure correcte, un nez droit, un menton rond, un galant sourire sur des dents blanches: un provençal avec ça, un peu noir de peau, les cheveux demi courts et frisant naturellement,—Buisson,** le tambourinaire. Toujours rasé, rien que des moustaches. Avec cela quelque chose de détraqué dans le regard, un vacillement par moment, qui pâlit l'œil noir; et alors une légère crispation nerveuse passant sur le visage. C'est la marque [Influence de la mère: douceur, courage au travail, timidité] de la lésion nerveuse qui augmentera plus tard, qui tournera son hérédité d'ivrognerie en folie homicide. Laisser deviner ainsi d'un bout à l'autre, l'inconnu qui s'exaspère en lui.—Je marquerai surtout

* Words between brackets were written by Zola in the interlinea.
** For the identity of Buisson, see, above, chapter 5.

cet inconnu à la fin, lorsqu'il tiendra Chaval sous son couteau, lorsqu'il verra [L'enfant fait ce qu'il n'a osé faire; analyser le coup sur Étienne] Jenlain tuer le petit soldat Jules, et enfin, et surtout (f. 8) lorsqu'il quitte la mine au dénouement, de peur de tuer Chaval, devenu porion. Tout cela très important. Dès le début, d'ailleurs, il faudra poser le côté détraqué.

Le côté physiologique doit être nettement établi dès les premiers chapitres. Il faut aussi parler de Gervaise, de la mère, de Coupeau, de Lantier, des inquiétudes d'Étienne renvoyé qui ne pourra plus donner des pièces de cent sous. Et cela je le dirai non dans le premier chapitre, que j'aime mieux laisser à Bonnemort, mais dans le chapitre du déjeuner, dans la causerie avec Catherine. Tout l'*Assommoir* résumé au fond de la mine.

En somme, Étienne, dans *Germinal* fait son éducation socialiste, apprend la révolte, qui jusque là n'a été qu'instinctive. La gifle, l'inconnu de violence qu'il découvre peu à peu en lui. Le nihiliste et Rasseneur lui enseignent le socialisme, la misère et la révolte des mineurs le soulèvent. Il faut aussi que son amour pour Catherine intervienne. Mais je ne voudrais pas d'un amour (f. 9) à la Goujet, platonique et pleurard. Il veut Catherine, et s'il ne la prend pas, c'est qu'il y a des obstacles. Idée de possession, avec un fond d'honnêteté, de mariage possible. Une ou deux délicatesses peut-être, mais l'idée du mâle lâché, contrarié par des timidités premières. Cela s'établira en écrivant. Ce que je ne dois pas perdre de vue, pour la vérité du personnage, c'est qu'il n'est pas un rêveur, un tendre, c'est qu'il obéit au contraire à des impulsions de sauvage, de nature inculte. Il veut Catherine, elle lui échappe, sa colère rentrée; il prend la Mouquette, la lâche, est sur le point d'avoir Catherine, qu'il ne prend pas, par un sentiment à analyser, et à la fin il l'a dans la mine. Il faut absolument qu'il l'ait. La satisfaction là-bas, au fond.

Avec les filles, il est un peu timide, avec des idées de violences, de les prendre et de se satisfaire. Les filles qu'il a eues, de la plus basse espèce, car il n'ose qu'avec (f. 10) celles-là. A Lille dans les maisons publiques ou les filles qu'il rencontre. N'a pas eu de maîtresse gentille, ouvrière. Laisser percer cela, le dire dans la causerie du déjeuner, et l'effet que lui produit la violence de Chaval renversant Catherine pour la baiser à la baiser (*sic*). Pourquoi n'a-t-il pas osé le premier? Ce sera là tout le livre.

Au point de vue de l'ivrognerie, ne boit pas, ne peut pas boire. Cela le rend fou, très malade, avec des idées de mort pour lui et pour les autres. Un rien le grise, et il change à terrifier, le masque, la voix, les idées. Il dit cela, [chez Rasseneur] quelque part. Puis, le griser une fois, la scène. Peut-être pendant la ducasse, ou dans un endroit où cela servirait au drame, où j'aurais besoin de l'avoir ainsi.

Comme éducation, très élémentaire. Sait lire et écrire, pas davantage. Supériorité pourtant chez les mineurs. Intelligence assez vive, mais obstruée (f. 11) d'idées toutes faites. Paris est resté au fond vague. Ne lit que quelques journaux, *le Siècle*, *le Rappel*, un journal de Lille, journaux que je déguiserai sous des titres inventés. N'a pas de livre, un ou deux peut-être. Peut sentir le besoin de savoir, sans pouvoir ni vouloir apprendre.

Enfin, le préparer pour le roman sur les chemins de fer, où il commettra un crime; et surtout le préparer pour le roman sur la Commune, où je le ferai passer, sans lui donner le livre entier. Il ne sera qu'une figure de second plan, un résultat des deux romans qu'il aura emplis. (Ce roman sur la Commune s'annonce comme une résultante, un dénouement où je ferai passer plusieurs des personnages des Rougon et des Macquart).

(f. 12) Étienne devient un des chefs de la grève. Plus intelligent, révolté par les abus, son caractère aide à le soulever. Il veut réformer, collectiviste autoritaire, ses études, sa demi-science, son affinement; ses luttes terribles contre ce qu'il sent qu'il faudrait savoir; son ambition et son naïf orgueil aussi; d'abord retenant la grève, puis emporté; et comme il n'est pas arrêté, soupçonné, popularité perdue, sourde rancune contre lui.—Tout un personnage central maintenant, beaucoup plus mouvementé. Un héros enfin. Et le contre-coup de son goût pour Catherine, sa lutte contre Chaval le traître qui l'exaspère, son examen de conscience et ses aveux secrets.

(f.24) CATHERINE MAHEU.—16 ans. Une figure fine, un teint superbe de rousse que le savon noir a déjà gâté, [yeux vert clair de source] est en train de gâter. La figure longue de la famille, mais délicate. La bouche trop grande, avec de très belles dents. Beaux cheveux roux, un peu durs et par trop drus. La ligne du cou très blanche, sous le visage qui se tanne; et, quand elle se déshabille, une apparition toute blanche, du lait; car le charbon entre moins là.—En somme, figure irrégulière et charmante, surtout lorsqu'elle est noire de charbon, et que ses yeux gris et ses dents blanches éclatent. Ses yeux dans le noir du visage, des yeux profonds, qui se mettent à luire comme des yeux de chatte. (Étienne ne la verra bien qu'au déjeuner)

Au moral, une bonne fille, un produit de la race et du milieu, une résignée. Bien de sa classe. Les pudeurs (f. 25) du milieu et pas d'autres. Se laisse très bien aller à un amant, comme sa mère s'est laissée aller.* Se déshabille le soir sans honte devant Étienne. S'abandonnerait à lui. Aimait vaguement Chaval, avant Étienne, et n'est troublée que par son goût pour Étienne joli garçon. Le regarde avec surprise, se laisserait prendre peut-être, si Chaval ne brusquait pas les choses; et reste combattue ensuite. Toute son analyse de passion part de là, sans pudeur plaquée, sans raffinements ni sentimentalités en dehors de sa classe.

Pour la grève, une résignée. N'entre pas dans cette question, qui regarde les hommes. Prend le parti de Chaval lorsqu'on le maltraite, sauve ensuite ses parents, plus tard s'abandonnerait à Étienne: en un mot, cède aux circonstances, selon sa nature. J'en fais (f. 26) en somme un produit et une victime du milieu.

Grande douceur et grand calme. C'est sa caractéristique. Avec une jolie gaieté dans le début.—Encore pas trop déformée par le milieu. Peut-être une légère déviation dans le bassin. *Anémique, des troubles dans ses fonctions de femme qui réagissent sur le caractère.* Cela est à régler.

Vis à vis de Chaval, grande peur. Le mâle qui l'a prise. Vis à vis des parents une obéissance frissonnante, elle ne s'est révoltée que sous la pression de Chaval, parce qu'elle le craint encore plus que ses parents.

* Here, Zola wrote and crossed out: N'a aussi qu'un seul.

Un peu indifférente pour ses frères et sœurs. La lutte pour la vie.

Silencieuse le plus souvent. Puis se répandant en bavardages tendres et (f. 27) jolis.—La montrer surtout avec les habitudes de la mine.

Aime beaucoup la danse à rester sur place [sa joie à la ducasse] les jambes brisées. Ce qui ne l'empêche pas de travailler le lendemain. Son adresse à pousser les berlines.

Amour n'allant pas trop dans le bleu surtout. Amour amitié pour Étienne, avec une pointe d'au-delà seulement. Le trouve joli, et *croit qu'elle serait plus heureuse avec lui*. L'idée du bonheur. Pas de phrase sentimentale. Des besoins et des satisfactions, autant morales que physiques.

Sait lire et écrire, c'est elle qui fait les comptes de la famille.

(f. 76) CÉCILE GRÉGOIRE, 18 ans.—Pas jolie, mais jeune et fraîche.

Enfant de gens déjà âgés. { Non, pas ce portrait, trop saine, trop bien portante. Voir le portrait au 1 de la partie 2.

Petite, maigre, anguleuse. Un visage torturé, le menton pointu, le nez [déjà mure à 18 ans, mais chair superbe] légèrement de travers, le front bombé et pas de cils, [les cheveux noirs]; blonde fade. Les parents la voient délicieuse, spirituelle et fine.

A été élevée à Lille jusqu'à dix-sept ans. Maintenant des professeurs de piano et de littérature viennent encore à Marchiennes. Volontaire, capricieuse, a voulu rentrer à la Réquillarde. Pas mauvaise pourtant, trop gâtée et gardant en elle un inconnu qu'elle ne dit pas.

D'abord a semblé s'éprendre de Paul. C'est presqu'elle qui a donné l'idée du mariage. Les parents n'en sont pas très contents, car ils craignent que Paul aille ailleurs et n'emmène leur fille. Pourtant, ils (f. 77) consentent comme toujours. Ils préféreraient qu'elle épousât quelqu'un fixé dans le pays. A la fin, je voudrais que la rupture vînt de la grève. Elle a été souffrante de l'assaut subi, elle ne veut pas quitter ses parents. Il faudra trouver quelque chose de plus vraisemblable. La faire romanesque peut-être, ayant rêvé un héros chez Paul, un homme qui allait écraser l'insurrection; et, désabusée, renonçant à lui. Cela lui donnerait un caractère.—Le mieux encore serait de la faire enfant gâtée, ne voulant plus de Paul, de même qu'elle le voulait, sans raison bien nette. Romanesque avec cela, et laisser deviner que c'est parce qu'elle ne le trouve pas assez héros.—Comme éducation, ignore tout, pourrait n'être pas à Lille, et avoir reçu toute son éducation chez elle, par des femmes. Cela coûte plus cher et l'explique mieux. De cette façon, elle est bien la résultante des faits et du milieu, dont j'ai besoin. Une capricieuse, une enfant gâtée, une ignorante, une romanesque.

(f. 81) SOUVARINE—Vingt-huit ans. Russe et nihiliste. Un petit jeune homme mince. Blond, cheveux courts,* figure douce encadrée d'une barbe légère [rasé] qui frise. Nez petit, mince; bouche fine, d'un rose de jeune fille, yeux vagues de slave, bleus, extrémités distinguées, [très peu d'accent]. Et une expression de douceur entêtée, avec des éclairs de sauvagerie. Petites dents blanches et pointues.

Exposant des plans monstrueux de destruction avec un calme tranquille. N'aime pas les femmes, a des petites mains et des petits pieds comme elles. Le mariage libre, pas de religion, etc.

Son histoire. Le faire passer avec son idée fixe, sans aucun autre intérêt dans l'action. A la fin, trouver son dénouement logique. (f. 82) Il est né d'une famille noble de province, près de Toula, famille riche, qui lui a coupé tous les vivres. Fond slave mystique. A fait ses études au gymnase de Toula, puis est allé faire sa médecine à Saint-Pétersbourg. à l'Université. Là, dans le mouvement socialiste, a cédé à la mode qui souffle, tous les jeunes gens apprenant un état, pour étudier le peuple, pour se rapprocher de lui, s'est fait mécanicien, a travaillé comme tel. Puis s'est trouvé mêlé à un complot de société secrète, un attentat contre un chef de la police. Histoire abominable de courage et de sauvagerie. Sa maîtresse y est restée. Est venu en France, après avoir réussi à s'échapper, la vache enragée mangée

* Instead of "blond", Zola first wrote "chatain," and instead of "courts" he first wrote "longs et flottants [bouclés] de poète."

par lui, puis est entré chez le mécanicien où Étienne faisait son apprentissage, dans l'industrie privée, car les grandes compagnies, les chemins de fer le repoussent, (f. 83) de peur qu'il ne porte les secrets en Russie. Comment plus tard il est engagé à la Cie de Montsou.

Un prince *raté*. Tout à fait différent du nihiliste russe, le vrai [le fils de pope, de petits bourgeois] qui ne veut l'extermination que contre le gouvernement, le despote et non contre le despote. Quelque part aussi parlera avec amertume de ses anciens amis qui tournent aux politiciens. Lui, aigri, dans l'exil, discipline (*sic*) de Bakounine et de Krapotchine. Aime les ouvriers par un esprit de justice, de fraternité presque religieuse, fait le rêve de vivre tous ensemble, en travaillant, en étudiant, en jouissant des arts; et non le rêve des ouvriers français qui veulent devenir bourgeois, ne plus rien faire et jouir. Est mal regardé par les ouvriers, comme étranger (Russe) et comme nature plus fine, distinguée.

(f. 84) A organisé une société secrète, aidé à un attentat. Préparation de bombes, chargement si dangereux; si l'on appuie, on est mort. Idée dans la mécanique plus tard, de confectionner des machines infernales. Quand on a tué le ministre de la sûreté, 3e section (78), Mesentzodf, on l'a filé pendant trois mois pour bien connaître ses habitudes. Ils ne l'ont pas tué chez sa maîtresse parce qu'ils ont eu peur qu'on vît là une jalousie, une vengeance. On l'a tué à la sortie d'une église, au milieu de la foule; celui qui l'a poignardé s'exerçait depuis un mois sur un gros pain, pour être sûr de ne pas le manquer. Il y avait des femmes parmi ceux qui le filaient. Le signal pour donner sa faction à un autre était par exemple de s'essuyer le front. Préparation d'un attentat. Un nihiliste se fait marchand de fromage, une nihiliste se fait passer pour sa femme, tandis que des nihilistes minent la rue, font un souterrain, pour faire sauter le pavé au moment où le tzar passera.—La terre sortie.

(f. 85) RASSENEUR. Trente-huit ans. A quitté la mine depuis trois ans, s'est remis, engraisse, refleurit.

Un gros homme, débonnaire, rasé, l'air d'un cabaretier

flamand, avec l'ouvrier mineur qui est resté par dessous. Son histoire : beau parleur, se mettant en avant, prenant la tête de toutes les réclamations, et congédié pour cela à la dernière grève. Sa femme tenait déjà un débit, et il n'a plus rien fait, il a réuni chez lui les mécontents, sa maison a prospéré. Il vit assez largement. Il est devenu ainsi un centre. Du reste, idée calme, un possibiliste, qui voit seulement la guerre aux abus, les réformes à faire, mais qui ne va pas jusqu'à un soulèvement politique. Plus doux qu'Étienne dont il sera jaloux, et dont il triomphera à la fin (la guerre entre les partis socialistes).

Des enfants qui traînent, mais qui ne me sont pas utiles. Sait à peine lire et ne sait que signer.

Son débit a pour titre : *A l'Avantage*, débit tenu par Rasseneur. (Le bal sera le bal du Bon Joyeux).

BIBLIOGRAPHY

Manuscripts, Bibliothèque Nationale, Fonds français, Nouvelles acquisitions:

10305–10308: *Germinal*, described in detail in our opening chapter, *q.v.*

10303: *La Fortune des Rougon*, but also includes the "Premier plan remis à l'éditeur A. Lacroix."

10345: *Notes diverses;* containing among other things: "Notes générales sur la marche de l'œuvre"; "Notes générales sur la nature de l'œuvre"; "Différences entre Balzac et moi"; early lists of novels to be included in *Les Rougon-Macquart.*

24510–24524: 15 volumes of correspondence, letters addressed to Émile Zola, arranged in alphabetical order.

Editions:

Émile Zola: *Les Œuvres complètes. Les Rougon Macquart, notes et commentaires* de Maurice Le Blond, Typographie François Bernouard, 50 vols., 1927–1929. *Germinal* is vol. 14 in this edition.

Germinal, 2 vols., Charpentier-Fasquelle.

Germinal, N.Y., Charles Scribner's Sons, 1951.

There are, of course, other editions including those of Le Club français du livre (1952), the Imprimerie Nationale (André Sauret, éditeur) with a preface by Julien Cain, 2 vols. 1953, and Le Livre de poche [s.d.]

Books and articles consulted:

Alexis, P., *Émile Zola. Notes d'un ami*, Charpentier, 1882.

Amicis, E. de, "Émile Zola" in *Studies of Paris* (trans. from the Italian by W. W. Cady), N.Y., G. P. Putnam's Sons, 1879.

Angell, N., Bernard, M., et al., *Présence de Zola*, Fasquelle, 1953.

Aubery, P., "Quelques sources du thème de l'action directe dans *Germinal*," *Symposium*, 1959.

Baillot, A., *Émile Zola, l'homme, le penseur, le poète*, Soc. fr. d'Imprimerie et de Librairie, 1925.

Barbusse, H., *Zola*, Gallimard, 1931.

Batilliat, M., *Émile Zola*, Rieder, 1931.

Bernard, M., *Zola par lui-même*, Ed. du Seuil, 1952.

Cain, J., "La Genèse de *Germinal*," *Le Figaro littéraire*, Oct. 3, 1953.

Cannac, R., *Netchaiev*, Payot, 1961.

Castelnau, J., *Zola*, Tallandier, 1946.

Cazaux, M., "Zola en Suède," *Revue de littérature comparée*; Oct.–Dec., 1953.

Céard, H., *Lettres inédites à Émile Zola*, pub. et annotées par C. A. Burns, Nizet [1958].

Chambron, J., "Réalisme et épopée chez Zola. De *l'Assommoir à Germinal*," *La Pensée*, sept.–oct. 1952.

Deffoux, L., *La Publication de "l'Assommoir"*, Malfère, 1931.

Deffoux, L. & Zavie, E., *Le Groupe de Médan*, Crès, 1926; nouvelle édition revue et augmentée, Crès [s.d.]

Dessignolle, E., *La Question sociale dans Émile Zola*, Clavreuil, 1905.

Dormoy, E., *Topographie souterraine du Bassin houiller de Valenciennes*, Imprimerie nationale, 1867.

Doucet, F., *L'Esthétique de Zola et son application à la critique*, Nizet & Bastard, 1923.

Duveau, G., *La Vie ouvrière en France sous le Second Empire*, Gallimard, 1946.

Faguet, E., "Émile Zola" in *Propos littéraires*, 3ᵉ série, Soc. fr. d'Imprimerie et de librairie, 1905.

Frandon, I. M., *Autour de "Germinal"—La Mine et les mineurs*, Geneva, Droz, 1955.

Gauthier, E. P., "New Light on Zola and Physiognomy," *Publ. Mod. Lang. Ass.*, June 1960.

Girard, M., "Situation d'Émile Zola," *Revue des sciences humaines*, avril–juin 1952.

Girard, M., "Positions politiques d'Émile Zola jusqu'à l'affaire Dreyfus," *Revue française de science politique*, juillet–sept., 1955.

Girard, M., "L'Univers de *Germinal*," *Revue des sciences humaines*, 1953.

Girard, M. & Hermies, V. d', "Émile Zola devant la critique tchèque," *Revue des études slaves*, 1950.

Girard, M. & Hermies, V. d', "Émile Zola devant la critique tchèque: la critique littéraire," *Revue des études slaves*, 1953.

Goncourt, E. de, *Journal, mémoires de la vie littéraire d'Edmond et Jules de Goncourt*, texte intégral établi et annoté par Robert Ricatte, Monaco. Ed. de l'Imprimerie nationale, [1956–57], 22v.

Grant, E. M., "Concerning the Sources of *Germinal*," *Romanic Review*, October 1958.

Grant, E. M., "La Source historique d'une scène de *Germinal*," *Revue d'histoire littéraire de la France*, janvier–mars, 1960.

Grant, E. M., "The Newspapers of *Germinal*," *The Modern Language Review*, January 1960.

Grant, E. M., "Marriage or Murder: Zola's Hesitations concerning Cécile Grégoire," *French Studies*, Jan. 1961.

Guyot, Y., *La Science économique*, Reinwald, 1881.

Guyot, Y., *Scènes de l'enfer social—La famille Pichot*, Rouff, 1882.

Hemmings, F. W. J., *Émile Zola*, Oxford, Clarendon Press, 1953.

Hemmings, F. W. J., "The Present Position in Zola Studies," *French Studies*, April 1956.

Hemmings, F. W. J., "Zola, *Le Bien public* and *Le Voltaire*," *Romanic Review*, April 1956.

Hemmings, F. W. J. & Niess, R. J., *Émile Zola. Salons*, Geneva, Droz, 1959.

Huysmans, J.-K. *Lettres inédites à Émile Zola*, publiées et annotées par P. Lambert, Geneva, Droz, 1953.

Huysmans, J.-K., *Les Sœurs Vatard*, Charpentier, 1879.

James, H., "Émile Zola," *The Atlantic Monthly*, August 1903—reprinted in *Notes on Novelists*, N.Y., Charles Scribner's Sons, 1914.

Josephson, M., *Zola and his Time*, N.Y., Macaulay, 1928.

Kayser, J., *Émile Zola: La République en marche*, 2 vols., Fasquelle, 1956.

Kleman, M. K., *Emil' Zola, sbornik statey*, Leningrad, 1934.

Lanoux, A., "Où en est Zola? En marge de *Germinal*," *Hommes et mondes*, août 1952.

Lanoux, A., "Style chez Zola," *L'Education nationale*, 16 Oct., 1952.

Lanoux, A., *Bonjour, Monsieur Zola*, Amiot-Dumont, 1954.

Laveleye, E. de, *Le Socialisme contemporain*, 2nd edit., Germer-Baillière, 1883.

Le Blond Zola, Denise, *Émile Zola raconté par sa fille*, Fasquelle, 1931.

Lepelletier, E., *Émile Zola—sa vie, son œuvre*, Merc. de France, 1908.

Leroy-Beaulieu, P., *La Question ouvrière au 19ᵉ siècle*, Charpentier, 1872.

Levasseur, E., *Questions ouvrières et industrielles en France sous la Troisième République*, Rousseau, 1907.

Loquet, F., "La Documentation géographique dans *Germinal*," *Revue des sciences humaines*, juill.–sept., 1955.

Louis, P., *Histoire de la classe ouvrière en France*, Libr. des sciences politiques et sociales, 1927.

Lukács, G., *Studies in European Realism. A sociological survey of the writings of Balzac, Stendhal, Zola, Tolstoy, Gorki and others*, London, Hillway, 1950.

Malot, H., *Sans famille*, Dentu, 1878.

Martineau, H., *Le Roman scientifique d'Émile Zola*, Baillière, 1907.

Massis, H., *Comment Zola composait ses romans*, Fasquelle, 1906.

Matthews, J. H. "Zola and the Marxists," *Symposium*, 1957.

Matthews, J. H., *Les Deux Zola*, Geneva, Droz, 1957.

Matthews, J. H., "*Things* in the naturalist Novel," *French Studies*, July 1960.

Matthews, J. H., "L'Impressionnisme chez Zola: *Le Ventre de Paris*," *Le Francais moderne*, juillet 1961.

Moreau, P., "*Germinal*" *d'Émile Zola, épopée et roman*, Centre de documentation universitaire, 1954, (A mimeographed "cours de Sorbonne").

Moreau, P., "*Le Germinal* d'Yves Guyot," *Revue d'histoire littéraire de la France*, avril–juin 1954.

Niess, R. J., *Émile Zola's Letters to J. Van Santen Kolff*, Washington University Studies, Saint Louis, 1940.

Patterson, J. G., *A Zola Dictionary*, N.Y., Dutton, 1912.

Robert, G., *Émile Zola. Principes et caractères généraux de son œuvre*, Les Belles Lettres, 1952.

Robert, G., "Trois textes inédits d'Émile Zola," *Revue des sciences humaines*, 1948.

Robert, G., "*La Terre*" *d'Émile Zola*, Les Belles Lettres, 1952.

Rod, Ed., "Émile Zola" in *Les Idées morales du temps présent*, Perrin, 1897.

Romains, Jules, *Zola et son exemple*, Flammarion, 1935.

Root, W. H., *German Criticism of Zola, 1875-1893*, N.Y., Columbia University Press, 1931.

Salvan, A. J., *Zola aux États-Unis*, Brown University Studies, Providence, R.I., 1943.

Salvan, A. J., *Émile Zola. Lettres inédites à Henry Céard*, Brown University Press, Providence, R.I., 1959.

Salvan, A. J., "Vingt messages inédits de Zola à Céard," *Les Cahiers naturalistes*, n° 19, 1961.

Seillière, E., *Émile Zola*, Grasset, 1923.

Sherard, R. H., *Émile Zola*, London, Chatto & Windus, 1893.

Simonin, L., *La Vie souterraine, ou les mines et les mineurs*, Hachette, 1867.

Stell, Georges (pseudonym for V. B. Flour de Saint-Genis), *Les Cahiers de doléances des mineurs français*. Bureaux du *Capitaliste*, 1883.

Talmeyr, M., *Le Grisou*, Dentu, 1880.

Tersen, M., "Sources et sens de *Germinal*," *La Pensée*, janv.–fév., 1961.

Testut, O., *L'Internationale: son origine, son but, son caractère . . .*, Lachaud, 1871.

Turnell, M. *The Art of French Fiction: Prévost, Stendhal, Zola, Maupassant, Mauriac, Proust*, N.Y., New Directions, 1959.

Van Tieghem, Ph., *Introduction à l'étude d'Émile Zola. "Germinal."* (*Documents inédits de la Bibliothèque Nationale*), Centre de documentation universitaire, 1954. (A mimeographed "Cours de Sorbonne").

Vizetelly, E. A., *Émile Zola. Novelist and Reformer*, London, J. Lane, 1904.

Vuillemin, E., *La Grève d'Anzin de février–mars–avril 1884*, Lille, Danel, 1884.

Walker, Ph. D., *A Structural Study of Zola's "Germinal,"* (unpublished doctoral dissertation), Yale University, 1956.

Walker, Ph. D., "Prophetic Myths in Zola," *Publ. Mod. Language Assoc.*, September 1959.

Weill, G., *Histoire du mouvement social en France 1856–1910*, Alcan, 1911.

Wenger, Jared, "The Art of the Flashlight: Violent Technique in *Les Rougon-Macquart*," *Publ. Mod. Language Assoc.*, December 1942.

Wenger, Jared, "Character-types of Scott, Balzac, Dickens, Zola," *Publ. Mod. Language Assoc.*, March 1947.

Wilson, A., *Émile Zola. An Introductory Study of his Novels*, N.Y., Wm. Morrow, 1952.

Yarmolinsky, A., *Road to Revolution*, London, Cassell & Co., 1957.

Zakarian, R. H., *A Study of the Sources of "Germinal,"* based upon an examination of Zola's manuscripts, notes, and their sources (unpublished doctoral dissertation), Northwestern University, 1960.

Zévaès, A., *Le Socialisme en France depuis 1871*, Charpentier-Fasquelle, 1908.

Zévaès, A., *Zola*, Éditions de la Nouvelle Revue critique, 1946.

Émile Zola. Exposition organisée pour le 50e anniversaire de sa mort, Bibliothèque Nationale, 1952.

Newspapers consulted:

Le Cri du peuple, Le Dix-neuvième Siècle, L'Écho de Paris, Égalité, L'Événement, L'Événement illustré, Le Figaro, La France, Le Gaulois, Gil Blas, L'Intransigeant, La Justice, La Liberté, La Marseillaise, Le Matin, Le Moniteur universel, Le National, Paris, La Patrie, Le Prolétariat, La République française, La République radicale, Le Réveil, Le Siècle, Le Télégraphe, La Vérité, Le Voltaire.

Periodicals consulted:

Les Annales politiques et littéraires, The Atlantic Monthly, Blackwood's Magazine, Contemporary Review, Le Correspondant, Le Figaro littéraire, L'Illustration, Le Journal des Débats, Longman's Magazine, Le Magasin pittoresque, The Nation, North American Review, Le Révolté, La Revue des revues, Revue contemporaine, Revue de Belgique, La Revue des Deux Mondes, Revue libérale, La Revue moderniste, Revue politique et littéraire, La Revue socialiste, La Vie moderne, La Vie populaire.

INDEX

Names of fictional characters and place names, whether real or fictional,
are not included.

Zola, E. Plans the *Rougon–Macquart*, 3; includes a novel on the mines, 3; his interest in nihilism, 5, 72–73; his admiration for Balzac, 5; his conversation with Goncourt, 7; with Turgenev, 5, 73, 77; his contact with Giard, 7, 8; with Roll, 8; he goes to Anzin, meets Basly, inspects the mines, 8–9; begins writing the novel, 9; finishes the composition, 11; his choice of a title, 12; his preliminary *Ébauche*, 16–24; qualities of his imagination, 22–24; his sources: (1) technical: "Mes notes sur Anzin," 26–28; Dormoy and Simonin, 28–30; Laveleye, 30–31, 77–78; Leroy-Beaulieu, 26, 146; Boëns–Boisseau, 33–34; (2) literary, 35–38; his plans for the opening chapter, 40–42; for the chapter on the night meeting, 43–44; for ch. 5, Part V, 44–45; for the violence before Hennebeau's house, 45–46; for the clash between miners and soldiers, 47–48; for the last Part, 48–49; his "trouvailles" in